MILITARY MEMOIRS

Edited by
Brigadier Peter Young
D.S.O., M.C., M.A., F.S.A., F.R.HIST.S.

Edward Costello

MILITARY MEMOIRS

Edward Costello

The Peninsular and Waterloo Campaigns

Edited by

ANTONY BRETT-JAMES

ARCHON BOOKS

1968

© Longmans, Green and Co Ltd 1967
First published 1967

This edition first published in the
United States of America by Archon Books, 1968,
Hamden, Connecticut

Printed in Great Britain by
W. & J. Mackay & Co Ltd, Chatham

SBN: 208 00630 3

Contents

General Introduction to the Series by Peter Young   vii

Introduction   xi

Adventures of a Soldier   I

Bibliography   164

Index of Persons   167

General Index   170

Portrait of Edward Costello   *frontispiece*
from the original edition of *Adventures of a Soldier*

Map of Spain and Portugal   xx–xxi

General Introduction
to the Series

by PETER YOUNG

Dr Johnson: *Every man thinks meanly of himself for not having been a soldier, or not having been at sea.*
Boswell: *Lord Mansfield does not.*
Dr Johnson: *Sir, if Lord Mansfield were in a company of admirals and generals who'd seen service he'd wish to creep under the table.*

None can doubt that Samuel Johnson, so formidable with tongue and pen, was also stout of heart. Yet it would be wrong to suppose that these remarks on military service were not inspired by a genuine sentiment. One suspects that he was a bit of a fire-eater at heart. For all his wisdom he could envy the exploits of less learned contemporaries who faced powder and shot. It is an attitude that endures even as late as the last half of the twentieth century.

It is the common lot of fighting men that they have little to show for their efforts. Their satisfaction seldom comes in the shape of material rewards, unless they are at the very top of their profession. They must be content with the private feeling that they have played their part. It may be no more complicated than the atavistic instinct to strike a blow for hearth and home, the grim satisfaction of the Gallic warrior who had killed a Roman.

But nowadays it is not given to everyone to be a soldier, or to serve in the air or on the seas. One earns no great reputation as a seer by predicting that the memoirs of those who serve in World War III will be somewhat brief, or that the struggle itself will be nasty. If people are still interested in wars, it may be better for them to satisfy their curiosity by pondering those of the past rather than provoking those of the future.

In planning a series of this sort there are a bewildering variety of factors to be considered. Of these perhaps the chief to be taken into account is the fundamental question: 'Why do people read Military History?' Is it because truth is more attractive than fiction? Baron de Marbot, although his tales had unquestionably improved in the telling, has an interest which Brigadier Gerard, despite the narrative skill of Conan Doyle, cannot rival. Marbot's memory could play him false in matters of detail, but not as to the sense of period. He brings to life the atmosphere of the Grand Army in which he served. Marbot, regrettably, is too well known, both in French and English, to parade with the veterans of this series. We have endeavoured to present memoirists who for one reason or another are relatively unknown to the English-speaking public.

In modern times memoir-writing seems to have become the prerogative of generals. One is not, however, without hopes of finding a voice or two from the ranks to conjure up the fields of Flanders or the deserts of North Africa. Of course, we have not rejected generals altogether. But on the whole we have tried to rescue 'old swordsmen' from oblivion rather than, say, a religious enthusiast like Colonel Blackader—more concerned with the salvation of his soul than the deployment of his battalion. The fighting soldier is more attractive than an officer with a distinguished series of staff appointments to his credit; the tented field has an appeal which the dull round of garrison life cannot rival.

If such knowing officers as Captains Kincaid and Mercer or Monsieur de la Colonie, or such hard-bitten foot soldiers as Rifleman Harris or Sergeant Wheeler do not appear here, it is only because their excellent narratives are comparatively well known and easy of access.

We have avoided those veterans who, their Napier at their elbow, submerge their personal recollections in a mass of ill-digested second-hand campaign history. These are the most maddening of all. What details they could have given us had they chosen to! One reads that Colonel So-and-so dined with General Such-and-such. But why can't the fellow go on to tell us whether the general kept a good table, or what sort of conversationalist he was? Was he liked by his men? There is all the difference in the world between Rifleman Harris, who gives us such a wonderful picture of General Robert Craufurd on the retreat to Corunna, and Captain William Bragge, who fought at Salamanca and whose Journal tells us exactly nothing about it!

The trouble is that memoirists take so much for granted. They assume that we know all about the military organisation and tactics of their day. And so we must just be thankful for small mercies. You will not get a fight on every page, but gradually a picture is built up. One comes to visualise the manners of a bygone age, to see how people then could endure the privations of a campaign, the rough surgery of the battlefield, or the administrative neglect of their commanders. In the end we come almost to speak their language, and to hear them speak.

When they are promoted or rewarded we can share their pleasure. '*C'était un des plus beaux jours de ma vie!*' Marbot naïvely remarks when recounting the successes of his younger days, and we are almost as pleased as he.

But if you prefer to read these adventures rather than to emulate them, that, too, is understandable.

'How sweet the music of a *distant* drum.'

Introduction

Edward Costello, born near Dublin on 26 October 1788, was apprenticed to a cabinet-maker, but soon tired of this and worked instead for his uncle, a shoemaker. Enthusiasm for a soldier's life led him to enlist in the Dublin Militia in 1806. Within two years Costello, now aged nineteen, volunteered into the 95th Rifles and joined the 1st Battalion at Colchester. Through not being trained in time in light infantry duty, he missed accompanying the regiment to Spain with Sir John Moore, but he rejoined it from the depot when Colonel Beckwith and his riflemen arrived back in England. March 1809 found the 1st Battalion sailing for Portugal to join Sir Arthur Wellesley's new expeditionary force charged with freeing the Peninsula from French domination. The 95th were brigaded with the 43rd and 52nd Regiments of Light Infantry under the command of Robert Craufurd. After taking part in the Light Brigade's celebrated forced march to the battlefield of Talavera, Costello spent six weeks in Elvas hospital with a severe bout of fever and was fortunate to recover when several hundred soldiers died of it.

A year later, in July 1810, 'Ned' Costello was wounded under the cap of his right knee, near Almeida and the River Coa, and he had a most painful journey to hospital, first using two rifles as crutches, then squashed with six other wounded riflemen in a tiny bullock cart, next in a boat down the River Mondego, and finally by ship to Lisbon. As a result of his wound Costello missed the battle of Busaco on 27 September, but was fit enough to rejoin his battalion when it reached the Lines of Torres Vedras a fortnight later and stood to the defence of the Lisbon base.

He gives us a grim account of the pursuit of Massena's army across Portugal—Santarem, Pombal, Condeixa, Sabugal—and of the battle of Fuentes de Oñoro early in May 1811. January of the following year sees Costello volunteering for the 'Forlorn Hope' at the siege of Ciudad Rodrigo, where he storms the breach, rushes along the ramparts and enters the central square. In April he joins the 'Forlorn Hope' again for the storming of the other great frontier fortress, Badajoz, has a dreadful time with siege ladders, up to his neck in water and nearly buried beneath corpses. Finally he is struck on the chest and knocked senseless, 'drenched with water and human gore'. A musket ball had passed through the lower part of his right leg.

Costello recovered in time to fight at Salamanca on 22 July 1812, but fatigue and hot weather caused his Badajoz wound to break out, and he was obliged to go into hospital before returning to the 95th in a village near Madrid. Wellington's main army, meanwhile, was besieging Burgos with inadequate means, and when it retreated south-west towards Portugal the Rifles also headed for Ciudad Rodrigo and the frontier. The Light Division spent the winter cantoned in and about the village of Alameda until the new campaign opened in May 1813 with the army marching north-east again through Salamanca and Burgos, now abandoned by the retreating French.

At the battle of Vittoria, Costello found himself fighting along a ridge, hotly engaged and lucky to avoid being hit by splintered rocks if not by bullets. At one point he thought he had received a mortal wound when a round-shot struck his pouch so violently that he was hurled several yards. He escaped unscathed, though his pouch was nearly ripped off. He had another close shave three months later when trying to swim with a little Spanish girl across the River Bidassoa. In her terror she squeezed him so tight that he went under twice, and was only just rescued in time by several of his companions. In his next engagement, high in the Pyrenees, Costello again believed himself mortally wounded when struck a hard blow in the stomach: this time the ball stuck in the brass serpent of his waist belt.

After the final advance to Toulouse in 1814, the battalion sailed from Bordeaux and reached Spithead on 22 July. Nine months were spent in Dover barracks. Here recruits joined the ranks; new clothing was issued; and when orders came to embark for Ostend to join Wellington's army assembling to oppose Napoleon after his return from Elba, the 95th were ready. With Picton's 5th Division, Costello marched out of Brussels to fight at Quatre Bras. He was taking aim at some French skirmishers when a ball struck his trigger finger and tore it off, while a second shot pierced his mess-tin. Not till the evening of 18 June did he reach Brussels, where he spent three days until a boat took him to Antwerp. Despite having the shattered finger taken off at the socket, within a few weeks the hardy Costello was able to rejoin his regiment at Clichy, outside Paris.

From early in 1816 they were quartered near Cambrai, and Costello fell in love with, and courted, a girl named Augustine Loude, but her father, who wanted her married to a Frenchman, intervened to thwart the marriage. Though unaware that she and Costello had been secretly married when she had eloped, he took steps to have the military authorities forbid the association. When the 95th embarked for England, Augustine remained with her uncle until Costello could get his discharge and send for her to join him.

It is at this point that we conclude Costello's *Adventures of a Soldier* in the present edition. He was not destined to enjoy with Augustine the happiness for which he hoped. When the 95th disembarked at Dover and marched to Shorncliffe, Costello was one of the sergeants and corporals who, by order of the Horse Guards, were discharged—in his case invalided out on account of wounds. While waiting at Chatham he was unexpectedly joined by Augustine, who gave birth to a child. Costello took them to London when he appeared before the Chelsea Board, but could not maintain his family on the pittance of sixpence a day allowed to him. Starvation faced them, so it was agreed that Augustine should return with the child to her uncle and endeavour to move her father to a reconciliation. Costello appealed to Wellington's brother, Dr Gerald Wellesley, rector of Chelsea, and was given five pounds for his Waterloo wound. This small sum just sufficed to take them across the Channel to Calais and thence to St Omer, where Costello took leave of his beloved Augustine and her infant for what proved to be the last time. After a precarious period of great poverty, he learnt in London of Augustine's death—'most likely owing to her father, as he remained inexorable to the last'.

Somehow Costello had been misinformed: Augustine did not die until October 1839. Indeed, she married a lime-burner named Wiart in 1822 and bore him three children. As for old Bernard Loude, the father, he lived on until 1843, dying at the age of eighty-five. The fate of the child born in London remains unknown. Costello himself was to marry again, and for some years he and his wife Charlotte lived in Hinden Street off the Vauxhall Road, London, together with their children.

Costello's military career was not over. In 1835, when war broke out in Spain between Queen Isabella and Don Carlos—she was only five at the time and her mother acted as Regent—the British Government issued an Order in Council authorising 'any person to engage during the next two years in the military and naval service of her Majesty Isabella II'. One of the ten thousand recruits enlisted was Edward Costello, who joined the British Legion commanded by Colonel De Lacy Evans. From being a sergeant Costello now found himself a captain in command of a rifle company, but he did not enjoy his service in northern Spain. 'The Legion,' he told his wife, 'is not a school for the young officer to acquire knowledge, nor the old to get credit. How different, indeed, were things carried on in the British Army: there, in the very height of the most desperate conflict, all was cool and collected, and every officer's word could be distinctly heard, at the slightest cessation of firing.'

Nor was the Peninsular veteran lucky in action, for on 5 May 1836 he was struck by two balls 'at the same moment, one grazing the skin of my left thigh, and the other entering under the right knee joint, passing downward through the ham, and out at the calf of the leg'. He was carried to the rear and on his leg being dressed Costello found that the ball had entered the old wound made by a French bullet at the action of Almeida, 24 July 1810. By the time he left Santander, having been pronounced unfit for further service by a medical board, the Legion was in a most disorganised and insubordinate state, the men being six months in arrears of pay and mutinous as a result.

In March 1838, after his return to England, Captain Costello was appointed a Yeoman Warder of the Tower of London. He was then forty-nine and served for over thirty years, until his death in the Salt Tower in July 1869. In Spain he had been awarded the Order of St Ferdinand; he survived to gain the Military General Service Medal with eleven clasps for his arduous campaigning across Portugal and Spain and over the Pyrenees into southern France. The Waterloo Medal had been granted to him in 1816.

His *Adventures of a Soldier; written by himself* was published in 1852 by Colburn & Co. of Great Marlborough Street, London, having already appeared in several issues of Colburn's *United Service Magazine*. Costello began his preface to the first edition on a modest note, and then went on:

Every man's life is a volume of change, felt and expressed according to his peculiar dispositions and feelings, which are as varied under a military as they can be under a civil life. Could the never to be forgotten Tom Crawley but give his own detail!—could Long Tom of Lincoln, once one of the smartest of our regiment, now the forlorn bone-picker of Knightsbridge, but pen his own eventful track— could Wilkie, Hetherington, Plunket, and many others of those humbler heroes, conquerors in such well-contested fields as Rodrigo, Badajoz, Salamanca, and Waterloo, etc., whose exploits form the principal attractions in this volume, and whose stubborn spirits and perforated bodies formed key-stones for the fame of our immortal

Wellington, whose standard might have found a sandy support but for the individual bravery of the soldiers of his invincible divisions: could they but recount their varied casts of fortune—who would fail to read their histories and help to rear a cypress to their memories?

With these considerations, I send this volume forth, trusting that the reader will bear in mind that he who wrote it was both actor and spectator in the scenes he has narrated, and feels assured that by their perusal, he will be enabled to guess at what is generally felt and experienced by the individual soldier.

In its lengthy review *The Athenaeum*, quoting several characteristic episodes, called it—

an excellent book of its class; a true and vivid picture of a soldier's life—a life of vicissitude and change, of incidents fearfully contrasted, of feasting and starving, of idleness and exhaustion, of fun, frolic, and 'the cat'; and by confining himself strictly to a personal narrative, Mr. Costello has contrived to make this, the last of so many military biographies, by no means the least welcome. . . . One merit of this work is its variety—we have tragedy, comedy, and farce all in one chapter. These fierce contrasts, indeed, seem especially characteristic of a campaign, during the progress of which there grew up amongst the common soldiers a sort of mad reckless indifference to good and ill, life and death, that is awful to contemplate, but without which perhaps men, unsustained by high principles, could never go through its horrors, its privations, and its sufferings.

The editor of the *United Service Journal and Naval and Military Magazine*, also published by Colburn, reviewed Costello's book in his November issue. The *Adventures* had already been serialised in this monthly during 1839 and 1840 and 'been received by all classes with the marked favour to which their extreme interest and graphic truth entitle them'. After drawing attention to some typographical errors and names misspelt, the reviewer added a personal complaint:

With our knowledge of the facts, we cannot overlook an omission which we should not have expected from the worthy old soldier towards whom we have proved our sincere interest, and, had we been consulted, should not have occurred—namely, the absence of all mention of the autobiographer's obligations to Mr. Meller, a gentleman now, we believe, studying for the bar, who served in the

Auxiliary Legion with Costello, and put together, from the vivid dictation and notes of the latter, the earlier papers of the narrative. This task, we are bound to say, Mr. Meller performed with spirit and fidelity, considering his want of intimate knowledge with the subject; and we conceive, that in doing him this justice, we are but discharging a duty which the hurry of publication alone may have caused the hero of this most striking story to omit.

No mention was made of Mr. Meller, the literary 'ghost', when a second edition appeared in 1852, but the same editor reviewed this in the *United Service Journal* and again drew on his personal knowledge of the author to comment: 'The frontispiece presents us with a capital portrait of Captain Costello, and every one will vouch for the likeness.'

Dressed in dark green jacket and trousers, with green-tufted black shako, black braid and buttons, black accoutrements, and bugle-horn badge, Costello was always proud of the 95th Rifles. And rightly so, for the three battalions, known by the French as 'those green fellows' or 'the grasshoppers', saw more fighting in Wellington's army than any other regiment, since at least one battalion was present at every major battle of the Peninsular War save Albuera. Furthermore, in addition to the great battles and sieges, the 95th were engaged in many affairs, the Light Division being employed as a covering force or else as advance-guard during pursuit of the enemy. Riflemen carried the Baker Rifle, invented by Ezekiel Baker, a London gunsmith: a shorter, lighter weapon than the smooth-bore Tower Musket nicknamed 'Brown Bess' with which the line battalions were armed; a more accurate weapon thanks to the seven grooves which made a quarter turn in the barrel, and with about thrice the effective range.

The famous Light Division was formed on 22 February 1810, initially by taking Robert Craufurd's brigade from the 3rd Division and then breaking it up into two brigades, each with companies of the 1st Battalion of the 95th, each having a battalion of Portuguese Caçadores (light infantry), and in one case the 1st Battalion of the 43rd, in the other the 1st Battalion of the 52nd, which at the present time constitute the First Greenjackets.

Like other *corps d'élite*, the Light Division sometimes aroused resentment and jealousy. Colonel Jonathan Leach, who served for many years in the 95th Rifles, was aware of this feeling and refers to it in his *Rough Sketches of the Life of an Old Soldier*:

Amongst a certain number (I hope a few only) of malcontents in the army, the very name of the 'Light Division', or the 'outposts', was sufficient to turn their ration wine into vinegar, and to spoil their appetite for that day's allowance of ration beef also. . . . Those invidious barkers and growlers, whether in the subaltern or in the higher ranks, in whose mouths was every uppermost—'Ah! the Light Division! what is the Light Division more than any other?'— should have been briefly answered thus—The Light Division never did affect to place itself on a pedestal, as being superior to its comrades in arms; nor, on the other hand, when the most honourable, danger-ous, harassing, and responsible post was allotted to it, and it was pushed across the Coa in the very teeth of Massena's numerous legions, which it watched night and day, month after month, along a difficult and extensive line of country, whilst the other divisions of the army were in cantonments behind the Coa, as perfectly at their ease, and as safe from surprise, as if they had been in a garrison in England,— could it have calculated on having its prominent services called in question by men, many of whom scarcely ever saw the Light Division in their lives, and were ignorant of the manner in which it was constantly employed in every successive campaign.

Colonel Leach also explains wherein lay the particular attributes of the Light Infantry in which he was so proud to have served:

Our corps gained the reputation, which it wrung from friends and foes, *not by aping the drill of grenadiers*, but by its activity and intelligence at the outposts; by being able to cope with, in all situations, the most experienced and best-trained light troops which the continent of Europe could produce; and by the deadly application of the rifle in action. . . . I will further assert, also, that when called on to storm the breaches at Monte Video, Ciudad Rodrigo, and Badajoz, the corps proved itself equally efficient in the form of grenadiers, as any of the other brave regiments employed on those occasions. . . .

The great and important points are to attain the most perfect use of the arms they bear, which can only be effected by constant and unremitting attention and practice; to become thorough master of all matters connected with outpost duties, pickets, flank patroles [*sic*], advanced and rear-guards; to direct the attention, and to practise the eye, to the selection of positions advantageous for posts and pickets; and to instil into the mind of the soldier, that he must act for himself, and on his own judgment, in taking every advantage of the ground on which it may be his lot to engage the enemy; and that, in the desultory nature of our warfare, it is impossible that an officer or sergeant can always be at his elbow to set him right.

French tactics had long highlighted the need for a British counterpart to the *voltigeurs* and *tirailleurs*, but not until the formation of a Rifle Corps under Colonel Coote Manningham at the beginning of the nineteenth century were adequate steps taken to meet the challenge. Under the farsighted and inspiring aegis of Sir John Moore, Manningham, Stewart and others introduced new training methods and a new spirit, especially in the relations between officers, N.C.O.s and the men they commanded. At Shorncliffe men were encouraged in individual initiative, in speed of movement, and were taught how to seize the advantage of ground as well as all the skills required for skirmishing and light infantry work: scouring tracts of country, reconnoitring woods and villages, advance- and rear-guards, and outpost duty.

No less important, and new, was the stress laid on marksmanship; indeed, men who excelled in this were rewarded with special cockades to wear on the cap. Recalling how he joined the 95th in July 1802 from another regiment, William Surtees writes:

Most of all I liked the shooting at the target. As recruits, we were first drilled at what is termed the horse, i.e. a machine to assist young riflemen in taking aim. At this I pleased my commanding officer so much the first time I tried, that he ordered me to the front, and told me to load, and fire at the target. I did, and made a pretty good shot, hitting pretty near the bull's eye; on which he made me load again and fire, and hitting that also, he made me go on till I had fired ten rounds, all of which hit the target, and two of which had struck the bull's eye. The distance indeed was only fifty yards, but for a recruit, that is, a person unaccustomed to rifle-shooting, he called it a wonderful exhibition, and in consequence he gave me sixpence out of his pocket, and ordered me home.

This officer was one of the best shots himself that I have almost ever seen. I have known him, and a soldier of the name of Smeaton, hold the target for each other at the distance of 150 yards, while the other fired at it, so steady and so accurate was both their shooting.

No pains were spared to make each individual rifleman a good and confident marksman instead of a shoulder-to-shoulder cog in a volley-firing machine.

Besides these military skills the particular *esprit de corps* was also destined to influence the entire British Army, though the process took all too long. Alike from Costello and from the memoirs of junior officers in the 95th such as Harry Smith and John Kincaid can be seen the good relations and atmosphere prevailing between officers and men. Officers had to set an example of conduct, had to get to know their troops as individuals, had to treat them as human beings; and to this end reward and encouragement were preferable to curses, prevention of crime far better than savage punishment. Education, indulgences, promotion, regimental medals and badges were available to those who distinguished themselves in a favourable way. In the 95th Rifles the good soldier was characterised by 'the most peaceable conduct in his quarters, and the most generous courage in the field'.

It cannot be said that an identical tone and attitude prevailed throughout the Light Division—its commander, the irascible Craufurd, often strayed from Sir John Moore's ideals; yet discipline was comparatively humane by the standards of the age. Edward Costello is a fine example of the best product of the system and the Rifle Corps.

The text of Costello's *Adventures of a Soldier* is here printed complete for the thirty years between 1788 and 1818, apart from the omission of an occasional historical survey, detailing troops positions and second-hand facts culled from Napier's history of the Peninsular campaigns, an account by a corporal of a battle in which Costello did not personally take part, and a French prisoner's account of his escape from the fortress of Almeida, related verbatim in fluent English even though Costello assures us that the Frenchman could speak only 'a little English'. From time to time in the footnotes I have quoted short extracts from the memoirs of other men who served in the 95th Rifles—Kincaid, Simmons, Leach and Harry Smith—because they confirm or amplify many of the episodes described by Costello.

Where Costello has misspelt the names of officers or of places, I have made the necessary correction, and the same applies to a few obvious omissions and errors by the printers of the original edition. Now and then I have altered the punctuation where the sense requires it, and where Costello mentions a town 'the name of which I forget', it has been possible to give the missing name. Within square brackets a few dates have been inserted, and also the meaning of several obsolete words. Costello's own footnotes are indicated by [E.C.]

ANTONY BRETT-JAMES

FRANCE

R. Garonne

nder

S. Jean de Luz
San Sebastian
S. Jean de Biassou

Bilbao

Bayonne
Arcangues
R. Nivelle
Vera
Lesaca
S. Estevan

Orthez

Toulouse

Tarbes

Medina del
Pomar
S. Milan
Vittoria
R. Zadora
La Puebla
Salvatierra
Pamplona

P Y R E N E E S

Burgos

A   I   N

MADRID

Getafe

Pinhel

R. Coa

Freixedas

Almeida
Villa
de Mula

R. Dos Casas

R. Agueda

Barba del Puerco

Fort Conception
Villar de Puerco
Alameda
Molina dos
Flores
Ciudad
Rodrigo

PORTUGAL

Gallegos
Marialva
Carpio

Villar Formoso
Fuentes de
Oñoro

S P A I N

Nave de Haver

El Bodon
Atalaya

Ituero

Fuente Guinaldo

Miles
0   5   10

S I E R R A   D E   G A T A

Souto

Sabugal

I

To give a young gentleman right education,
The army's the only good school in the nation.

SWIFT

It has ever been the fashion in story-telling to begin, I believe, with the birth of the hero, and as I do not forget, for a moment, that I am my own, I can only modestly say with young Norval[1] I am,

> . . . of parentage obscure
> Who nought can boast, but my desire to be
> A soldier.

I was born at the town of Mount Mellick, Queen's County, Ireland, on the 26th October 1788. When I was seven years old my father removed to Dublin, where he had been appointed to the situation of tide waiter.[2] As soon as I became a good-sized youth, my father bound me apprentice to a cabinet-maker, in King William Street, in the aforesaid city; but urged by a roving and restless spirit, I soon grew tired of my occupation, which I left one morning early 'without beat of drum'.

I next went to live with an uncle, a shoemaker, who employed several men to work in his business. Among these was an old soldier, who had lost a leg, fighting under Sir Ralph Abercromby, in Egypt [1801]. From this old blade, I think it was, I first acquired that martial ardour that so frequently infects young men in time of war. There was, indeed, no resisting the old pensioner's description of glory. I became red-hot for a soldier's life, and although rejected as too young for the regulars, I 'listed', as it is technically called, in the Dublin Militia on the 17th of June 1806.

At the latter end of the following year, our regiment was stationed at Londonderry, in the north of Ireland, where I volunteered into the

---

[1] The infant son, by her first husband, of Lady Randolph. Norval, exposed at birth because of his father's hatred, was found in a basket by a shepherd, Old Norval, who brought him up as his own son. From *Douglas* (1757), a tragedy by John Home (1722–1808).

[2] A customs officer who boards ships on arrival, in order to enforce regulations.

95th, since made the 'Rifle Brigade'. It was rather singular, but I remember I was the only volunteer from the regiment who joined the Rifles.

After receiving my bounty of the eighteen guineas (£4 of which were deducted for my kit, which I was to have on joining), the sum allowed at that time to those who volunteered from the militia, I took the mail coach for Dublin, where I found a recruiting party of my new regiment, consisting of one sergeant, a corporal and six privates. I must say I felt highly delighted with the smart appearance of the men, as well as with their green uniform. The sergeant proposed that I should remain in Dublin, being as it were almost a native of that city, from which circumstance he thought I might materially assist in raising recruits.

Recruiting, on the pay of a private soldier, is anything but pleasant, and particularly if he be confined to the mere shilling a day, doled out to him once a week, for he not unfrequently spends it all the first night he receives it. I myself had woefully experienced this, having been frequently for days without food, through my irregularities and my unwillingness to acquaint my friends that I was so near them.

I was crawling about one day in this manner, heartily tired of my first sample of military life, garbed in an old green jacket of the sergeant's, when I was accosted by a smart young fellow. After eyeing me rather shrewdly from head to foot for several seconds, 'I say, green boy,' said he, 'do you belong to the Croppies?[1] D——me, but I like your dress. What bounty do you give?'

'Eighteen guineas,' replied I.

'Come then,' said he, 'tip us a shilling. I'm your man.' Unfortunately for me, I had not a farthing, for I had eaten nothing for that and the whole of the previous day. However, knowing that we received two pounds for every recruit, I hurried into a public house near at hand, and requested of the landlord to lend me a shilling, telling him the use for which I wanted it. This he very kindly did, and I handed it over to the recruit, who, chucking it instantly on the counter, called for the worth of it in whiskey. While we remained drinking, the sergeant, whom I had sent for, arrived, and supplying us with money, the recruit passed the doctor and was sworn in for our corps.

His name was Wilkie, he was an Englishman; his father having

---

[1] The name given to Irish sympathisers with the French Revolution.

been sent for from Manchester to superintend a glass manufactory in Dublin, accounted for his being here. He was a fine young fellow of about five feet eight inches in height, and possessed all the genuine elements of a soldier, that is, was quarrelsome, generous and brave, of which qualities he gave us a specimen the evening he enlisted, by quilting [*thrashing*] a pair of coal-heavers. After a few days, he introduced me to his family, consisting of his parents and a sister, a remarkably pretty girl of about seventeen. Had war not claimed me with her iron grasp as her proselyte, I, no doubt, should have interwoven my destinies with the silken web of Cupid, who, very naturally, when my youth and early passions are considered, for I was but nineteen, tapped me very seriously on the shoulder.

I, however, went on recruiting, and the two pounds I received for enlisting Wilkie, I handed over to my landlady in advance for future food, which my last misfortune had taught me to value. This precaution, as is generally the case, was now no longer necessary, for in a short time after, we enlisted so many recruits, that money became very plentiful, and I was enabled to get coloured clothes. While we remained in Dublin, I became a constant visitor at the house of Wilkie's father, and the young lady I have alluded to, not disapproving of my advances, a serious attachment followed. But my stay threatened to be speedily terminated, as the sergeant and his party received orders to join his regiment immediately, then at Colchester,

Mars and Cupid *beat to arms,*

and placed me in the predicament of the donkey betwixt the haystacks. I became bewildered as to which to take, both being, as it were, necessary to the calls of my nature.

At last, the time for parting arrived, which took place after a little private snivelling and simpering, and the usual vows of eternal fidelity, passion and remembrance—which last I have kept to this day. She and her mother accompanied Wilkie and myself towards the Pigeon House, Ringsend,[1] and in something more than twenty-four hours, we found ourselves cheek by jowl with the quays of Liverpool. It was past midnight when *we* cast anchor. We were ordered to remain on board; but Wilkie's and my own anxiety to see the place took advantage of a loop-hole in the waterman's pocket, and we got ashore in our coloured clothes; from the lateness of the hour, however, we

---

[1] A district of Dublin, near the mouth of the Liffey.

were obliged to take lodgings in a cellar. We had not been long settled and asleep below stairs, before I was awoke by the bright glare of a bull's-eye lanthorn staring me full in the face, and some five or six rough sailors all armed to the teeth, standing before us.

The first thing they did was to feel our hands, which, finding to be rather soft, one remarked to the other, that we had never been sailors, though nevertheless they took us as lawful prey. Wilkie, at first, wanted to fight with them, but was persuaded by half a dozen *bull dogs*, and some cutlasses to walk quietly to the tender, in which we most probably should have taken a voyage, but, for one thing, we had been *sea-sick* and were *sick of the sea*, and on being examined by the officer on board the next morning, we gladly sent for our sergeant, who, claiming us, accordingly, we were liberated.

Our party continued their march, and Wilkie, whom for more reasons than one I was growing exceedingly attached to, was always my companion and many a scrape he got me into. He was continually in hot water; on several occasions and particularly at Lichfield where we were caged, for kicking up disturbances amongst some Irish recruits in which, however, I supported my friend, we were detained for want of means to pay for the damage done to a public house, the scene of riot. Sergeant Crooks (for that was our sergeant's name) had not unfortunately the means to satisfy this demand, having nothing but the men's bare allowance to carry us to London. Meanwhile, we remained in the cage, which was in a very conspicuous part of the market-place.

The fact of an Irishman being there, seemed to have aroused all the little brats and blackguards of the neighbourhood (my countrymen were not so plentifully scattered then as they are now), and every minute of the day we were annoyed by, 'I say Paddy, Hilloa Paddy, which way does the bull run?' Taking both of us for Irish, the young devils kept twirling their fingers on their noses, even through the bars of the cage. The poor sergeant, who was a mild good fellow, arranged matters, after all, with the magistrates; the money was to be sent to the injured parties as soon as we joined the regiment, and deducted from our pay—which was done accordingly.

Wilkie, however, continued his pranks, and once while in London when on a visit to St Paul's Cathedral, stopped the pendulum of the clock, and set the bells ringing; for this we were again imprisoned, but escaped this time, by paying a fine of five shillings for being drunk, after which nothing occurred till we arrived at Colchester. Here I joined the 1st battalion, then under the command of Colonel Beckwith, after known as General Sir Sidney Beckwith,[1] and was attached to Captain Glass's company.

Shortly after my arrival, the regiment was ordered to Spain, the campaign having then commenced. But not being perfect in my exercises, I was left behind as depot, until time and practice had made me a greater proficient in Light Infantry duty. Although this was a necessary consequence to a mere recruit, at that time, I felt not a little mortification at being prevented sharing in the glory, which I believed the regiment about to reap.

As it was, however, I had no great reason to complain. I became an adept in my drill, and a tolerable shot along with some other recruits, before the regiment returned. This took place in the month of January 1809, at Hythe, where we were at that time stationed, the depot having moved from Colchester.

The Rifle regiment, it is well known, had distinguished itself, and had suffered severely, especially in the retreat to Corunna under the gallant Moore. From thence, they had embarked for England, where, on their landing, they presented a most deplorable sight. The appearance of the men was squalid and miserable in the extreme. There was scarcely a man amongst them, who had not lost some of his appointments, and many, owing to the horrors of that celebrated retreat, were even without rifles. Their clothing, too, was in tatters, and in such an absolute state of filth as to swarm with vermin. New clothing was immediately served out and the old ordered to be burnt, which order was put into execution at the back of our barracks amid the jest of the men, who congratulated each other on thus getting effectually rid of those myriads of enemies, that had proved such a source of personal discomfort to them abroad.

---

1 Beckwith was an outstanding commanding officer and a well-loved 'character'. He had served in India as early as 1791, and with the 95th had taken part in expeditions to Copenhagen, Hanover and Denmark before going to the Peninsula. His final post, as a lieutenant-general, was C.-in-C. at Bombay in 1829.

II

Shortly after the return of the regiment, I was drafted into the company commanded by Captain Peter O'Hare; a man whose eccentric habits were equalled only by his extremely ugly countenance. Peter, for that was the cognomen by which he was generally known to the men, was as brave as a lion; and had risen, it was said, to his present commission from the ranks.[1]

While here, he got in tow with a young lady of Hythe, whom he was in the habit frequently of escorting about the barracks and the neighbouring heights. This the men as often took advantage of, and throwing themselves in his way, when arm-in-arm with the lady, would ask any favour they might have required of him. This Peter, who we presumed had an eye to the opinion and future requital of, perhaps, his own wishes upon the fair one herself, would always readily grant; until, at last, through their importunities he became awake to the scheme, and swore he would flog the first man who made another attempt of the kind, when the lady was present.

A rather humorous adventure, which came to my knowledge through his servant, occurred while here. One day at Hythe with a dinner party, at which the young lady was present, he chanced, unintentionally, to give offence to some Militia officer, one of the party; the consequence was, that the next morning he received, what he perhaps supposed a *billet-doux*, but which, to his surprise, turned out to be a challenge. He was sitting shaving himself when the note was delivered to him by his servant, and of course dropped the razor to peruse it.

'John,' said he, calling his man back, 'who brought this? Faith, it's a challenge'.

'A gentleman!' replied John, 'now waiting at the door.'

'Oh, then,' says Peter, 'tell the gentleman that I am going to Spain, and that if he follows me, he'll not find me behind a hedge; and with my compliments, tell him also to take back this bit of paper to the

---

[1] O'Hare, whose name appears frequently in Costello's memoirs, had joined the Rifle Corps from the 69th Foot in 1800, and had been badly wounded at Buenos Aires during the campaign in South America. He served with great bravery in the battles of Rolica, Vimeiro, Corunna, Busaco and Fuentes de Oñoro, and was eventually killed in the storming of Badajoz, April 1812.

humbug who sent it; for by Jove!' he continued, closing the door, 'captain's commissions are not to be got every day!'

Our commanding officer, who was considered as one of the most humane of the whole army, was an excellent man, and well deserving of his fame; he seldom had recourse to the 'cats', thinking, perhaps, with a great deal of truth, that it was necessary only in extreme cases. The plan of punishment, generally adopted by him, was to put the offender on extra drill with all his accoutrements on. When, however, the men became incorrigible, he would order a six-pound shot to be affixed to the leg, with a long chain attached to it, and so oblige them to trail it about with them.

We had in our regiment, at this time, a man of the name of Tom Crawley, who was always getting into scrapes, and who was one of those singular characters with which every regiment abounds. To enormous strength, and great meekness of temper, he added an infinity of dry humour, which I shall better illustrate by introducing him to the reader at once, as bearing no little part in my career—in which he first became known to me as one of the 'incorrigibles'. Tom, however, made light of every punishment, even of the 'six-pounder', which he would generally chuck under his arm as if it were a mere toy. To obviate this, another move was made by our Colonel, which was the obliging him to wear a kind of long smock-frock, with a green cross painted on the back and front of it. The barrack in which we were, being only temporary, presented no outward wall to prevent our free intercourse with the town where Tom was a general favourite. Tom used, therefore, at night, while under disgrace, to take advantage of the dusk, and steal by the sentries into the town. Here, of course, his strange dress elicited innumerable queries.

'Arrah and sure!' Tom would reply with a knowing side leer of the eye, 'sure and is it not the new regulation of the Duke of York,[1] and musn't all the likes of me, that are Catholics in our regiment, wear the cross on their dress!'

The first parade we had after our men had received their new equipments, was imprinted upon my memory from a circumstance attending it, that was well calculated to make an impression upon the mind of a youthful soldier, such as I then was; and to inspire that *esprit de corps* in a regiment, which is absolutely essential to even disciplined valour. I had previously, more than once, heard a man of

[1] Commander-in-Chief of the British Army from 1795 to 1809 and again from 1811 until his death in 1827.

the name of Tom Plunket eulogised by the men for his courage. He was a smart, well-made fellow, about the middle height, in the prime of manhood; with a clear grey eye, and handsome countenance; and was a general favourite with both officers and men, besides being the best shot in the regiment.

On the occasion I have above alluded to, we were formed into hollow square, and ordered to face inwards; as we knew it was not a punishment parade, we naturally expected some address from the commanding officer, and wondering in our own minds what was coming, when Colonel Beckwith broke the silence by calling out:

'Private Thomas Plunket, step into the square.' All eyes, it is needless to say, were fixed upon Plunket, as he halted with his rifle shouldered, in the finest position of military attention, within a few paces of his officer.

'Here, men,' exclaimed the commanding officer, pointing to Plunket, 'here stands a pattern for the battalion!' Then addressing Tom, he added, 'I have ordered a medal for you, in approval of your late gallant conduct at Corunna. Present yourself, Sir, to the master tailor and get on a corporal's stripes, and I will see you do not want higher promotion, as you continue to deserve it. I love to reward conduct such as yours has hitherto been!'

Making his salute, Tom retired, when we formed into column and marched back to our barracks, duly fired with a love of emulation to deserve the praise that had been bestowed on the fortunate Plunket. I have since often thought of the judicious conduct pursued by our Colonel in the foregoing instance, as I am convinced that it was attended with the happiest effects among many of the men, and, perhaps, indeed, induced much of that spirit of personal gallantry and daring for which our corps afterwards became celebrated.

Our regiment was shortly afterwards raised to one thousand strong, chiefly through volunteering from the Militia, our common medium of supply at the time at which I write, and it is justly due to the Militia regiments, to say, that in the knowledge and exercise of their military duties, during the war, they were very little inferior to the troops of the line. The men who joined our battalion, were in general a fine set of young fellows, and chiefly the *élite* of the light companies of the different provincial corps.

For his qualifications, as before stated, Tom Plunket, with a few others, was selected to recruit from the Lincoln Militia, which lay at Hythe, while we remained in temporary barracks on the heights.

While the volunteering went on, the Militia colonels were ordered to give their men full liberty to do as they liked, and the better to obtain the object in view, barrels of beer with the heads knocked in, were, by order of government, placed in the different streets of the town, for those to partake of who chose. The butts, consequently, were dipped into by every kind of person with utensils of every description. This we must not wonder at, when we consider the double thirst those times gave rise to, 'Barclay' as well as 'Glory'.

Tom's manner of attack was rather singular, but joined to the profusion of government, very efficacious. The Rifles, from the dark colour of their uniforms, and the total absence of all ornament, had gained the nick-name of 'Sweeps', an appellation, which, nevertheless, held out a kind of temptation to the 'wide awake' of the squads. The pipe clay and button stick were always hateful to the eyes of all soldiers; but to none so much as to the Riflemen, who looked upon them as fitted only for men less useful than themselves. This, Tom took advantage of on all occasions. He was the soul of every company he mixed in, and amongst his other accomplishments, numbered that of dancing excellently.

One day, the better to attract the 'awkwards', he commenced a shuffle on the head of one of the aforesaid barrels of beer, to the infinite amusement of a very large crowd; in the course of a few steps, however, the head suddenly gave way, and soused Tom up to his neck in the liquid. The whole crowd laughed uproariously. But Tom, whose head only was to be seen, stared very gravely round the edge of the cask, then suddenly recovering himself, and bolting out of the butt, he made his way instantly to the public-house chimney, which having ascended some distance and descended, he as quickly reappeared amongst the crowd.

'There now,' said he, giving himself a Newfoundland shake, that opened a wide and instantaneous circle of militia men, 'there now,' he exclaimed, 'd—n your pipe clay, now I'm ready for the grand parade!'

I must now notice an order that arrived for our immediate embarkation for Portugal, to join the army under Sir Arthur Wellesley. We went on board the transports lying for us at Dover in March 1809, in the best of spirits; such, in fact, as sportsmen feel in anticipation of the pleasures of the chase.

Shipboard, though perhaps not quite so forlorn as Doctor Johnson has portrayed it,[1] soon becomes sufficiently irksome and unpleasant

---

[1] In Boswell's *Life*, Dr Johnson is more than once quoted as inveighing against

to those not accustomed to it, especially when three or four hundred men are crowded into a small vessel. Our officers, who were mostly a jolly set of fellows, had recourse to various expedients to while away the time on our voyage. Among these was one extremely popular, and that was getting Plunket to dance a hornpipe to the music of our band upon the quarter-deck. Tom danced it famously; and the beating of his feet in the 'double shuffle' used to draw the loudest plaudits from our men and the crew of the vessel.

As I have already been induced to mention Plunket, while we are now on our voyage to Portugal, I will introduce a sketch of his life, which well known as it is to many individuals formerly in the regiment, possibly may not form an unamusing episode in my own.

III

When I'm in want I'll thankfully receive
Because I'm poor; but not because I'm brave.
TOM PLUNKET TO THE LIFE

Plunket's first career in arms was in South America with General Whitelocke,[1] where he acquired the reputation, in his company, of a good soldier. It was at the retreat of Corunna, some years afterwards, that an opportunity particularly presented itself of getting distinguished, and which Tom took in the nick of time. The rear-guard of the British, partly composed of the Light Brigade, notwithstanding the gallantry of some of our cavalry, were exceedingly pressed by the

life on board ship. After one such outburst, of 10 April 1778, Boswell comments: 'His abhorrence of the profession of sailor was uniformly violent.'

[1] Lieutenant-General John Whitelocke (1757–1833) was in command of a force sent in 1807 to retake Buenos Aires. His disastrous failure to assault the town, and the treaty he was obliged to conclude, led to his being cashiered by court-martial.

French horse, who were vastly superior to us in that arm. In the neighbourhood of Astorga, in particular, they made several determined charges. In these onsets, a French general, named Colbert,[1] was remarkably active, as well as conspicuous, from riding a grey horse, and, though frequently aimed at by our men, seemed to bear a charmed life, as he invariably escaped. In one of the French charges, headed by this officer, our General, Sir Edward Paget, rode up to the rifles, and offered any man his purse who would shoot this daring Frenchman, whom he pointed out.[2] Plunket immediately started from his company, and running about a hundred yards nearer to the enemy, he threw himself on his back on the road, which was covered with snow, placing his foot in the sling of his rifle, and taking a deliberate aim, shot General Colbert. His Trumpet-Major riding up to him, shared the same fate, from Tom's unerring rifle.[3] Our men, who had been anxiously watching Tom, immediately cheered him; and he had just time, by running in upon the rearmost sections, to escape some dozen troopers who made chase after him. Our General immediately gave Tom the purse he had promised, with encomiums upon his gallantry, and promised to recommend him to his Colonel, which he did in high terms to Colonel Beckwith. A few days afterwards, when the French attacked Sir John Moore's position at Corunna, Plunket again became noted for his cool bravery and daring, especially in making some admirable shots, by which they lost many officers.

But the truth must be told. Like all heroes, Tom had his faults. Among these, in particular, was one which, in its destructive consequences, was calculated to counterbalance in a soldier a thousand virtues. In other words, Tom was a thirsty soul, and exceedingly fond of a 'drop'. This was his unfortunate failing through life, and but for which he must have got on in the service.

One deplorable instance of insubordination, arising from this vice,

[1] Auguste-Marie-François Colbert (1777–1809) had served in Italy and Egypt, and distinguished himself at Austerlitz and Jena.

[2] Sir William Cope, in *The History of the Rifle Brigade*, casts doubt on Paget having bribed a soldier 'to slay a chivalrous and brave enemy. . . . It is quite possible that General Paget flung his purse (or some of its contents) to Tom Plunket, in admiration of two such unerring shots in the midst of a hot fight. But this is a very different matter from the previous offer of it.'

[3] Kincaid writes: 'Plunket was not less daring in his humble capacity than the great man he had just brought to the dust. He was a bold, active, athletic Irishman, and a deadly shot; but the curse of his country was upon him.'

I well remember, which took place at Campo Mayor, after the battle of Talavera. Tom had been promoted to the rank of sergeant, and was in the Hon. Captain Stewart's company. One morning, when the company was on private parade, Tom appeared quite tipsy, and, in giving the words of command for inspection, previous to the arrival of the officers, he set the men laughing. The pay-sergeant, his superior in rank, immediately ordered him to desist. Tom refused, and, while an altercation was going on, Captain Stewart came up, who, perceiving the state he was in, put him under arrest, and ordered him to be confined to his quarters.

Here he was no sooner left alone than, conceiving that a great indignity had been placed upon him, thoughts of vengeance immediately suggested themselves to his mind. Under the influence of intoxication that man, who, when sober, was noted for his good humour and humanity, now conceived the diabolical intention of shooting his Captain. He immediately barricaded the door of the room, and then set about loading some ten or twelve rifles, belonging to men, then on fatigue duty. Taking up one of these, and cocking it, he placed himself at an open window for the avowed purpose, as he stated to several of the men, of shooting Captain Stewart as he passed.

Fortunately the Captain got notice of the danger of going near the house, while several of the men, by coaxing and force, alternatively, endeavoured without effect to get into the room Tom had barred. At length the unfortunate Plunket was induced to relent on the appearance of a Lieutenant of the company named Johnston, who was a great favourite with the men, among whom he was known by a very familiar nickname. The door was opened and Tom made prisoner.

Although Tom was a general favourite, and his conduct had resulted from the madness of intoxication, his insubordination was too glaring to stand a chance of being passed over. He was brought to a regimental court-martial, found guilty, and sentenced to be reduced to the ranks, and to receive three hundred lashes. Poor Plunket, when he had recovered his reason, after the commission of his crime, had experienced and expressed the most unfeigned contrition, so that when sentence became known, there was a general sorrow felt for him throughout the regiment, particularly on account of the corporal punishment. In this feeling, I believe, the officers participated almost as much as the men.

At length the time arrived when the bravest soldier of our battalion was to suffer the penalty of his crime in the presence of those very men before whom he had been held up as a pattern but some few short months before. The square was formed for punishment: there was a tree in the centre to which the culprit was to be tied, and close to which he stood with folded arms and downcast eyes, in front of his guard. The surgeon stood by, while the buglers were busily engaged untangling the strings of the cats.

There was a solemn stillness on that parade that was remarkable; a pensiveness on the features of both officers and men, deeper than usual, as though the honour of the profession was to suffer in the person of the prisoner. Flogging is at all times a disgusting subject of contemplation: in the present instance, it seemed doubly so, now that a gallant, and until within a few days, an honoured and respected man was to suffer.

The sentence of the court-martial was read by the adjutant in a loud voice. Poor Tom, who had the commiseration of the whole regiment, looked deadly pale. That countenance which the brunt of the fiercest battle had been unable to turn from its ruddy hue—that countenance which the fear of death could not change—was now blanched in dread of a worse fate.

'Buglers, do your duty,' exclaimed Colonel Beckwith, in a voice husky with emotion, I thought, as the men seemed to hesitate in their business of stripping and binding the prisoner to the tree. This, however, was soon accomplished, Tom only once attempting to catch the eye of his colonel with an imploring glance, while he exclaimed in broken accents—

'Colonel, you won't, will you? You won't—you cannot mean to flog *me*!'

The appeal, although it went to the heart of every one present, was vain. Colonel Beckwith betrayed much uneasiness; I beheld him give a slight start at the commencement of the punishment; but his sense of duty became paramount the moment he beheld the punishing bugler laying on rather lighter than was common.

'Do your duty, Sir, fairly!' he uttered in a loud voice.

The first man had bestowed his quantum of punishment, twenty-five lashes, when he was succeeded by another. This man, as if determined that his reputation as a flogger should not suffer, however his victim might, laid on like a hardened hand. Plunket's sufferings were becoming intense: he bit his lip to stifle the utterance of his pangs; but nature, too strong for suppression, gave place more than once to a half-agonized cry, that seemed to thrill through the very blood in my veins. Happily this wretched scene was destined to a brief termination: at the thirty-fifth lash, the Colonel ordered the punishment to cease, and the prisoner to be taken down. When this was done, he addressed Plunket: 'You see, Sir, now, how very easy it is to commit a blackguard's crime, but how difficult it is to take his punishment.'

So ended the most memorable punishment-scene I have ever witnessed. It has usually been contended, by those averse to the system of flogging, common in our army, that it destroys the pride and spirit of the man. That it has had that effect, in many instances, I have myself witnessed, where the character of the soldier was not previously depraved. But with reference to Plunket, he appeared soon to get over the recollection of his former disgrace. He got into favour with his officers again, and, notwithstanding little fits of inebriety, was made corporal, and went through the sanguinary scenes of the Peninsula, unscathed from shot or steel. His usual luck, however, forsook him at Waterloo, where a ball struck the peak of his cap and tore his forehead across, leaving a very ugly scar. I recollect having gone wounded at the time to the rear, where I saw him under the hands of the surgeon.

After Waterloo, he was invalided to England, where he passed the board at Chelsea; but only being awarded the pittance of sixpence a day for his wound and long services, he felt disgusted, and expressed himself to the Lords Commissioners in a way that induced them to strike him off the list altogether. The following day he started off for Ireland, where he duly arrived in rags and wretchedness. To relieve himself, he again enlisted in either the 31st or 32nd regiment of the line, then quartered somewhere in the north.

While wearing a red coat, he had a singular meeting with his former Colonel, then General Sir Sidney Beckwith, which I have often heard him relate. It is customary, as the reader may probably be aware, to have half-yearly inspections of our regiments at home. Shortly after Tom's having enlisted, it so happened, on one of the above occasions, when his regiment was formed for inspection, that the duty devolved upon his old commander, Sir Sidney, who was in command of the district.

In walking down the front rank scrutinising the appearance of the men, the General suddenly came to Tom, distinguished as he was by two medals on his breast.

'Do my eyes deceive me?' said Sir Sidney. 'Surely you are Tom Plunket, formerly of my own regiment.'

'What's left of me, Sir,' replied Tom, who was seldom deficient in a prompt reply.

'And what has again brought you into the service?' inquired Sir Sidney. 'I thought you had passed the board at Chelsea?'

'So I did,' said Tom; 'but they only allowed me sixpence a day, Sir; so I told them to keep it for the young soldiers, as it wasn't enough for the old, who had seen all the tough work out.'

'Ha! the old thing, Tom, I perceive,' observed Sir Sidney, shaking his head; then immediately remarked to the Colonel of the regiment, as he proceeded down the ranks—'One of my bravest soldiers.'

The same day the General dined at the officers' mess, when Tom was sent for after dinner.

'Here, Plunket, I have sent for you to give us a toast,' observed Sir Sidney, as he handed him a glass of wine.

'Then, Sir, here's to the immortal memory of the poor fellows who fell in the Peninsula, Sir,' said Tom.

The toast was drunk by all with much solemnity, when Tom was dismissed with a present from Sir Sidney. The following day Tom was made a corporal, and shortly afterwards, through the medium, I believe, of Sir Sidney, went up and passed the pension board at Kilmainham, which granted him a shilling a day.

But I had forgotten to mention, in its place, an event common in man's life—I mean his marriage. Shortly after the battle of Waterloo, Tom had wedded a lady remarkable for being deficient in one essential to beauty—she actually had no *face*, or, at all events, was so *defaced*, it amounted to the same thing. This slight flaw in the beauty of Tom's wife, who

Had gallantly follow'd the camp through the war,

arose from the bursting of an ammunition-waggon at Quatre Bras, near to which the lady stood, and by which her countenance was rendered a blue, shapeless, noseless mass. This event was duly commemorated by the government, who allowed the heroine a shilling a day pension, in allusion to which Tom used facetiously to say—'It was an ill blowing up of powder that blew nobody good.'

The story of Tom Plunket, already narrated at greater length than I had intended, draws fast to a close. Imbued with roving inclinations, partly owing to his nature, and more perhaps to his profession, for nothing more unsettles a man than the ever-changing chequered course of a soldier's life, he at one time determined to become a settler in Canada, and, accordingly, accepted the offer held out by government to all pensioners, of allowing them so much land, and giving them four years' pay for their pensions. Plunket, ever eager for the handling of cash, got two years' pay down here, and started off with some two or three hundred others to try their fortune. This proved to be a very miserable one: Tom was not a man to rusticate on the other side of the Atlantic amid privations, and with the recollection of old England fresh in his mind.

Before a year had elapsed, he returned to England with his wife, and, by way of apology to his friends, stated his grant of land was so wild and swampy that it made him quite melancholy, looking at it in a morning out of the chinks of a wretched log hut he had managed to erect upon his estate. He returned home swearing loudly against forest-land, a swampy soil, and a bad climate, having, of course, duly forfeited his own pension for ever.

The last time I saw Tom Plunket was in Burton Crescent, most picturesquely habited, and selling matches. I did not disdain to speak to an old comrade who had been less fortunate in 'life's march' than myself. I asked him how he got on, when with one of his usual cheerful smiles he informed me, that the match-selling business kept him on his legs.

'I should have thought, Tom, you had seen enough of *firing*,' I remarked, 'without endeavouring to live by it now.'

'A man must do something these hard times for bread,' replied Tom, as he passed his hand thoughtfully across the furrow made by the bullet at Waterloo.

Poor Tom! I felt for him. I was sorry to see him neglected; others, whose service were many days' march behind his, were taken better care of. But Tom's incorrigible failing was his own stumbling-block.

I did not, however, leave him my mere reflection, but giving him a portion of that coin he so well knew how to get rid of, I wished him success in his new business, and went my way, musing on the strange vicissitudes of a soldier's life.[1]

[1] A few months back, while on duty at the Tower, one of the warders informed me a most extraordinary lady was anxious to see me, when, to my astonishment, Mrs Plunket stood before me, and while she held a handkerchief by one hand close to that part where her nose formerly stood, with her other hand she squeezed mine, and in the most plaintive tone told me of poor Tom's death. It appeared that herself and Plunket, who usually tramped through different parts of the country, and procured a livelihood selling needles and tapes, while passing through a street in Colchester, suddenly staggering a few paces fell down and expired. The death of Tom and the sight of Mrs Plunket, whose extraordinary countenance excited disgust as well as pity, spread like wildfire through the town, and it came to the ears of several retired officers living in that city,

Alas! the brave too oft are doom'd to bear,
The gripes of poverty, the stings of care.

But after this digressive sketch, it is high time to return to my own career in the field that was just now commencing. Returning to shipboard, from whence I conducted the peruser of this veritable narrative, allow me to say, that after a tolerably pleasant voyage we anchored off Lisbon [*28 June 1809*]. From thence, in a few days, we proceeded in open boats up the River Tagus, and landed about four miles from Santarem, where we encamped for the night.

On the following morning, we marched into the city of Santarem amid the cheers of its inhabitants, who welcomed us with loud cries of '*Viva os Ingleses valerosos!*' Long live the brave English!

Here we immediately became brigaded with the 43rd and 52nd regiments of Light Infantry, under the command of Major-General Craufurd.[1]

IV

On the third day after our arrival at Santarem, we commenced a series of forced marches to join the main army under Sir Arthur Wellesley, at Talavera, then almost hourly expecting an engagement with the French corps commanded by Marshal Victor. Our men suffered dreadfully on the route, chiefly from excessive fatigue and the heat of the weather, it being the melting month of July. The brain fever soon commenced, making fearful ravages in our ranks, and

---

who happened to read my description of him; the result was that a handsome collection was set on foot, and the amount of twenty pounds was collected for the widow. The lady of a colonel also, entirely out of her own pocket, paid for the funeral of poor Tom, with a handsome tombstone to perpetuate his memory. This she told me with many sobs. Thus ended the career of the gallant but unfortunate Plunket. [*E.C.*]

[1] Robert Craufurd (1764–1812) had served in India and Ireland, Switzerland and Holland before commanding the Light Brigade in 1807 at Buenos Aires.

many men dropped by the road-side and died. One day I saw two men of the 52nd, unable to bear their sufferings, actually put a period to their existence by shooting themselves.[1]

The greatest efforts possible were made by Major-General Craufurd to arrive in time to join the Commander-in-Chief, previously to a battle being fought. The excellent orders our Brigadier issued for maintaining order and discipline on the line of march on this occasion, though exceedingly unpopular at first, have since become justly celebrated in the service. No man, on any pretext whatever, was allowed to fall out of the ranks without a pass from the officer of his company, and then only on indispensable occasions.

This pass, however, was not a complete security, for on the return of the stragglers to camp, the orderly sergeants were compelled to parade them before their regimental-surgeons, when, if pronounced as skulkers, they were instantly tried by a drum-head court martial, and punished accordingly; thus, frequently, when almost dying with thirst, we were obliged to pass springs of the finest water by the road-side untasted. But all this apparent severity, as we afterwards learnt, was considered as absolutely essential to the great purpose General Craufurd had in view—dispatch. If the General found a man fall out without a pass, his plan was to take his ramrod and ride off. It was not unfrequently you might see him rid into camp with a dozen ramrods, when the adjutant of each regiment was ordered to find

---

[1] As the reader may not be aware of the weight each rifleman had to carry during this long and harassing march, this, too, by men considered the lightest troops in our service, they are as follows: Knapsack and straps, two shirts, two pair of stockings, one pair of shoes, ditto soles and heels, three brushes, box of blacking, razor, soap-box and strap, and also at the time an extra pair of trousers, a mess-tin, centre-tin and lid, haversack and canteen, greatcoat and blanket, a powder-flask filled, a ball bag containing thirty loose balls, a small wooden mallet used to hammer the ball into the muzzle of our rifles; belt and pouch, the latter containing fifty rounds of ammunition, sword-belt and rifle, besides other odds and ends, that at all times are required for a service-soldier. Each squad had also to carry four bill-hooks, that weighed six pounds each, so that every other day each man had to carry it; thus equipped, with from seventy to eighty pounds weight, this, too, in the melting month of July. Not content with the above, the General gave strict orders for each man to have his canteen filled with water before commencing this day's march every morning. Through being thus overloaded, four hundred of the battalion died a few months after our arrival, without a single shot being fired. But the survivors soon found out the cause of this mortality, as I don't think there was a man in the regiment five years after, before we left the country, could show a single shirt or a pair of shoes in his knapsack. [E.C.]

those that had no ramrods, each of which received two dozen lashes.

Fortunately for us, our longest halt took place during the heat of the day, and our longest marches were made at night; at this time, therefore, it was a usual scene to see a number of men who had been flogged, with their knapsacks on their heads, and their bodies enveloped in the loose great coats—to ease the wounds inflicted by the lash. But yet with all this, strange as it may appear, Craufurd maintained a popularity among the men, who, on every other occasion, always found him to be their best friend.

A few days before we came to Malpartida de Placencia, we were going through a small town, the name of which I forget [Coria], when in passing the gaol, a man looking through one of the high barred windows of the building vociferated, in accents not to be mistaken—

'Od's blood and 'ounds, boys, are you English?'

On several of our men answering in the affirmative, the prisoner exclaimed, in a tone that set our men in a roar of laughter—

'Oh! by Jasus, the Spaniards have poked me into this hole for getting a drop of wine, boys;—get me out, pray.'

When we halted about half a mile on the other side, Colonel Beckwith sent, and obtained the man's release. He proved to be one of the 23rd Light Dragoons, who had been taken prisoner by the French, but had made his escape in the dress of a peasant; when, in passing through this place, he had been incarcerated on a charge of taking some wine from a man without paying for it. Much merriment was excited by his appearance, and the droll and earnest manner in which he narrated his adventures.

On the following day, we bivouacked near Malpartida de Placencia, when a report reached our corps that a battle had been fought at Talavera, and that the English had been beaten and dispersed. Although I believe few of us gave credit to the story, still it created some uneasiness amongst men and officers. Its effect, however, upon our brigadier was to make him hurry forward with, if possible, increased speed. Our bivouac was immediately broken up. We got under arms, and leaving the sick of the brigade behind us in the town under charge of a subaltern from each regiment, we commenced one of the longest marches, with scarcely a halt or pause, in the military records of any country. To use the words of our admirable historian of the Peninsular War,[1] we 'passed over sixty-two miles and in the hottest season of the

[1] *History of the War in the Peninsula and in the South of France from 1807 to 1814* (1828–40) by Colonel, later Major-General, Sir William Napier.

year in twenty-six hours'. As Colonel Napier justly observes, 'Had
the historian Gibbon known of such a march, he would have spared
his sneer about "the delicacy of modern soldiers".'

As we approached Talavera, we learned for a fact, that a battle
had been fought from the crowds of disorderly Spanish soldiery we
continued to meet upon the road; some few of them were wounded.
These men were part of General Cuesta's army that had been beaten
by the French on the 27th, and who chose to give the most disastrous
account of the English army, which they stated was completely destroyed. We could not but remark, that these Spaniards, whom we
knew to be a disorganised crew, had not forgotten to help themselves
to plunder in their flight, as most of them carried some article or other
to which they could have little claim, such as hams, cheese and fowls.
Some, although infantry-men, rode on excellent horses, while others
drove mules, carrying sacks of flour, etc. Never was seen such a
thoroughly demoralised wreck of an army.

As we advanced nearer to the scene of action the reports became
less formidable, until the heights of Talavera burst upon our sight,
and we hailed, with three loud huzzas, the news that the British, in the
action of the preceding day with the French, had been victorious.

Our bugles struck up merrily as we crossed the field of battle
early in the morning, on the 29th July. The scene, however, was most
appalling, especially to the young soldiers; we had partaken in no
encounter as yet, and here had missed the interest which blunted the
feelings of the men engaged. We 'raw ones', indeed, had as yet
scarcely seen the enemy, and recognised no comrades among the
fallen. The ice still remained to be broken which the experience of one
engagement would have done effectually. The field of action had
occupied an extensive valley, situated between two ranges of hills,
on which the British and French armies were posted. It was now
strewn with all the wreck of the recent battle. The dead and dying,
to the amount of some thousands, conquerors and conquered, lay
diversely in little heaps, interspersed with dismounted guns, and
shattered ammunition-waggons, while broken horse-trappings, and
blood-stained shakos, and other torn paraphernalia of military pomp
and distinction, completed the reality of the battle scene.

The long grass which had taken fire during the action was still
burning, and added dreadfully to the sufferings of the wounded and
dying of both armies; their cries for assistance were horrifying, and
hundreds might have been seen exerting the last remnant of their
strength, crawling to places of safety.

In the midst of this, it was that I saw, for the first time, our immortal chief, Sir Arthur Wellesley. I also then beheld that deformed-looking lump of pride, ignorance and treachery, General Cuesta.[1] He was the most murderous-looking old man I ever saw.

On our arrival we were immediately ordered upon outpost duty: in executing which we had to throw out a line of sentinels facing the French position. Another and a more painful duty that devolved upon us, was to carry the wounded men into the town of Talavera. Many of these poor fellows, I remarked, were dreadfully burnt.

In consequence of the increasing weakness of the British army at this period, the ranks of which were daily thinned through the scantiness and wretched quality of the food with which they were, of necessity, supplied, as well perhaps as by the accession of strength which the French had received, Lord Wellington[2] was induced to retire. After retracing, for a few days, the route by which we had arrived, our brigade was left by the main army encamped upon a rocky eminence partly surrounded by wood, and overlooking the River Tagus. It was a wild and beautiful scene, with several corn-fields in our immediate neighbourhood.

Our living here became truly savage. Although we remained at this place for two or three weeks, I think we scarcely received half a dozen rations during that period, but existed, as we could, by our own ingenuity. Fortunately for us, as regards meat, there were some droves of pigs that were taken into the woods to feed, and which fattened upon the acorns. To these animals, that were generally under the charge of some Spaniards, we were obliged to have recourse for food. For bread we took the corn from the fields, and, having no proper means of winnowing and grinding it, were obliged as a substitute to rub out the ears between our hands, and then pound them between stones to make into dough, such as it was. From this latter wretched practice, we christened the place 'Dough Boy Hill', a name by which it is well remembered by the men of our division.[3]

1 General Don Gregorio García de la Cuesta (1740–1812) commanded the Spanish army in the Talavera campaign of 1809.

2 After the battle of Talavera, Sir Arthur Wellesley was created Viscount Wellington on 4 September 1809; he became Earl of Wellington on 28 February 1812, Marquess of Wellington on 3 October of the same year, and Duke of Wellington on 11 May 1814. He was promoted to field-marshal on 3 July 1813, in recognition of his victory at the battle of Vittoria.

3 Harry Smith says it was so called 'from our having nothing to eat for three weeks but dough and goat's flesh, and very little of either'. Simmons writes:

From the preceding place we marched to Campo Mayor [11 September]; we remained here three months, during which time a dreadful mortality took place. In our regiment, alone, the flux and brain fever reigned to so frightful an extent, that three hundred men died in hospital. I myself was seized with the prevailing fever shortly after our arrival, and was sent to the Convent of St Paul, the general hospital at Elvas.

I could not help remarking the manner of cure adopted by our doctors; it principally consisted in throwing cold water from canteens or mess kettles as often as possible over the bodies of the patients; this in many cases was effectual, and I think cured me.

I, however, had a narrow squeak for my life, though I fortunately recovered after an illness of nearly six weeks, thanks to my good constitution, but none to the brute of an orderly, who, during the delirium of the fever, beat me once most furiously with a broom stick. On leaving the hospital with other convalescents, I was sent to the Bomb Proof Barracks, where it frequently became our duty to see the dead interred. This was a most horrible office, and obliged us to attend at the hospital to receive the bodies, which were conveyed away in cart-loads at a time to the ground appropriated for their burial. This lay outside the town beneath the ramparts, and was so very small for the purpose required, that we were obliged to get large oblong and deep holes excavated, in which two stout Portuguese were employed to pack the bodies, heads and heels together, to save room. For this duty these two brutes seemed duly born—for never before did I see two such ruffianly looking fellows.

It was singularly revolting to witness how the pair went to work when handing the bodies from the hospital to the cart; each carried a skin of vinegar, with which they first soused themselves over the neck and face; this done, with one jerk they jilted a single corpse at a time across their shoulders, naked as it was born, and bolted off to the cart, into which it was pitched as if it had been a log of wood. The women, however, who fell victims to the epidemic were generally sewed in a wrapper of calico or some such thing, but they partook of the same hole as the opposite sex, and otherwise were as little privileged. Many were the scores of my poor comrades I thus saw

---

'A more appropriate name for it would have been *Starvation* Hill, as a small quantity of goat's flesh and a little coarse pea-flour was all we obtained here daily. The flour was made up into little cakes by each individual and put upon a thin stone over a fire until sufficiently done.'

committed to their first parent, and many were the coarse jests the gravediggers made over their obsequies.

While I was confined in hospital, the brigade marched and took up their cantonments between Ciudad Rodrigo and Almeida. In the beginning of February about three hundred convalescents, among whom I was one, were marched, under charge of an officer of the German Legion, to join their respective regiments. Nothing of any consequence, in the march of our party, occurred, with the exception of a very narrow escape I had of being provosted, or in other words flogged. As the anecdote serves to show the light in which the Germans regarded this description of punishment during the war, I will detail it.

The men being from different regiments, and under the command of a foreigner, some availed themselves of what they considered a fair opportunity of pilfering from the country people as we pursued our march, and I am sorry to say that drunkenness and robbery were not unfrequent. The German officer, as is usual under such circumstances, experienced great difficulty in keeping the skulkers and disorderly from lingering in the rear. In compliment to my steadiness, he had made me an acting corporal, with strict orders to make the rear men of our detachment keep up. Just before we arrived at the town of Viseu, then occupied by the Foot Guards, and the headquarters of the Commander-in-Chief,[1] I came up to some of our party who were doing their best to empty a pig-skin of wine they had stolen. Being dreadfully fatigued and thirsty, I had not sufficient restraint upon myself to refuse the invitation held out to me to drink, which I did, and so became a partner in the crime. I was in the act of taking the jug of wine from my lips, when a party of the 16th Light Dragoons rode up and made us prisoners; the peasant, from whom the wine had been taken, having made his complaint at headquarters. We were imprisoned, nine of us in number, in Viseu. The second day, the Hon. Captain Pakenham,[2] of the Adjutant-General's department,

1 From January to 27 April 1810.

2 The Honourable Captain Pakenham was a brother-in-law to the Duke of Wellington. This gentleman, who belonged to my regiment, was much beloved by us all. He was also so considerate! On every occasion when the fresh arrival of necessaries, meat, wine, etc., brought the men in crowds about the stores, he invariably would abide his turn, and, as though he were one of ourselves, oblige every new-comer, whatever his rank, to submit to the same. This, though mere justice, for its rare occurrence with the other officers, was never forgotten by the men. Since his return from the Peninsula I have been told he was ordered to New Orleans, where he was killed. [E.C.]

paid us a visit, and told us he had had great difficulty in saving us from being hanged. Although this was probably said to frighten, still it was not altogether a joke, as a man of the name of Maguire of the 27th regiment, who had been with me in hospital, was hung for stopping and robbing a Portuguese of a few *vintems*.[1]

As it was, the German officer in charge of the detachment received orders, on leaving Viseu, to see that we received two dozen each from the Provost-Marshal every morning, until we rejoined our regiments. This comfortable kind of a breakfast I was not much inclined to relish, particularly as we had seven days' march to get through before we reached our battalion. The following day, the eight culprits and myself were summoned during a halt, to appear before the German, expecting to be punished. We were, however, agreeably deceived by the officer addressing us as follows, to the best of my recollection, in broken English:

'I have been told to have you mens flogged, for a crime dat is very bad and disgraceful to de soldier—robbing de people you come paid to fight for. But we do not flog in my country, so I shall not flog you, it not being de manner of my people; I shall give you all to your Colonels; if they like to flog you, they may.'

Being thus relieved, each of us saluted the kind German and retired. From that moment, I have always entertained a high respect for our Germans, which indeed they ever showed themselves deserving of, from the British, not only on account of their humanity and general good feeling to us, but from their determined bravery and discipline in the field. As cavalry, they were the finest and most efficient I ever saw in action; and I had many opportunities of judging, as some troops of them generally did duty with us during the war. Indeed, while alluding to the cavalry of the German Legion, I cannot help remarking on the care and fondness with which they regarded their horses. A German soldier seldom thought of food or rest for the night until his horse had been provided for. The noble animals, themselves, seemed perfectly aware of this attention on the part of their riders, and I have often been amused by seeing some of the horses of the Germans run after their masters with all the playfulness of a dog. The consequence of this attention to their horses was, they were in condition when those of our own cavalry were dying, or otherwise in very deplorable state; this, without wishing to throw a disparage-

[1] About a penny, since one Portuguese dollar equalled 40 *vintems*, equivalent to 4s. 6d. at the time.

ment upon our own countrymen, I attributed to the difference of custom between the two countries. We never saw a German vidette or express galloping furiously, that we did not immediately know there was work for someone to do. While on outpost duty their vigilance was most admirable.

V

I rejoined my regiment at Barba del Puerco, a small village near the banks of the River Coa, on the other side of which the enemy had taken up their position. Our regiment was cantoned in the surrounding villages, while nightly we mounted a captain's picquet on a height facing a bridge, on the other side of which the French had thrown out their advanced sentry. Two of our sentries were posted on the bridge, while a third was stationed half-way down the steep, to keep up the communication with our picquet above.

On the 19th of March, the company to which I belonged was on picquet. It was a fine, though windy night, a fleecy scud occasionally obscuring the light of the moon. About twelve o'clock, while our men were mostly asleep, we were suddenly woke by the rifle reports of our sentries, and the French drums playing their advance 'rub-a-dub-dub', which our men designated with the name of 'old trousers'.[1] I was now, as it were, but a young sleepy-headed boy, and as yet had been scarcely aroused to a true sense of the profession I had embraced. I had never been under the fire of a French musket, and I felt an indescribable thrill on this occasion. The chilly hour of the night and peculiar inclination to sleep, at the time, had sunk my senses below

[1] Kincaid explains this as 'a name given by our soldiers to the point of war which is beat by the French drummers in advancing to the charge. I have, when skirmishing in a wood, and a French regiment coming up to the relief of the opposing skirmishers, often heard the drum long before we saw them, and, on those occasions, our riflemen immediately began calling to each other, from behind the different bushes, "Holloa there! look sharp! for damme me, but here comes old trousers!" '

zero. But I was speedily startled out of my lethargy by the whizzing of the enemies' bullets, as they greeted my astonished hearing. My surprise soon, however, gave place to perfect recollection, and in less than a minute we were all under arms, the balls of the French whistling about us as a column came rushing over the bridge to force our position. Captain O'Hare, with his characteristic coolness, immediately gave us the word to 'seek cover', and we threw ourselves forward among the rocky and broken ground, from whence we kept up a galling fire upon those who had commenced storming our heights.

We were exceedingly hard pressed when three companies of our regiment, under Colonel Beckwith, came up to our relief, and the contest for a while was both doubtful and bloody. But, after about half an hour's hard fighting, the enemy were obliged to retreat with much precipitation, and under a close and murderous fire from us. During this brief conflict some incidents occurred that, perhaps, are worth mentioning. Colonel Beckwith actually employed himself, at one time, in heaving large fragments of stone upon the French as they attempted to ascend the acclivity on which we were placed, and, while so engaged, got a musket-shot through his cap.

Another officer of ours, the adjutant, Lieutenant Stewart, a fine tall fellow, was engaged in a personal contest with two of three grenadiers, a number of whom had managed to ascend the hill on our right; at this critical moment one of our men, named Ballard, fortunately came to his aid, and shot one of his assailants, at which the other instantly surrendered. The above gallant officer, however, afterwards fell on our advance from Santarem the following year [*March 1811*].

This was, I believe, the first and last time the French ever attempted surprising a rifle picquet.

Both our sentries at the bridge were taken prisoners, one of them badly wounded. A rather interesting recollection is attached to one of them, named Meagher [?*Maher*], who, when the exchange of prisoners took place in 1814, returned to England and rejoined us at Dover. He was with us in France at the time of Waterloo, which, however, he was not present at on account of the following circumstance.

A quarrel had originated a few nights before the battle of Waterloo in a wine-house at Brussels, between some of our men, and the Belgian gens-d'armes; the consequence was, that the inhabitants were forced to send for the guards. These, of course, were soon on the spot, but were as soon attacked and beaten back by the Belgians, who would have driven them into the guard-house but for Meagher, who, suddenly turning to the assailants, levelled his rifle and shot the foremost through the body; on this, the whole of the gens-d'armes retreated, not, however, till after Meagher had received a cut on the side of the neck. For this affair he was put into prison, and a general court-martial honourably acquitted him, not until the battle had been fought which for ever destroyed Napoleon's hopes. Our company, to which Meagher belonged, soon after presented a requisition to Captain Leach, who then commanded us, and through his intercession, Meagher obtained a Waterloo medal.

Shortly after this attempted surprise, we quitted Barba del Puerco [*29 April*] for the town of Gallegos, situated some five or six miles from Ciudad Rodrigo.

The following laughable incident occurred to me while we lay at Gallegos: I happened to be acquainted with General Craufurd's private servant, a German, chiefly through my being employed as orderly to the brigadier. At times when an opportunity offered, we used to take a glass of wine together upon the most convivial terms. One morning, however, when I thought the brigadier had gone out, as was his usual custom, I went to his room to ask the valet to partake of some wine which I had received from the patron of the house. On opening the door, I unhesitatingly went in, and beheld, as I imagined, the individual I wanted in a morning-gown looking out of the window. It entered into my head to surprise my servant friend, so, as he had not been disturbed by my approach, I stepped softly up to his rear, and with a sudden laugh, gave him a smart slap on the back. But my consternation and surprise may be better imagined than described, when the gentleman in the dressing-gown, starting round with a 'Who the devil is that?' disclosed—not the merry phiz of the valet, but the stern features of General Craufurd himself.

I thought I should have sunk through the ground at the moment, had it have opened to swallow me. I could only attempt to explain the mistake I had made, in a very humble way, as I gradually retreated to the door.

'And where did you get the wine from, Sir?' inquired the General, with a good-humoured smile; for he observed the fright I was in.

I informed him.

'Well, well, you may go,' said the General; 'but, pray, Sir, never again do me the honour to take me for my servant.'

I needed not the permission to vanish in a moment. And many a laugh and jest were created at my expense afterwards among the men, as the circumstance got circulated by the valet.

We were here joined by the 1st and 3rd regiment of the Portuguese Caçadores.[1] These fellows I never had any opinion of from the very first moment I saw them. They were the dirtiest and noisiest brutes I ever came across. Historians of the day have given them great credit; but during the whole of the Peninsular War, or, at least, the time they were with us, I never knew them to perform one gallant act. On the line of march they often reminded me of a band of strollers. They were very fond of gambling, and every halt we made was sure to find them squatted, and with cards in their hands.

One of these regiments was placed under the command of a captain of ours, named Elder, a brave officer, who was made Colonel of the 3rd; and being afterwards severely wounded at Badajoz, returned to England; at the same period, also, we were incorporated with the 14th and 16th Light Dragoons, together with the 3rd regiment of German Hussars, and Captain Bull's troop of horse artillery.

The French had now commenced laying siege to Rodrigo, and we were terribly harassed by the severity of our duty, being both day and night accoutred and under arms; indeed, we were daily expecting an attack.

A section of our rifles usually mounted picquet with a troop of dragoons, and occupied, accordingly, three different points—Carpio, Molina dos Flores and Marialva; all about two miles nearer to Rodrigo. Bull's troop of artillery remained always near a church, in the centre of the village of Gallegos, and at all times kept a gun ready loaded with blank carriage, and a sentry near it, watching a beacon erected on a hill, about a mile from the village. A vidette and one of our riflemen were placed near the beacon in case of the picquets being attacked, to give alarm by discharging his piece into the combustibles, and so setting it on fire; or, in case of its not igniting, to ride round it three times, with his cap mounted on his sword, at which signal the gun was instantly fired, and the whole division were immediately under arms.

As I have remarked, we were greatly harassed; our picquets and the French were constantly in the habit of firing at each other, and scarce a day passed without some of the men being brought in, either killed or wounded. We had not yet established that understanding with the enemy, which avoided unnecessary bloodshed at the outposts which afterwards tended much to humanize the war.

Meanwhile the siege of Rodrigo was vigorously carried on by the

[1] Light Infantry. The word literally means 'hunters' or 'huntsmen'.

French. The weather was intensely hot, and we delighted in bathing
in a small river that flowed between the beacon-hill and the village.
Many of us, while so amusing ourselves, would take these opportunities to wash our shirts in the running stream, laying them out to
dry on the sand. Frequently, however, when thus employed, the
alarm gun would be fired, and in a moment we might be observed,
like so many water sprites, jumping out of the stream and hurrying
on the wet shirts, actually wringing, and throwing them over our
shoulders, while we fell in with our comrades. It was rather surprising,
that I never felt any ill effects from these wet habiliments; but the
men, from constant exposure, had become as hardy as the soil itself.

From the novelty, however, of the picquet duty, the men preferred it always to any other: as we amused ourselves generally at
night watching the shells exchanged between the besieged and the
assailants, the sight was very beautiful, sometimes as many as seven
or eight-and-twenty crossing each other, like so many comets.

Once [26 June] we were visited by the Duke himself, who, although
his headquarters were at the time at Viseu, distant somewhat about
twenty leagues, had come on a reconnoitring excursion to our outline
picquets. While on sentry one day I recollect his Grace placing his
telescope on my shoulders to take a view of the enemy's position. Our
intelligence was chiefly derived from deserters, a number of whom
daily came over to us, and gave information that Ciudad could not
hold out much longer.

One day we were unusually alarmed by an extraordinary bustle in
the French camp; being on the advanced picquet, I could distinctly
hear the cheering of men and firing of cannon: the whole of our
division was ordered to fall in, and it was not until the morning following, that we learned that it originated in the news from Paris of the
Emperor's marriage with the Archduchess Marie Louise of Austria
[2 April 1810].

We now daily held ourselves in expectation of an attack, and
were under arms every morning at one o'clock, five minutes only
being allowed for the whole division to fall in. But we seldom took
our accoutrements off, and used both to sleep and to cook with them
on. The baggage was paraded every morning half a mile to the rear,
and every other precaution taken by the Brigadier for an orderly
retreat, as the French were in our front and in overwhelming force,
while our division was scarcely more than four thousand strong. One
of the General's stratagems to make our small force appear more
numerous in the eyes of the French, was to draw the regiments up in

rank entire. After, however, several months of severe hardship at Gallegos, General Craufurd was at last obliged to change his ground, and we retreated to Alamada, a little town about two miles in our rear, and on the main road leading to the fortified town of Almeida: we remained here a few days, and took a French spy, who had passed among us as a lemonade-merchant. His indifference and carelessness in accepting remuneration for his beverage, which was in constant request, together with his laughing one day very significantly when one of our men was swearing at the French for the trouble they caused, induced a sergeant to apprehend him. He was brought before General Craufurd, and on his being searched, letters were found upon him that proved him to be a French Colonel. He was sent to the rear: how, indeed, he managed to escape the doom he had rendered himself liable to, I know not.

A few mornings after this, the French came down in great force, and we were obliged to retire. This we did slowly, covered by Captain Ross's guns and our rifles, assisted also by a few troops of the 14th and 16th Dragoons and 3rd German Hussars. We retired with very little loss, for a distance of four or five miles, to Fort Conception in front of the little town of Val de Mula. Here we went into cantonments. We were now close on the borders of Portugal, which is here divided from Spain only by a small stream—at this spot, so narrow, that in some places it may be jumped over. We daily mounted a picquet of two companies at the fort, which was a beautiful work, in the shape of a star.

VI

A few days after our arrival at Val de Mula, a part of the division formed a night expedition to surprise and cut off one or two French regiments that nightly occupied an advanced position on our right, retiring every morning about daylight. The rifles got under arms at ten o'clock at night, and were soon afterwards joined by several companies of the 43rd and 52nd regiments, together with one or two troops of the 14th Light Dragoons, and some of our favourite Germans. We soon guessed that some secret enterprise was about to be undertaken, as strict orders were issued to keep the men from talking, and to make them refrain from lighting their pipes, lest our approach should be noticed by the enemy. Even the wheels of two of Captain Ross's guns that accompanied us were muffled round with haybands to prevent their creaking.

In this disposition we proceeded in the direction of the left of the enemy's position which rested on Villar de Puerco. We had all loaded before marching, and were anxiously looking forward to the result, when a whispering order was given to enter a large field of standing corn and to throw ourselves on the ground. There we anxiously waited the first dawn of day for the expected engagement. At length the cold grey of the morning appeared faintly in the east, when the commands were given with scarce a pause between to 'fall in', 'double', and 'extend'. This was accomplished in a moment, and forward we ran through the corn-field up to an eminence, looking down from which we beheld a gallant skirmish on the plain beneath. The 14th Dragoons were in the act of charging a body of French infantry, who had, however, thrown themselves into square. The cavalry cheered forward in gallant style, but the French, veteran-like stood firm to meet the onset, pouring in, at the same time, a close running fire that emptied many saddles. Lieutenant-Colonel Talbot, who headed the charge, fell almost immediately together with the quartermaster and from sixteen to eighteen privates. After an unavailing attempt to shake the square, the cavalry was obliged to retire— a movement which the enemy on their part immediately imitated. An attempt was made to annoy them with our guns, but in consequence of their smallness, being but light field-pieces, our shots were attended with very little effect.

The following day, we buried Colonel Talbot and the quartermaster close to the porch of the little chapel in the village we occupied —a somewhat romantic-looking spot for a soldier's grave. The miscarriage of our enterprise, it was generally rumoured, had brought our General into bad odour at headquarters; indeed, for some days after, I thought he wore a troubled look, as though he took our failure to heart.

As I have already remarked, two of our companies alternately did duty in front of our position, at Fort Conception. The orders issued to the officer commanding the picquet were to blow up the fort immediately on the approach of the enemy, for which purpose it was undermined in several places by the artillerymen, who were left to fire the mines when the order should be given.

On the morning of the 19th of July, our company and another were on duty at this point, and it was generally expected we should be attacked on the morrow. I think the intelligence was brought by a deserter. The fort contained a great quantity of good English rum and biscuit, which Captain O'Hare allowed the men of both companies to help themselves to and fill their canteens, upon their promise, which they kept, not to get drunk. The following morning, before it was scarcely light, the enemy proved the correctness of our anticipations by advancing upon us in heavy columns, preceded by their light troops. The command was instantly given to fire the mines, and we retired upon our division. A few minutes after our quitting the fort, its beautiful proportions, which had excited the admiration of so many beholders, was broken, as by the shock of an earthquake, into a blackened heap of ruin.

We retreated under the walls of Almeida, where we halted until the 23rd, when at night we experienced a storm that for violence, while it lasted, exceeded anything I had ever before beheld. The lightning, thunder, wind, and rain were absolutely awful. With a few other men, I had sought shelter in the hollow of a rock, where we were not a little amazed at the numbers of snakes and lizards which the occasional gleams of lightning exhibited to us running about in all directions, as though the tempest had the effect of bringing them all from their holes.

At break of day, the music that we were now getting quite accustomed to—*i.e.* the cracking of the rifles of our outline picquet, gave intelligence of the enemy's advance. Our company was immediately ordered to support them. Captain O'Hare accordingly placed us behind some dilapidated walls; we waited the approach of the picquet then under the Hon. Captain Stewart engaged about half a mile in our front, and slowly retreating upon us. They had already, as it afterwards appeared, several men killed, while Lieutenant M'Cullock had been wounded and taken prisoner with a number of others. We could distinctly see the enemy's columns in great force, but had little time for observation, as our advance ran in upon us followed by the French tirailleurs, with whom we were speedily and hotly engaged. The right wing of the 52nd regiment, at this period, was drawn up about one hundred yards in our rear behind a low wall, when a shell, which with several others was thrown amongst us from

the town, burst so near, that it killed several of our men, and buried
a sergeant so completely in mud, but without hurting him, that we
were obliged to drag him out of the heap, to prevent his being
taken by the enemy[1]—at this moment also Lieutenant Coane who
stood close to me received a shot through the body. My old
Captain, O'Hare, perceiving him roll his eyes and stagger, caught
him by the arm, saying in a rather soft tone to the men about
him:

'Take that poor boy to the rear, he does not know what is the
matter with him,' and with the same characteristic coolness he continued his duties. While hotly engaged, however, with the French
infantry in our front, one or two troops of their hussars which, from
the similarity of uniform, we had taken for our German hussars,
whipped on our left flank between our company and the wing of the
52nd, when a cry of "The French cavalry are upon us" came too late
as they charged in amongst us. Taken thus unprepared, we could
oppose but little or no resistance, and our men were trampled down
and sabred, on every side. A French dragoon had seized me by the
collar, while several others, as they passed, cut at me with their swords.
The man who had collared me had his sabre's point at my breast,
when a volley was fired from our rear by the 52nd, who by this time
had discovered their mistake, which tumbled the horse of my captor.
He fell heavily with the animal on his leg, dragging me down with
him.

It was but for a moment nevertheless: determined to have one brief
struggle for liberty, I freed myself from the dragoon's grasp, and
dealing him a severe blow on the head with the butt of my rifle, I
rushed up to the wall of our 52nd, which I was in the act of clearing
at a jump, when I received a shot under the cap of my right knee and
instantly fell. In this emergency, there seemed a speedy prospect of
my again falling into the hands of the French, as the division was
in rapid retreat, but a comrade of the name of Little instantly dragged
me over the wall, and was proceeding as quick as possible with me,
on his back, towards the bridge of the Coa, over which our men were
fast pouring, when he, poor fellow! also received a shot, which passing
through his arm smashed the bone, and finally lodged itself in my

1 I must here remark, that these shells were thrown at us by mistake, as the
town was in the possession of our friends the Portuguese, under the command
of Colonel Cox, a British officer, who from our position being near the enemy,
as well as our green dress, must have mistaken us for the latter. Almeida was
afterwards taken by the French. [E.C.]

33

thigh, where it has ever since remained.[1] In this extremity, Little was obliged to abandon me, but urged by a strong desire to escape imprisonment, I made another desperate effort, and managed to get over the bridge, from the other side of which Captain Ross's guns were in full roar, covering our retreat; in this crippled state and faint through loss of blood, I made a second appeal to a comrade, who assisted me to ascend a hill on the other side of the river.

On the summit, we found a chapel which had been converted into a temporary hospital, where a number of wounded men were being taken to have their wounds dressed by the surgeons. Fortunately, I had not long to wait for my turn, for as we momentarily expected the coming of the French, everything was done with the greatest dispatch.

In this affair our company sustained a very severe loss; our return was, "one officer, Lieutenant Coane, quite a youth, dangerously wounded, eleven file killed and wounded, and forty-five taken prisoners".

My old Captain O'Hare had only eleven men on parade next day. The preceding facts will serve to show the unmilitary reader, that skirmishes are frequently more partially destructive to riflemen than general actions, although attended with but little of their celebrity. For my own part, I was never nearer death, excepting on the night we took Badajoz [6 April 1812].

I must not forget a singular escape that occurred: a man of the name of Charity, of my own company, when the cavalry first rushed upon us, had fallen, wounded in the head by a sabre; while on the ground, he received another severe sword slash on the seat of honour, and a shot through the arm, the latter, no doubt, from the 52nd. Yet after all this, he managed to escape, and

Clothed in scarlet lived to tell the tale,

as a pensioner in Chelsea Hospital.

Having no mules nor waggons to accommodate us, the surgeons advised all who were by any means capable of moving, to get on as quick as they could to Pinhel.

There were of our regiment about seventy or eighty disabled, a number of those hobbled onwards assisting each other by turns.

We commenced our slow and painful march, and by the help of a

Strange as it may appear, this ball may be this hour felt with as much ease as the first day it entered, forty-two years back. [E.C.]

couple of rifles that served as crutches, I managed to reach the first village where the Juiz [de Fora] or chief magistrate selected and put the worst of our wounded into bullock carts. Amongst those I fortunately was one; and although crammed with six others into a wretched little vehicle, scarcely capable of accommodating more than two, I thought it a blessing for which I could not feel sufficiently thankful.

In this manner, we were dragged along all night, and by the following daylight we halted at another village, where I felt so dreadfully faint from loss of blood and my confined position, that I could not move at all. While refreshing our parched lips with some water that had been eagerly demanded, Lord Wellington and some of his staff galloped up. Glancing his eye at us for a moment, and seeing our crowded condition in the carts, he instantly gave an order to one of his aides-de-camp to obtain additional conveyance from the Juiz de Fora, and also bread and wine. His Lordship then rode off towards Almeida.

Although neither bread nor wine made their appearance, a few additional carts were procured, into one of which I was transferred with four other men.

We again continued our march, until we came into a stream of water where we halted;[1] here we lost a most excellent officer, a Lieutenant Pratt,[2] who was wounded through the neck, and at first appeared to be doing very well. He was seated on one of the men's knapsacks conversing with some of his wounded brother officers, when he was suddenly seized with a violent fit of coughing, and almost instantly began pumping a quantity of blood from the wound. I never before saw so much come from any man.

It appeared that the ball, which went through his neck, had passed so close to the carotid artery, that the exertion of coughing had burst

---

[1] They reached the Mondego at Pinhel on 31 July.

[2] Among the officers wounded was the present Sir H. Smith, his brother Tom also. The former being on the staff had a *cedan* with two mules to carry him; the latter was packed with the men in bullock-carts. [*E.C.*]

Harry Smith writes: 'In collecting transport for the wounded, a sedan chair between two mules was brought, the property of some gentleman in the neighbourhood, and, fortunately for me, I was the only person who could ride in it, and by laying my leg on the one seat and sitting on the other, I rode comparatively easy to the poor fellows in the wretched bullock-carts, who suffered excruciating agony, poor brother Tom (who was very severely wounded above the knee) amongst the rest.'

it, and it became impossible to stop the hæmorrhage. He bled to death, and warm as he was, they covered him in the sand and proceeded.[1] After we had been driven some few miles further, one of my wounded comrades, who was shot through the body, and whose end seemed momentarily approaching, at length in a dying state relaxed his hold from the cart sides and fell across me as I lay at the bottom, whilst foam mixed with blood kept running from his mouth. This with his glass eyes fixed on mine made me feel very uncomfortable. Being weak and wounded myself, I had not power to move him, and in this situation, the horrors of which survived for some time in my mind, death put an end to his sufferings, but without granting me any respite for some hours. His struggles having ceased, however, I was enabled to recover myself a little, and called to the driver to remove the body. But the scoundrel of a Portuguese, who kept as much ahead of the bullocks as possible, was so afraid of the French, that I could get no other answer from him than 'Non quireo', 'Don't bother me', and a significant shrug of the shoulder, which bespoke even more than his words.

At length we arrived at Freixedas on the road to Coimbra, where we found the 1st division encamped outside the town. Here I got rid of my dead comrade, and we had our wounds dressed. The Guards, who belonged to the 1st division,[2] behaved to us with a kindness which I never can forget; as we had no men of our own to attend to us, forty of their number, under an officer, were ordered to supply our wants until we arrived at Lisbon.

[1] Simmons writes: 'Pratt went ashore to get some milk for our breakfast, as we rested, to give the rowers breathing time. I suppose the exertion he used, the day being very hot, had assisted to remove the slough in the wound in his throat, the carotid artery being injured; he died instantly from one gush of blood.' Pratt was interred at Coimbra.

[2] 1st Coldstream and 1st Scots Guards.

VII

From Freixeda we pursued our way to Mondego, and from thence we passed in boats down the river through Coimbra, to the sea-port of Figueira. Sick and ill as I was, I well recollect the exquisite scenery that met our gaze on the banks of that beautiful river, as we floated over its surface to our destination.

The heat of the weather was intense and dreadfully affected our wounds. The scarcity of doctors too, and the fear of falling into the hands of the enemy, spurred everyone forward, and so took up the moments that the surgeons had not time sufficient nor opportunity to look after us. The consequence was, that this neglect caused maggots to be engendered in the sores, and the bandages, when withdrawn, brought away on them lumps of putrid flesh and maggots. Many died on board, and numbers were reduced in consequence to the necessity of amputation. By care and syringing sweet oil into my wounds, I however had managed to get rid of them.

At Figueira we embarked on board some transports that there waited our arrival, and we sailed for Lisbon, where, in a short time, we landed, and borne on stretchers by some men of the Ordenança or Portuguese Militia, were conveyed to the hospital.

From regular and kind treatment there, I soon recovered; and the British army retired towards Lisbon.

It may perhaps be necessary, before I continue my personal narrative, to observe, that Lord Wellington, finding his numbers greatly unequal to the enemy, was obliged to retreat. This, it is well known, he directed in a very skilful manner, having long before anticipated the probability of such an event by the erection of the lines of Torres Vedras. During the retreat, his Lordship ordered the people of the country to accompany the troops, and to destroy all those things which they could not carry with them. By this precaution, Massena's army, on the track of the British and Portuguese, through want of food and necessaries, were reduced to the greatest privations, of which the Marshal bitterly complained in his dispatches of that period.

Perhaps few events in the Peninsular War reflect more credit upon Lord Wellington, as a commander, than the admirable manner in which he had thus drawn an overwhelming force of the French into actual famine, in front of works that afforded security and plenty to his own comparatively small force.

In a few weeks after our arrival at Lisbon, I became sufficiently recovered to leave the hospital and was accordingly transferred to Belem, a place much noted amongst us for every species of skulk, but better known to my fellow soldiers as the 'Belem Rangers'. The chief part of the 58th and 87th regiments, the latter I believe from the severe loss they had sustained at Talavera, were doing duty there.

Belem itself is about two miles from Lisbon, but contiguous to it, or, as the suburbs of London are to the city. I was here, as it were, quite at my ease; and usually spent my time rambling about the quays. The port was thronged with shipping, bringing troops and stores from England, and if I recollect rightly, the *Hibernia*, the *Caledonia*, and the *Britannia*, and other ships of war lay in the bay; at all events, we constantly intermixed with the sailors, and were mostly coupled with them; some recognising old friends—town-mates; and others, nearer and dearer ties, and forming new links and acquaintances; this the peculiarity of our situations naturally tended to strengthen, fighting as we were in the same cause, though on different elements. . . .

Among the officers of our battalion that had been wounded at Almeida, was one Captain Mitchell, who having received a ball through the arm, was transferred with us to Lisbon: when sufficiently recovered, he one morning came to the convalescent barrack to muster those who were willing and able to rejoin their regiments. Amongst others selected, was a man named Billy M'Nabb, of our corps, a most notorious skulker and a Methodist. He had scarcely ever done duty with his company, but had remained sneaking about the hospital as an orderly; and occasionally preaching and praying to the drunken soldiers in the streets of Lisbon. Captain Mitchell, however, had made up his mind that M'Nabb should see the enemy before he returned to England, and as a 'persuasive', when Billy most violently resisted the summons, ordered him to be tied to the bullock cart, amid the jeers of the soldiers, and conveyed back to his regiment. But it was only for a short period, as Billy got tired of the 'sight', and took the earliest opportunity to decamp, for he suddenly disappeared from among us, and but for my having seen him since preaching in the streets of London, should have been inclined to think he never returned home at all.

The morning that the convalescents fell in to start for the main army, we were joined by a batch of recruits, chiefly intended for the 68th and 85th regiments. They were a squad of plump, rosy-cheeked, smart-looking fellows, and like ourselves, each of them had been provided with five days' rations in advance; consisting of salt pork, biscuits, and rum, the first of which they cooked ready for the march.

Their officer in command was an astonishing man, nearly seven feet high. I shall never forget him: by his high-cheeked bones and dark complexion, I took him at first to be a foreigner; but as soon as he spoke, his broad accent declared him to be a North Briton, as far north as could be. He seemed well acquainted with every theory, or that part of a campaign which is generally digested at home; and as a sample of this, he ordered his men, in accordance with the regulations of Dundas,[1] the then Commander-in-Chief, to halt and rest ten minutes or a quarter of an hour at the end of every three miles.

'Coom, men,' he would say, pulling out his gold watch, 'ye ken, I suppose, yer three miles is up, set ye down and eat a pound, the mair ye tak into yer stomachs the less ye'll carry on yer backs.' This over, the watch would be again in requisition, and it would be, 'Coom men, yer quarter of an hour is nearly up, ye maun aye be ganging again'; and the men, of course, would fall in. By thus halting every three miles, and eating a pound each time, before we reached Jafra, at the end of the second day's march, the men had 'pounded' the whole of their five days' rations, and some of them began to growl most confoundedly from the want of provisions. Wishing to know the cause, he sent for the sergeant, and desired him to inquire, when the latter informed him.

'Hoot mon, ye dinna say that, do ye? Tell them all to fall in. I fear I maun chop a wee logic with them.'

'Oh ye hungry hounds,' he exclaimed, when the men appeared before him. 'Ye dinna ken the grand army yet; not content now, ye maun aye whistle then, for ye waunna get in ten days then what your hungry maws have now devoor'd in twa!' saying which, he placed himself at their head, to direct their movements when on the march. I used to liken him to a kite, while the files of short men after him reminded me of the tail. His shoulders were so broad and yet so skinny and square, and his height so convenient, that without stirring a peg from the front section he would wave his sword and look over their heads down the ranks and see every manœuvre.

Amongst the convalescents, but very recently from Cockneyshire, was a man named Josias Hetherington. This fellow was one of the

[1] General Sir David Dundas (1735–1820), Commander-in-Chief in 1809, was the author of *Principles of Military Movements, chiefly applicable to Infantry* (1788).

queerest I ever met with, and I verily believe had seen *service* before, but amongst gipsies, prigs [*knavish beggars*], gaol-birds, and travelling showmen. There was not a move but what he was up to, and in addition to these, he was an excellent ventriloquist, and terrified the inhabitants as we went along, whenever an occasion offered.

I think it was on the third day's march, we had stopped for the night in a small village, and as it happened, Josh and I got billeted in the same house together. Outside our quarters in front of the house was a small square (every town, village and pig-stye in Portugal has one), in the middle of which and while we were cooking our rations the inhabitants had commenced a fandango [*dance*]. This also is usual on Sundays in Portugal. Attracted by the whistle and a small drum beaten by a short, dumpy, ugly-looking lump of a Portuguese, Josh and I would occasionally run down to join, and leave our pots beside the Patrone's wood fire as close as we could to the red embers. But invariably, when we came in to take a peep at the boiling progress, we found our utensils moved aside and the contents as cold as charity. Josh looked at me, and I at Josh, the same as to say, 'Who the blazes moves our meat, about so?' Josh, however, hearing footsteps on the stairs, popped me and himself after into a kind of pantry. I partially closed the door, and there we stood watching.

In a few minutes in came the Patrone or lady of the house, and looking about her a little, bounced to our little utensils, and was proceeding to purloin the meat, muttering something to herself at the same moment. But she had scarcely put a hand to it, when a voice as if from the pot plainly told her to 'Sperum poco' (wait a little.) The old woman frisked up, looked doubtful, *crossed herself*, and with the courage *this* afforded, again attacked the pot. But the same words, only quick and smart as a rifle shot, sent her reeling and screeching to the corner of the kitchen. 'Oh Santa Maria! oh Jesu, oh la deos! Pedro aye el demonia ei in panello, (the devil's in the pot), Santa Maria ora—ora—ora—ora pro nobis!' and the good soul went off in a Portuguese fit.

Josh and I, scarcely able to contain our mirth, rushed out of the house instantly and joined in the crowd, which her screams were collecting about the doorway. The old Patrone, when she recovered, was off in a twinkling to the Priest and the Alcalde [*magistrate*], but it was all in vain, the billet could not be changed, for the whole village equally feared the devil, and we held quiet possession till the next morning, and might have carried away the house for what the old Patrone cared, for she left her domicile and never returned till we had marched out of the place.

The following day, 12th October 1810, I rejoined my regiment encamped near a small village on the lines of Torres Vedras, called Arruda, where I found my old Captain [O'Hare], who despite his severe loss, had scraped together a snug company, partly from men who had made their escape from the French after the affair at Almeida, but chiefly from a batch of recruits that joined our first battalion with the third of our regiment that came from England while I was in hospital. Arruda was a pretty little place enough until we mounted our picquets, when the men dreadfully defaced it, perhaps from a belief that the French might enter—a pleasure they never had.

The inhabitants whose fears had been enhanced by its exposed situation had nearly all evacuated the place, taking with them only the most portable and valuable of their effects, and leaving the houses, as it were, furnished and tenantless. The change was the more extraordinary from the circumstance of its pleasant site having for many years made it a country resort for the rich citizens of Lisbon.

For a few days after our arrival, it presented a picture of most wanton desolation. Furniture of a most splendid description in many instances was laid open to the spoliation of the soldiery. Elegant looking-glasses wrenched from the mantelpieces were wantonly broken to obtain bits to shave by, and their encasures, with chairs, tables, &c. &c., used as common firewood for the picquets; an Israelite would have gloated over the gilded embers, and have deemed perhaps one of them as under the value of what our united fireplaces might have been reduced to. These proceedings, however, unravel the secret of spending 'half a crown out of sixpence a day', and the philosophical reader will perhaps admit of the plea, that if we had not, the French would have done it for us, an event which we expected, though it fortunately never was realized.

Tom Crawley was particularly pre-eminent in this havoc; his enormous strength and length fitting him especially for the pulling down and 'breaking up' department.

Our company was one night on picquet at Arruda; we had, as usual, made a blazing fire close to the stable of a large house, which in the morning we had noticed contained a very handsome carriage (the only one by the by that I had ever seen in Portugal). Rather late in the evening we missed Tom—who, by the way, had a great love of exploring the houses of the village, and whom we imagined to be employed in his favourite amusement, 'looking for wine'. After having consumed sundry chairs to keep alive our fire, we found it necessary to obtain fresh fuel, and while consulting where it was to come from, one man, with an oath, proposed to burn the Portuguese coach. The novelty of the thing among our thoughtless fellows was received with acclamations, and as our officers were absent in a house close by, several started up on their legs for the purpose. The stable-doors were immediately opened, and the coach wheeled backwards into the large blazing fire. 'This will make a jolly roast!' exclaimed several of the men, as the paint and paneling began to crack under the influence of the heat. Our scamps were laughing and enjoying what they called a capital joke, but just as the flames were beginning to curl up around the devoted vehicle, a roar like that of a bull came from its interior, and threw us for a moment into consternation: immediately afterwards one of the glasses was dashed out, and Tom Crawley's big head was thrust through the window, amid shouts of laughter from the men, as he cried out—'Oh bad luck to your sowls! are you going to burn me alive?' At the same moment, urged powerfully by the heat of his berth, he made the most violent efforts to open the door, which from the handle being heated, was a difficult and painful operation. We had some trouble ere we could extricate the poor fellow, and then not before he was severely scorched. It afterwards appeared he had gone half tipsy into the carriage, and was taking a snooze, when he was so warmly awoke. After this occurrence, Crawley used to boast of going to sleep with one eye open.

At this period the French soldiers and ourselves began to establish a very amicable feeling, apart from duty in the field. It was a common thing for us to meet each other daily at the houses between our lines, when perhaps both parties would be in search of wine and food. In one of the houses so situated, I remember once finding Crawley in a drunken state in company with a couple of French soldiers. I was mortified by the merriment his appearance had excited, and could with difficulty get him away, as he stripped, and offered to fight the whole three of us for laughing at him.

VIII

About the middle of November the enemy retired, and we made a movement to follow them towards Santarem, which they immediately occupied and strongly fortified. As soon as we came in sight of their works, our battalion received orders to cross a river (the Rio Mayor), which discharged itself into the Tagus, about half a mile lower down on our right. While executing this movement, we met with rather a warm reception, which became more intense as we attempted to get a peep into their position; we however were obliged in turn to retreat, and finally took up our cantonments at a place called Valle. The regiment was distributed in companies on the houses on both sides of the main road, that to which I was attached being in an old wine-store near the bridge crossing the Mayor.

On this bridge we had double sentries, and abbatis of fallen trees. But the better to foil the incursions of the enemy, the arches had been undermined, and the powder secured from the wet by bullocks' hides, trained ready for explosion.

About two hundred yards in front of this were the French outlying sentries, and a little in their rear, on a slight eminence, their camp ground, which they had very beautifully built over with ranges of huts.

About three or four miles to our left, and divided from us by the Rio Mayor, rose the pretty town of Santarem; its towers and steeples peering up from the summit of a hill, studded on all sides with groves of olive-trees. The prospect from it must have been very 'soul-stirring', as the two armies lay within shell range, although they never interfered with each other for the whole of the four or five months that we were there; during this time we were flanked on the left and right by the 43rd and 52nd regiments, and enjoyed the most uninterrupted repose, almost our sole employment being to watch the French movements.

Some of the men, for want of better pastime, succeeded in constructing a still, with which they managed to make spirits from a quantity of dried grapes found in the old wine-house; a discovery, however, soon took place, much to our chagrin, and the still was destroyed by our old Captain, Peter O'Hare.

The sanguinary nature of the Portuguese during the whole period of the war was notorious. When crossed or excited, nothing but the shedding of blood could allay their passion. It was always with the greatest difficulty that we could preserve our French prisoners from being butchered by them even in cold blood. They would hang upon the rear of a detachment with prisoners like so many carrion birds, waiting every opportunity to satiate their love of vengeance; and it required all the firmness and vigilance of our troops to keep them in check. It was well known that even our men fell in stepping between them and the French, whom they had marked out as victims. Indeed it was not unfrequent for our own men to suffer from the consequences of their ferocity, and I myself, while at Valle, had a narrow escape. I had crossed the hills to purchase some necessaries at the quarters of the 52nd regiment, and on my return fell in with several of the soldiers of the 3rd Caçadores; one of them, a fierce-looking scoundrel, evinced a great inclination to quarrel, the more particularly as he perceived that I was unarmed and alone. Having replied rather sharply to some abuse they had cast upon the English, by reflecting on their countrymen in return, he flew into a rage, drew his bayonet, and made a rush at me, which I avoided by stepping aside, and tripping him head foremost on the ground; I was in the act of seizing his bayonet, when a number of his comrades came up, to whom he related, in exaggerated terms, the cause of our disagreement. Before he had half concluded, a general cry arose of 'kill the English dog', and the whole drawing their bayonets, were advancing upon me when a party of the 52nd came up, the tables were turned, and the Caçadores fled in all directions.

Among other laughable circumstances that made the time pass gaily while we remained here, was a ghost story, in which Tom Crawley cut rather a conspicuous figure. We had accoutred ourselves, as was our custom before laying down for the night's repose, when in rushed Tom Crawley like a distracted man.

'Bring me some salt and water for the love of God, boys!' he immediately demanded; 'I have seen a ghost.'

'What sort of ghost, Crawley?' sung out a dozen voices from the men, who immediately became alive to the fun.

'Oh, a Portuguese ghost, as sure as the Lord,' replied Crawley. 'Give me a little water with some salt in it.'

This salt, I must explain to the uninitiated, according to a vulgar superstition in Ireland, is absolutely necessary to be drunk by those who have seen a phantom before seeing a light, as a neglect of the precaution was sure to be followed by an evil influence. As soon, therefore, as a tin measure was brought to the agitated Tom (not filled, indeed, with salt and water, but, I am sorry to say, a much more objectionable liquid), Crawley drank it off with as much avidity as if his future salvation depended on it: the men, meanwhile, nearly convulsed with laughter at Tom's credulity.

At length, something like silence being restored, Crawley took a seat, at the same time making many wry faces (that were sufficiently accounted for by the potion he had swallowed). He then told us, in a very solemn manner, that he had distinctly seen the semblance of a Caçadore in Colonel Elder's regiment, the 3rd Caçadores, who used to sell our men rum on the retreat from Almeida, and who was afterwards killed at the battle of Busaco [27 September 1810].

'But did you not speak to it?' inquired Jack Murphy.

'You know I can't talk Portuguese,' replied Crawley.

'A ghost can talk any language; he would have spoken English to you if you had talked to him,' observed another.

'But I was in too great a fright to talk at all to him till he vanished away among the trees.'

Poor Tom Crawley! His ghost story afforded us ample amusement for many weeks afterwards, although I remember it caused his grog to be stopped, for having woke the Captain of our company in an adjoining room by the noise he had occasioned by his spiritual narration.

There is nothing, not even flogging, damps the spirit of a service-soldier more than stopping his grog, particularly a man of Crawley's temperament, for like his renowned prototype (Nautical Jack), if he were allowed three wishes, the first would be all the rum in the world, the second all the tobacco, and the third would be for more rum. During our stay here, the commissary had ovens made, and a number of our men employed baking bread, something after the fashion of our quartern loaf, one of which was allowed each man every four days. One day while the company was being served out with rations of salt beef and a hot four-pound loaf, and the commissary was busy in serving out rum from a barrel turned on the end, with the head knocked in, while the quarter-master was calling over the name of each man, when Crawley's name was called—stopped by order of Captain O'Hare, was the answer. Had sentence of death been pronounced, it could not have sounded more harsh; but Tom had a little philosophy. This trial put it to the test, for while he kept peeping over the men's shoulders, anxiously watching each man receive his portion of rum, I also observed him poking his thumb into different parts of the hot loaf, while he gradually kept edging himself through the men, until he got close to the rum barrel, and quietly putting his loaf under his arm, remained stationary, until the commissary turned round to speak to one of the men, when raising his arm in flopped the loaf into the rum-barrel, while he lustily began damning the awkward fellows who pushed, and caused the accident, no doubt wishing the loaf to remain soaking in the barrel as long as possible; but seeing the commissary about taking the bread out, he instantly dived his arm into the barrel, shoving the loaf to the bottom, then drawing it out dripping, as well as his coat-sleeve, and looking the commissary seriously in the face, begun cursing his misfortune, saying: 'Faith, Sir, I'll have a hot meal for the next four days, anyhow; if salt junk and hot rum don't blister a poor devil's guts, I don't know what will.' The good-natured commissary, who looked on the whole as a pure accident, handed Tom an extra half loaf, which he instantly squeezed against the wet one, lest a drop of the precious liquor should fall to the ground, and walked away, humming as he went:

'Oh, love is the soul of a neat Irishman', &c.

About this period we had a regiment of Brunswickers[1] sent to join our division, and one of our least amusing duties soon consisted in watching them, to prevent their deserting to the enemy. It was the prevalence of this honourable propensity among them, I believe, that induced Lord Wellington to distribute their force among the different divisions of the army. These 'death and glory men', as we used to term them, from their badge of the skull and cross-bones which was worn on their shakos and accoutrements, were dressed in dark green, which but too frequently enabled them to steal past our guards and join the French, with whom many of their connexions were. Among other attributes with which these allies were gifted, was a *canine* appetite, that induced them to kill and eat all the dogs they could privately lay hold of. By this means the different dogs of the division disappeared before the Germans with a celerity truly astonishing, and we were in ignorance of their fate until the fact became openly proclaimed and acknowledged. Among other animals thus 'potted for consumption' was a dog which, from its having

---

[1] In November 1810 the Brunswick Oels Jäger arrived from England. Leach writes: 'They deserted to the French in such numbers that we had a *lease* of them but for a few weeks. Lord Wellington caused several of them who had been taken in the attempt to desert to the enemy to be tried and shot.'

attached itself to our regiment, we had christened 'Rifle'. Rifle could never be induced to leave us, and upon one or two occasions when we had lost it, had always managed to rejoin us again. We used often to joke among ourselves at Rifle's antipathy to a red coat, and his decided preference to green; but although, poor fellow! he had survived many of our skirmishes, in which he used to run about barking and expressing his delight as much as a dog could, it was only, after all, to be devoured by the insatiable jaws of the Brunswickers.

We had in the company a sergeant of the name of Fleming, a tall athletic brave fellow from the Lake of Killarney. One night, being posted in picquet, he unluckily came in collision with one of the Brunswick officers, and suspecting his intentions to bolt to the enemy, knocked him down with his rifle and otherwise maltreated him. The result was that Fleming was tried by a brigade court-martial, convicted for the assault, and sentenced to be reduced to the ranks and to receive a corporal punishment of five hundred lashes. This put us all on the alert, and the officers also, by whom he was very much liked. The division being formed by order of General Craufurd, the prisoner was brought to the centre of the square, and the minutes of the court-martial read aloud, Fleming proceeded to strip, while the men stood attentively yet sullenly awaiting the result. The General now addressed him, saying:

'Prisoner Fleming, the offence which you have been guilty of is of so heinous a nature, that could it be proved to be wilfully committed, it would be most unpardonable; but the excellent character for gallantry and honourable conduct, given of you by your officers, is such that I take the responsibility on myself, relying on the plea made by you. I shall not flog you, therefore, but your stripes will be cut off, and I trust your future conduct will testify that the discretion I now use is not misplaced; and I here,' proceeded the General, turning round to the division, 'take the opportunity of declaring, that if any of those gentlemen (meaning the Brunswickers,) have a wish to go over to the enemy, let them express it, and I give my word of honour I will grant them a pass to that effect instantly, for we are better without such.'

Fleming was shortly afterwards reinstated, but, poor fellow! he was destined to an early though a more honourable fate, and fell leading on the ladder party, in the forlorn hope at Badajoz.

All this time, and for a great part of that in which we were quartered here, a very friendly intercourse was carried on between the French and ourselves. We frequently met them bathing in the Rio Mayor, and would as often have swimming and even jumping matches. In these games, however, we mostly beat them, but that was attributed, perhaps, to their half-starved, distressed condition. This our stolen intercourses soon made us more awake to, until at length, touched with pity, our men went so far as to share with them the ration biscuits, which we were occasionally supplied with from England, by our shipping; indeed we buried all national hostility in our anxiety to assist and relieve them. Tobacco was in great request; we used to carry some of ours to them, while they in return would bring us a little brandy. Their 'réveille' was our summons as well as theirs, and although our old Captain seldom troubled us to fall in at the 'réveille', it was not unusual to find the rear of our army under arms, and, perhaps, expecting an attack. But the Captain knew his customers, for though playful as lambs, we were watchful as leopards. . . .

IX

In the month of February, General Craufurd went to England on leave, and the command of the light division, during his absence, devolved upon Major-General Sir William Erskine.

On the night of the 5th March we were suddenly ordered to fall in, as intelligence had reached us that the French were evacuating Santarem. This was soon ascertained to be the fact, and we immediately commenced an advance, crossing the bridge in our front at three o'clock on the morning of the 6th.

Ours being the senior Captain of the regiment, the company, as was usual, were in the advance, when some of the front files suddenly came within a few yards of what appeared to be a French sentinel, leaning against a wall that ran along from the bridge. One of our fellows fired, but perceiving no movement made, we all rushed up, and discovered him to be, what our money-changers at home have so great a horror of, 'a man of straw', or a piece of sacking stuffed and accoutred. This afforded a fit theme for joking, as we carried our 'prisoner' with us until we came to Santarem.

Our march was uninterrupted, and over a bold thickly wooded

country, much cut up, however, by the retreating enemy; about mid-day we entered Santarem, where a sight of a most horrifying description offered itself. The streets and houses presented a mass of desolation and filth, which, in some degree, contaminated the air around, while to add to the picture, numbers of half-starved looking Frenchmen were grouped about in knots, and exhibiting the loath-some appearance of disease. The faces of many of these poor fellows were dreadfully swollen and white. Our men were moved to pity at the scene, and threw them biscuits as we passed through the town.

Massena had not the means of conveyance for the whole of his sick, and had been obliged to leave these to their fate. This, indeed, would have been soon decided had the Portuguese first come up with them.

At every mile the enemy, on their retreat, had fixed finger posts with directions to the road the 'grande armée' had taken; they sufficiently directed us also. But after all, these were of little service, for straggling groups of the unfortunate enemy strewed the road as we advanced over it. The poor fellows at first would greet the English with a faint hope of protection, and turned up their swollen and pallid countenances to us with expressions that needed not words to explain them. But we were obliged to pass on and leave them, for aught I know, to be butchered by the inhabitants, who fearfully retaliated for all the scenes we had witnessed. At night we encamped on the out-skirts of a small village, the name I do not recollect, but the sights within it I never can forget.

In searching for a stream from which I might procure water, I fell upon a small fountain, close to which lay two or three murdered Portuguese; their brains and blood, which seemed freshly to have oozed from their mangled remains, had even streamed into the spring, and turned me away with disgust from the water. Proceeding onward, I observed a gaunt ghastly figure in a cloak stealing towards a group of cadaverous-looking Frenchmen—on his getting a little nearer to them, he suddenly spat in his hands and throwing his cloak aside, produced a heavy club, with which, I suppose, he was going to beat their brains out. Struck with horror, I instantly seized the stick from his half-famished grasp, drove him away, and assisted by one or two comrades got the poor men into a house, and pursued my search.

As I, however, approached into the Plaza, the desolation thickened; all the havoc that can possibly be imagined in so small a compass lay before me—murdered and violated women—shrieking and dying children—and, indeed, all that had possessed life in the village lay quivering in the last agony of slaughter and awful vengeance.

These became every-day scenes until we overtook the French rear-guard at Pombal, which we did on the 11th; my company had been hurried forward by the cavalry, each dragoon mounting a rifle-man behind him on his horse—a method of riding peculiarly galling to the infantry, but which we frequently had to experience during the war. From the friction alone produced on the legs and seat by the dragoon's saddle-bags, it was some time before the foot-soldier, when placed upon his legs, could move with anything like dispatch. Besides, this method of riding was generally attended by the loss of the men's mess-tins, which became shaken off by the jolting. There were, indeed, few of our men who would not have preferred marching twice the distance on foot to being thus carried.[1]

We first got sight of the enemy about two miles from the town of Pombal. They had possession of a wood, from which, however, we soon managed to drive them. They retired in great disorder in the direction of the town. The long straight road that led to Pombal became filled for some hundred yards with the confused masses of the French; but their distress was still further increased by the arrival of Brigade-Major Mellish, who came up, at the time, with a couple of Ross's guns, and commenced playing upon them. It soon became a complete rout with the enemy, and they pressed pell-mell over the bridge of the river between us and the town. They suffered con-siderably in this business—the ground was strewed with their dead, and as we followed we found several poor fellows at the bridge badly wounded by the rifles, and many dissevered legs and arms, the latter, no doubt, caused by Ross's two pieces.

It was during the preceding skirmish that, for the first time, I heard the words that afterwards became so common in our regiment, 'kill a Frenchman for yourself'. Its origin was as follows: Two men of known daring, named Palmer and Tracey, during our approach to the bridge, seeing a French sergeant fall, ran up to claim the meed of conquest, by relieving him of any valuables he might be possessed of. They were quarrelling as to the appropriation of the spoil, when Palmer, who was a known excellent shot, told Tracey to go 'and kill a Frenchman for himself', as he had shot this man.

---

[1] With regard to knapsacks, of which so much has been spoken, I cannot see why they could not be carried by the quartermaster of commissariat, and given out with the same ease as the rations. This I apply only to the Rifles and other light troops, who, being always exposed and in advance, have need of all their energies and activity to render them fully effective. [E.C.]

This circumstance afterwards gave birth to a little gasconade [*boasting*] in the regiment, that every rifleman could and ought to kill a Frenchman in action. From the period of the above occurrence, Palmer received the nick-name of the 'man-killer', until a singular circumstance, that occurred at the siege of Badajoz, gave him a new title. In relieving picquet in the trenches, many of our men, instead of going quietly through the trenches or parallels in front of the walls of the town, used to show their contempt of danger by jumping out of them and running across in the face of the enemy's fire. In executing this feat one day with some others, a cannon-shot fired by the French struck the ground first, and then hit Palmer on the back, and he fell, as we thought, killed upon the spot. To our surprise, however, in a moment he jumped up unhurt, the ball having glanced off his knap-sack. In commemoration of this event, he was afterwards known by the appellation of 'the bomb-proof man'.

It must be borne in mind that my own company only were present here, and we had to sustain, at a great disadvantage, a smart fire from the different houses, occupied by the rear-guard of the enemy. As soon as we crossed the bridge we took possession of the houses opposite those held by the French, from which we kept up a brisk fire out of the windows. Tired, however, with this cross work, several of our men dashed into one of the French holds and found it crowded with the enemy, who to the number of thirty or forty quietly surrendered themselves prisoners. I recollect Sergeant Fleming, who was the first to mount the stairs, bundling them neck and crop over the staircase. Lieutenant Hopwood, however, fell severely wounded in the thigh on entering the house. We maintained the conflict until the remainder of the regiment came up, and then drove the enemy entirely out of their cover.

In the eagerness of pursuit, however, we had suffered severely: as our men followed the enemy a considerable distance out of the town, galling them terribly in the street, when perceiving how few our numbers were, being supported by a single troop only of our German Hussars,[1] they turned round and made it a hard matter for us to escape

---

[1] 1st Hussars of the King's German Legion. Kincaid says they were 'deserved favourites' of the Light Division. 'In starting from a swampy couch and bowling along the road long ere dawn of day, it was one of the romances of a soldier's life to hear them chanting their national war songs—some three or four voices leading and the whole squadron joining in the chorus. They were no less daring in the field than they were surpassingly good at outpost duty.' One May day in 1813 the Hussars were so affected by British cheering when the Light Division

the consequences of our temerity. Several of the men were out-flanked and taken prisoners, and for myself, I had to run a great risk, and should certainly have been killed or captured, but for the gallantry of a German dragoon, who riding up, dragged me behind him, and galloped away amidst a volley of shots, unhurt.

At night, the French, who had posted themselves partly under cover of a wood, threw shells into the town of Pombal, of which we had possession, and succeeded in setting it on fire in several places. We nevertheless remained for the night, and sold by auction among the officers and men some baggage which we had taken, snugly packed on a grey horse, from one of the Generals; among other valuables it contained were two beautiful gold medals, which we presented to our old Captain; we divided the proceeds, which amounted to six dollars to each man of the company.

In the morning, the French continued their retreat, and we were again in pursuit. After crossing a well-wooded hill, we came up with them at Redinha, a small town situated in the hollow of rather a difficult pass—the company ascending a hill covered with pine-trees, on the right of our battalion.

From its eminence, I remember to have seen one of the finest views of the two armies I ever witnessed. The rifles were extended in the distance for perhaps two miles, and rapidly on the advance to the enemy's position. These were followed by our heavy columns, whose heads were just emerging from a wood about a quarter of a mile in our rear. Everything seemed conducted with the order and regu-larity of a field day. Meanwhile the rear columns of the French were slowly retiring, but in a few minutes the scene became exceedingly animated by our artillery opening their fire upon the retreating forces.

This was the signal for us to set to work. We instantly moved down from our lofty station, and were soon engaged skirmishing and en-deavouring to out-flank and drive in their light troops, which, after a hard struggle, we at length accomplished, but not before many men had fallen on both sides. The enemy, however, although they slowly retired, continually turned, making temporary stands, whenever the ground seemed favourable.

One affecting circumstance that took place in this action made a deep impression on my memory. A French officer whom we had

turned out to line the road and greet their old friends that many of the singing, pipe-smoking Germans burst into tears. 'Oh!' they said, 'we are always glad to see the old *lighty* division, who will ever live in our hearts.'

observed very conspicuously cheering on his men, had fallen by a rifle-shot through the thigh, when two of our buglers ran forward for the purpose of easing him of his money. This, I must observe, the French generally kept concealed in a kind of belt round their waists. As soon therefore as the buglers came up to him, they commenced quarrelling as to which of them should possess his property. The more readily to disencumber him of his belt, each of them had fallen on his knees over the poor Frenchman, and one of the buglers had drawn a knife to cut the strap that secured the hoped-for treasure, then the other endeavouring to restrain him brought on a scuffle, during, which, I am sorry to relate, the knife entered the body of the wounded man, and he expired on the spot. I had arrived just in time to perceive the occurrence, and could with difficulty restrain myself from shooting the owner of the knife on the spot, until he told me it was purely accidental.

After pursuing the enemy through the town, where we took a number of prisoners (among whom were some of my own company, taken the day before) in a water-mill, we encamped at night on the side of an extensive hill. The country, here also, was well wooded and watered, and exceedingly picturesque, as was also the position occupied by the enemy. We were encamped on a range of heights, while the French lay below in a beautiful valley; the outlying sentries of both armies being not more than two hundred yards apart.

This night our company, with Captain Balvaird's, formed the outlying picquet. As we had had no rations for two days previous, we were soon busily employed in cooking what we had taken from the prisoners; during this ceremony, a man of the name of Humphrey Allen, a tall powerful fellow, whom we had also nick-named 'Long Tom of Lincoln', came up from the rear, where, during the preceding skirmish, he had been employed taking the wounded. On asking to be allowed to join one of the messes, he was immediately refused, on account of his having gone out of action with the wounded, when the care of them devolved upon the buglers or bandsmen alone. This, I must remark, was at first a common excuse for getting from under fire and soon became marked with indignation by the brave men; at length, during the latter part of the campaign, no good soldier would venture, under so frivolous a pretence, so to expose himself to the indignation of his comrades, excepting for any very extreme cases. In the preceding instance, however, Allen proved himself more daring than humane.

Taking up his rifle, very coolly observing that he would soon get something to eat if a Frenchman had it: walked quietly down to our outlying picquets, and taking deliberate aim, shot one of the French sentries on the spot: in an instant he was across the field to where he fell, and having hoisted him on his shoulders, was in the act of bearing him back to our line, which the French perceiving, not only fired, but pursued him, and compelled him to drop his prize.

A general alarm, meanwhile, was occasioned by this firing, and before it could be checked, Colonel Beckwith came down, and having traced its origin, sent for Allen.

'Why, Zur,' replied Tom, to the inquiry of the Colonel, 'I arn't had nought to eat these two days, and thought as how I might find summut in the Frencher's knapsack.'

Although he had been guilty of a cruelty which no law of arms could justify, he managed to escape with a severe reprimand.[1]

In the course of an hour after, being on sentry at our advance posts, I was leisurely sauntering up and down, occasionally looking about me, and stooping to cull some flowers that grew in the field which divided us from the enemy. It was just at the close of the evening, or between the lights. The French sentry, who advanced occasionally seemingly for the same purpose, at last came so near, that I feared he was up to some manœuvre, or about to fire at me; with this, I instantly cocked my rifle, and was awaiting his approach, when he suddenly rushed towards me, bellowing out in French, 'Déserteur! Déserteur!' Of course, at the words I allowed him to approach, which he did, exclaiming, 'Je suis allemand', and instantly turning on his quondam comrades, fired into them. The report of his fire caused the picquets of both parties to fall in, and the whole line of sentries again to be engaged. However, he stuck by me all the time, shaking his fist at them, and leading and firing with all the jaw-breaking oaths that the French and his native German could supply him with.

Colonel Beckwith, a second time alarmed, was soon amongst us swearing also, at what he supposed to be another Lincoln job, but he returned rather pleased, chatting to the deserter.

---

[1] Any of my readers passing through Knightsbridge may chance to observe a tall military figure, bent with years, a bag thrown over his shoulders, stooping to pick up bones, etc.; this person is no other than the once redoubtable Humphrey Allen, at that time one of the smartest and finest-looking men in our Rifles. [E.C.]

X

The French got under arms before the dawn of the morning, and we as usual followed, keeping them well on before us.

In the course of the noon we passed through the pretty little town of Condeixa, which the enemy had fired in several places. The main street was completely blocked by the flames darting across the road from the opposite houses. To enable the troops to pass, we were obliged to 'break' a way through some dry walls. This caused a temporary halt, during which the chief part of the division gallantly employed themselves extricating the unfortunate inhabitants from the burning houses. Tom Crawley (forgetful of the coach) made use of his great strength to some purpose, and chucked some five or six old people, whom he had brought forth on his shoulders, over a wall as he supposed, out of immediate danger. Tom, however, who should have 'looked' before he made the old ones 'leap', was not aware that close to their descent was a large well, into which, to their great terror, he had very nearly dropped the terrified and screeching sufferers.

Having cleared the houses 'a way', we proceeded to Casal Nova, where we came up with the incendiaries, whom we found perfectly prepared to receive us. The country all about was greatly intercepted by old walls, and afforded excellent facilities for skirmishing. In a few seconds some of our division was observed moving upon our right, and we were ordered instantly to extend, and at it we went. After several hours' hard fighting, kept up with great spirit on both sides, we compelled the enemy to retire, but not before we had lost an excellent officer in the person of Major Stewart, who received a shot through the body.[1] He was led by two buglers to the rear, where he died shortly after. The death of this officer gave a step to my old Captain O'Hare, who obtained the majority.

In this skirmish Lieutenant Strode also received a severe [*mortal*]

---

[1] Leach comments in his *Rough Sketches*: 'By his death the regiment was deprived of an officer who thoroughly understood the command of light troops, and was quite at home at outpost duty. He had a quick and accurate eye in taking advantage of ground, was devoted to the particular nature of our service, and his mind soared far above the uninteresting minutiae of barrack-yard drill— the exact distance from button to button on the soldier's jacket, the width of his leather stock, and other matters of the kind.'

wound. This officer in action always carried a rifle, for the skilful use of which he was celebrated.[1] A man of our company named Pat Mahon received three balls on the hip at the same instant, and so close together that a dollar might have covered the three holes they made.

The enemy still continued the retreat, their skirmishers, at times, making short stands to keep our rifles in check, and a few of their rear sections occasionally pouring a running fire into us. We drove them, however, through the village of Casal Nova. Some of the French for a few minutes here availed themselves of pieces of dilapidated walls, but as soon as we commenced out-flanking them, they all retreated, with the exception of one man, who, to our surprise, remained loading and firing as if he had a whole division to back him. I scarcely know what could have induced me to fire at this poor fellow alone, and exposed as he was to at least twenty other shots; but my blood was up, through his having once aimed at me, his ball whizzing close by as I approached. Be that as it may, I had got within fifty yards when I fired. In an instant I was beside him, the shot had entered his head, and he had fallen in the act of loading, the fusil tightly grasped in his left hand, while his right clutched the ramrod. A few quick turns of the eye as it rolled its dying glances on mine turned my whole blood within me, and I reproached myself as his destroyer. An indescribable uneasiness came over me, I felt almost like a criminal. I knelt to give him a little wine from a small calabash, which hung at my side, and was wiping the foam from his lips, when a heavy groan drew my attention aside, and turning round my head I beheld, stretched near him and close to the wall, another wounded Frenchman, a sergeant. 'Hélas,' exclaimed the wounded man, the big tears suddenly gushing down his sun-burnt countenance, as he pointed with his finger to my victim, 'vous avez tué mon pauvre frère' (you have killed my poor brother), and indeed such was the melancholy fact.

The sergeant, a stout heavy man, had fallen, his thigh broken by a

---

[1] I have often felt surprised that our officers have not generally adopted the plan of carrying a rifle when in action; the defence it would afford to the individual himself in its superiority over the sword or the pistol, which latter are mere toys in the field, would, I imagine, bear its own argument. The additional strength also it must give to the efficiency of the regiments generally, from the number it would add to each volley (in the proportion of fifty to a regiment), and the confidence it must inspire in the officers, would, one should think, carry everything before it, nor can it prevent any officer in keeping his eye on his as all riflemen, while in action, use their own judgment by getting under cover, consequently out of sight. [E.C.]

shot. The younger brother, unable to carry him off the field, had remained, apparently with the intention of perishing by his side.

We halted for the night on an adjacent hill, about a mile in advance. The French also took up their position opposite us. The picquets of both armies occupied a beautiful ravine, that sloped between us. I took advantage of the few moments' leisure our position afforded to return to the French sergeant. But I found him and his brother both as naked as they were born, perforated with innumerable wounds, no doubt administered by the Portuguese. I turned back to the camp, but in a very poor humour with myself, though I could not well close my eyes to the magnificent scene around me. The sun had set, its light had been supplanted by burning villages, and fires that on vale and mountain correctly pointed out where the hostile divisions were extended.

The following morning, the French continued their march of havoc, and we closed after them, village after village giving flaming proofs of their continued atrocities. Passing through one which had been fired by reason, as we were informed, of its having been the quarters of Marshal Ney and staff—an appalling instance of vengeance here occurred. The parents of one of our Caçadores had lived in this village, and immediately we entered, he rushed to the house where they resided. On reaching the doorway, the soldier hesitated a few seconds, but the door was open, and stretched across the threshold he beheld the mangled bodies of his father and mother, the blood still warm and reeking through the bayonet stabs, while an only sister lay breathing her last, and exhibiting dreadful proofs of the brutality with which she had been violated. The unhappy man staggered, frenzied with grief, and stared wildly around him; till suddenly burying all other feelings in the maddening passion of revenge, he rushed forth from what had probably been once a happy home. His first act was to dash at some French prisoners that unfortunately were near the spot, guarded by some of our dragoons. These he attacked with the fury of a madman. One he shot and another he wounded, and he would have sacrificed a third, had not the guard made him prisoner. On the circumstances being made known to the General, he was liberated.

Outside the village, and on a gentle slope, we came to the enemy's camp ground, which they had been obliged to quit so precipitately as to have left their fires lighted. We noticed a goat, which, by its frisking and jumping about, I supposed to have been a pet of some French officer. Whenever we went near, it would step aside, until some of the men levelled their rifles and shot it; swords were out in a moment, and the little animal, skin and all, dissected. I was just apportioning the hind quarter, when who should ride near, but Lord Wellington and staff; for a while I felt as if the noose were already round my neck, until the Colonel coming up, re-established my serenity, and congratulated us on our lucky chance; for this kindness we shared our booty with him that same night.

We had suffered dreadfully throughout the previous week; many of our men from weakness, and through want of rations, having been unable to keep up with their regiments, Colonel Beckwith, in the hearing of many of us, took this opportunity of making it known to the Commander-in-Chief, who immediately promised we should have the first rations that came up. We then marched to some high ground, from whence we could distinctly see the French camp at a place called Foz d'Arouce, their fires lighted preparatory to passing the night there. It was determined, however, that they should not enjoy it so easily. Our battalion was instantly ordered to the attack, before proceeding to which, I will introduce to my readers a squad of 'gentlemen', who joined us a few evenings preceding. We had been reinforced by a fresh batch of recruits from England, a number of whom had been drafted into our company. These fellows' rosy cheeks and plump appearance, with their new dresses, formed a bright relief and amusing contrast to our fierce embrowned visages, covered with whisker and mustachio, as we then were, and our clothing patched and of all colours. As these newcomers were now about to go through the ordeal of fire, for the first time in their lives, Major O'Hare thought proper to say a few words by way of advice to them, on so momentous an occasion; accordingly, he gave the command, 'Recruits to the front.'

Some ten or twelve immediately stepped forward, wondering, no doubt, what they were wanted for. 'Do you see those men on that plain?' asked the Major, as he pointed to the French camp. On several of the men answering 'Ees, Zur!' Major O'Hare, with a dry laugh, continued, 'Well then, those are the French, and our enemies. You must kill those fellows, and not allow them to kill you. You must learn and do as these old birds here do,' pointing to us, 'and get cover where you can. Recollect, recruits, you come here to kill, and not be killed. Bear this in mind: if you don't kill the French they'll kill you.' —'Ees, Zur!' said they again.

The Major's logic, although it elicited roars of laughter from the old soldiers, I believe had more effect with the recruits than if Demosthenes had risen for the purpose. Immediately after this out went our muzzle stoppers, and sallying down the slope on which we had been drawn up, at the enemy we went. Our battalion was soon hotly engaged, assisted by some light companies of the Guards, belonging to the 1st division. The night was fast setting in, but we soon succeeded in beating the enemy out of their camp ground, and we dashed at them as they retired crowding with precipitation over a bridge which crossed the river in their rear. Before two-thirds of their force had accomplished this, the bridge, by some irregularity, was blown up, and great numbers also were drowned in attempting to ford the stream.

At their camp ground many of our men came in for a bit of a wind-fall, as the French, in their hurry to place the river between us and them, had left their meat and pots on the fires. This afforded a happy regale to some of our unfortunate hungry stomachs, the more especially as the food thus come by was eaten with a sense of having been fairly earned.

During the foregoing skirmish and while very closely engaged, I perceived a horse, gaily bedizened with French trappings, galloping about, as though looking for an owner, and I managed to catch it by the bridle. A minute afterwards my prize received a shot, probably intended for myself, but which stretched the poor animal dead beside me.

The night was passed on the French camp ground. At the fire round which we thronged were two wounded Frenchmen; it was a satisfaction to mark the care and attention which they received at the hands of our men. One of the prisoners, whom I found to be a very intelligent fellow, gave me interesting accounts of the state and proceedings of Massena's troops, which, as it much amused us at the period, possibly may prove equally entertaining to the reader.

'At the time that Massena and his troops,' said he, 'lay at Santarem, we had encouraged hopes of driving the English into Lisbon, or the sea; but finding these unavailing, it was given up in despair, and the army prepared, at about the beginning of the spring of 1811, to retire back through the country into Spain.

'The batteries and other works which for several months our men had been erecting, were destroyed, and leaving behind us a great number of our sick, whom we had no means of conveying away, we shared the last of our provisions, amounting to about ten biscuits each man amongst us, and we prepared to retreat.

'The troops were in a most distressed state, reduced to half their numbers, almost naked and without provisions, for most of them consumed in a few days the whole of their scanty allowance. They could not expect aid from any of their comrades, for all were without, and the country around us devastated by both parties; our wants, however, urged us to plunder, and we wandered in strong parties from the regiment, and meeting with every species of resistance, gave blow for blow.

'The guerillas followed us everywhere: they fled in the front and harassed us on our flanks, so that not an hour passed but we were obliged to be on the alert to save our lives; out of this arose every cruelty which ensued, and made our retreat almost unparalleled for devastation and bloodshed. Meanwhile the British troops came on in our rear, their light divisions harassing us night and day, and completing the wreck that never will be forgotten while Portugal retains its name.'

We continued to occupy the same spot the whole of the following day, waiting very anxiously for the promised supply of rations; one day's rations, however, to our exceeding joy, made their appearance in the evening of the 16th. The following being the morning of St Patrick's Day, the whole of our battalion, English and Irish, duly celebrated the event by a proper attention to greens, and not having shamrocks, leaves, grass and boughs of trees were substituted: thus ornamented we commenced our march.

Just before we arrived at the River Ceira, the waters of which flowed over the body of many an unfortunate French soldier, we came upon a sight which was enough to make the 'Humane Society'[1] declare eternal war against the men of the wooden shoes.

This was some two or three hundred donkeys and mules, which the enemy, unable to drive off, had maimed and hamstrung. The poor animals looked up to us as if for vengeance, and every mute appeal was sternly fulfilled, for they struck home to the feelings of us all.

We continued our march for about two leagues, when the battalion halted upon a hill covered with pine-trees. At the bottom of this and near our advanced posts, flowed the River Alva, on the opposite side of which the retreating army lay encamped. We had halted, and refreshed ourselves, with the notion that we should spend the night there quietly, but we were doomed to be miserably undeceived, as a fresh order was given for us to fall in, the artillery coming up, and

[1] The Royal Humane Society was founded in 1774 with the object of saving life from drowning and of restoring by means of artificial respiration people who appeared to be drowned.

commenced playing on the enemy's masses, and our division was ordered to cross the river. Lord Wellington certainly was determined to allow the French no rest if possible, and indeed, if truth be added, ourselves as little. A pontoon was thrown over the river for the division to cross, while others forded the stream a little higher up on our right. The enemy retired in excellent order, and we pursued until both halted for the night. The place we occupied was a little village called Melo, where we remained during the following day, having had one ration only for the last four days. Never let it be said that John Bull cannot fight upon an empty stomach. If ever one division of our army proved this more than another, I certainly think it was the light one. *Light* enough we were at this and at other periods, Heaven knows. While thus impelled by hunger, myself and Wilkie searching about for something to devour, proceeded down a lane, where we came upon the body of an elderly woman. She was lying in the middle of the road, dressed in white, and, from the hands being bound together in a praying attitude, and the general appearance of the corpse, it was evident that she had been taken out for the purpose of burial, as it is the custom in that country to inter them in full dress, and without a coffin: the arrival of the French no doubt had obliged her attendants to abandon her.

The reader is expecting perhaps, that we set to work and nibbled the old woman, but let me assure him we did nothing of the kind, though we thought many and many a time, and growled sadly that we had not provided ourselves with a bit from the donkeys.

The corpse had round its neck a set of beads with a gold cross at the end, which Wilkie very 'piously' put into his pocket.

We still, however, continued our prowling, and stumbled at last on a small cottage, into which we entered, in full hopes of having made a substantial discovery.

An old emaciated half-starved looking hag sat squatted by some extinguished embers, like the last survivor of a universal wreck. She was indeed the only living inhabitant we had seen in the village, and remained squatted by the embers, as if permitted that privilege only to recount her tale. The old soul continued a fixture until Wilkie, suspecting something, pressed her to move. 'Non hai nada!' screamed the old lady. 'Non hai nada!' (there is nothing).

'Oh, but there is,' replied my comrade; until growing furious, he upset the old woman from her position, and out rolled a loaf of bread from under her, as natural as if it had been an egg from under a hen. Wilkie pounced at it instantly, and the miserable old creature burst into tears, and screamed herself almost into fits. Her cries in a few seconds brought in her daughter, who unable to keep herself concealed at this agonizing appeal of her parent, rushed forward to her assistance. Never before did I see such a pitiful pair, both were almost cadaverous with want, and begged hard for the loaf. But we were all of us half starved, and at last Wilkie and myself, unable to contain ourselves any longer, willingly shared it with them.

We were engaged daily with the enemy until we came to Freixedas, on the 28th March, on which day we lost our gallant adjutant, Lieutenant Stewart, who fell by a musket shot.[1]

On the 1st of April we again came up with the enemy, who held possession of the town of Sabugal, where they seemed inclined to make a final stand.

The town is situated partly upon a hill, with some woodland interspersed about, while the rapid River Coa winds between it and the Lisbon side of the country.

On the day of the 3rd an attack upon the enemy was commenced by our battalions, when through some mistake, we were left almost unsupported; after crossing the river, we advanced up the hill, on the other side, and under a fleecy shower of rain soon became hotly engaged with the French. They were at least four or five times our number, and compelled us to retire twice before their overwhelming masses. Led on, however, by our gallant Colonel, we fixed swords, and came to the charge and drove them up the hills before us. There a strong reserve was prepared for our reception. A third time we were obliged to give ground, until our second brigade coming to our aid, we again dashed at them, carried the position, and after a hard contest, obliged the enemy to retreat with the utmost precipitation, leaving behind them a howitzer, which had been twice taken and retaken.

No one that day could have observed our Colonel during the heat of the action, and not have admired his cool and soldier-like bearing. 'Steady, lads—show no hurry,' was his cheering exhortation, accompanied by a smile when we were obliged to retreat, the blood, at the same time, flowing copiously from a wound he had received across his

---

[1] Kincaid says that Stewart was shot through the head from a window. 'We placed his body in a chest, and buried it in front of Colonel Beckwith's quarters.' Leach writes of Stewart: 'He was open-hearted, manly, friendly, and independent, a most gallant and zealous officer, and much devoted to his own corps. He neither cringed to, nor worshipped any man, but did his duty manfully, and with impartiality—two qualities inestimable in adjutants. By the soldiers he was idolised, and very justly.'

forehead. Never, perhaps, in any action did the Rifles display more consummate tact and resolution than in this. Lord Wellington was too just to pass over their services on this occasion, and in general orders passed a high encomium upon the gallantry of Colonel Beckwith, and the brigade under his command. We lost a fine young fellow, an officer, Lieutenant the Honourable Duncan Arbuthnot, whose head was smashed by a round-shot.

At the conclusion of the battle the rain poured down in torrents, and obliged us to take such shelter as the walls and trees around afforded. The enemy, meanwhile, were in rapid retreat, and we should, in all probability, have continued in pursuit, but for the exhausted state of the men.

While endeavouring to obtain shelter, Lord Wellington rode up, and knowing the chief business of the day had fallen upon our brigade, he ordered us into the town. We arrived just in time to prevent the 5th division from supplanting us, and they consequently were obliged to retrace their steps, which they did with much grumbling and discontent. It was dark before we got into the house appropriated to us. Myself and one or two others turned into a small square room, the floor of which was covered with straw. Though wetted through to the skin I soon fell into a sound sleep, but was, however, quickly awakened by a hurried exclamation from a man who had just entered the room with a light. On looking around for the cause of his surprise, I beheld a stiff and naked corpse placed upright against the walls of the room, brutally defaced; at the same moment, and in the act of turning, I placed my hand on the clammy features of another body, partly concealed under the straw, and across which I had actually been sleeping; we found four bodies altogether, evidently Portuguese, and all of them bearing the usual proofs of French retaliation.

The next day Massena evacuated Portugal, with the exception of Almeida, and in a short time we ourselves crossed the frontiers and took up our old quarters at Gallegos; here we found many of our acquaintances of the preceding year, and the enemy having retired upon Ciudad Rodrigo, we were suffered for a while to recruit our strength.

Some weeks after our arrival at Gallegos, the battalion had orders to prepare for marching at an hour's notice, and to leave their knapsacks behind. This was announced by Colonel Beckwith on the afternoon parade, who at the same time desired those who were sick or weakly to fall out, as a forced march was to be undertaken to prevent the French throwing supplies into Rodrigo. On hearing this several skulkers in the regiment fell out of the ranks, but were obliged to fall in again.

Passing down the regiment, Colonel Beckwith, attracted by the evident looks of ill health of a man named Burke, noted for his daring courage, very humanely advised him to remain behind, 'For you look very ill, Burke,' said the Colonel. 'No Sir,' replied Burke, casting a look of contempt on the skulkers, 'I certainly am not well, but I still have the heart of a man, and will keep up with my comrades as long as my legs will carry me.' The Colonel evinced a melancholy, but evident satisfaction, at this manly reply. 'I am sorry,' said he, 'that the sneaking propensities of others should compel a brave man to act against himself.' This brave fellow Burke was afterwards one of the forlorn hope at Ciudad Rodrigo, Badajoz, and San Sebastian, through the successive horrors of which he lived to fall mortally wounded at Quatre Bras, just previous to the battle of Waterloo.

Our expeditionary party marched early in the morning. We took the direction of Rodrigo, fording the River Agueda in our way. We were doomed to have only our march for our trouble—the expected convoy of the enemy had escaped us; so that, harassed to death, we had the pleasure of retracing our steps not a whit wiser than we went. In recrossing the river, a poor fellow of our company, spent with fatigue, was carried off his legs and drowned. Another would have shared the same fate, but for Brigade-Major Mellish, who, by swimming his horse to his assistance, saved the man.

XI

On the 4th May, about half-past nine o'clock, A.M., our advance videttes were observed circling, one to the right, and the other to the left, at a trot, by which information was conveyed that bodies of infantry and cavalry were advancing. The bugle immediately sounded the 'assemblée', and our division quickly assembled on its alarm post, on the Gallegos road. My company was attached to the 14th Light

Dragoons, then under the orders of General Slade, who commanded the cavalry brigade. He ordered them to take ground to the right, and deploy into line in the rear of a rivulet, which flowed between us and the French. In a few minutes the enemy's cavalry were discovered emerging from a wood in our front, where they had formed in close columns and halted, throwing out strong bodies of skirmishers.

A sharp conflict ensued betwixt the cavalries, yet the enemy were evidently awaiting the concentration of their advancing columns from Ciudad Rodrigo. General Slade now ordered the whole of us to retire, which the cavalry did in echelons of squadrons, and covering us on the road towards Nave de Haver, which was quietly effected; the enemy still holding their old position near the wood. One squadron of the 14th was stationed on the verge of another wood, on the right of Fuentes, as an advanced picquet, but was withdrawn at the close of the evening, and joined the regiments in bivouac within some stone wall enclosures, near Villar Formoso.

During the night some of the dragoons discovered the resting-place of a sutler, who had just arrived from Abrantes with a string of mules laden with rum, wine, aguardiente [*brandy*], &c. &c., and sardines, a species of red-herring, which was then considered a great luxury. News of such a neighbour flew on eagle wings through the camp, but in low whispers, lest the slumbers of the chief should be disturbed, and check their merry-making. The secret, however, was soon discovered, no doubt occasioned by the uproarious bursts of merriment and songs which pealed from fire to fire. Although these were the general characteristics of the British soldier on the eve of a battle, on this occasion they were heightened by the liquor, and were louder than usual, while the officers awakened from their slumbers could not for some moments conceive the cause of what they heard. General Slade, however, with lungs that roused the camp, as though a thirteen-inch shell had exploded amongst them, called for the Regimental Sergeant-Major Sharp, who, on making his appearance, was discovered to have partaken too freely of the sutler's strong waters, and was immediately place in arrest. A non-commissioned officer was ordered to bundle off both sutler and mules to some distance, placing a line of sentries that no one might come in or go out of the camp. The noise and hilarity soon ceased, the merry-makers dispersed, and a few minutes found them outstretched and asleep under cover of the dry walls.

Early on the morning of the 5th, our company was ordered to join the battalions; we did so, and took up our position to the left of the ruins of Fort Conception, which, as I before mentioned, had

65

been previously destroyed, as it lay near the main road to Almeida, the siege of which place the French seemed anxious to raise.

While things were in this state, at an early hour General Craufurd made his reappearance amongst us from England [4 May], and was welcomed with much enthusiasm by the division; although a strict disciplinarian, the men knew his value in the field too well not to testify their satisfaction at his return. The Caçadores, particularly, caused much laughter among us by shouting out in Portuguese, the moment they caught sight of him, 'Long live General Craufurd, who takes care of our bellies!' meaning by this exclamation they got their rations regularly, while under his command; the General seemed highly pleased, and bowed repeatedly with his hat off as he rode down the ranks.

The whole of the British were under arms at day-break, earnestly expecting, from the movements of the enemy, that an attack would be made; this suspense was but short, for very soon a heavy cannonading was heard on our right, in which direction we were immediately ordered. While moving accordingly we passed the Guards of the 1st division, entrenched behind the town of Fuentes; we immediately occupied some old dry walls considerably in advance, and facing the enemy's left, a fine extended plain laying between us, with a wood on the French side, of which the enemy had possession. In front of this a regiment of cavalry was conspicuously formed, a troop of which came trotting leisurely towards us to reconnoitre our position.

This movement induced a corresponding one from some of our dragoons, when both parties threw out their videttes, and remained halted with some four hundred yards of ground between them.

One of their videttes, after being posted facing an English dragoon, of the 14th or 16th (for we had only those two light dragoon regiments with us at the time, and the German Hussars), displayed an instance of individual gallantry, in which the French, to do them justice, were seldom wanting. Waving his long straight sword, the Frenchman rode within sixty yards of our dragoon, and challenged him to single combat. We immediately expected to see our cavalry man engage his opponent, sword in hand. Instead of this, however, he unslung his carbine and fired at the Frenchman, who, not a whit dismayed, shouted out so that every one could hear him, 'Venez avec le sabre: je suis prêt pour Napoléon et la belle France.' Having vainly endeavoured to induce the Englishman to a personal conflict, and after having endured two or three shots from his carbine, the Frenchman rode proudly back to his ground, cheered even by our own men.

We were much amused by his gallantry, while we hissed our own dragoon, who, it was afterwards stated, for the credit of the gallant regiment he belonged to, was a recruit.

Just after the preceding occurrence, a smart action had commenced in the wood before-mentioned, and our company was ordered to take ground to the front, where the 85th regiment were very roughly handled by the enemy. This was the first time since their arrival in the country that they had been engaged. Opposed, with their conspicuous red dresses, to the old trained French tirailleurs, it is no wonder that the gallant 85th should have suffered so severely. When we came up, however, our practised fellows, in their dark clothing, from the murderous nature of our arms, soon turned back the advancing French, who commenced gradually retreating before us, until they got through the wood on the plain that leads to Nave de Haver.

We had no sooner beaten back the enemy than a loud cheering to the right attracted our attention, and we perceived our 1st Heavy Dragoons charge a French cavalry regiment. As this was the first charge of cavalry most of us had ever seen, we were all naturally much interested on the occasion. The French skirmishers who were extended against us seemed to participate in the same feeling, as both parties suspended firing while the affair of dragoons was going on. The English and French cavalry met in the most gallant manner, and with the greatest show of resolution. The first shock, when they came in collision, seemed terrific, and many men and horses fell on both sides. They had ridden through and past each other, and now they wheeled round again. This was followed by a second charge, accompanied by some very pretty sabre-practice, by which many saddles were emptied, and English and French chargers were soon seen galloping about the field without riders. These immediately occupied the attention of the French skirmishers and ourselves, and we were soon engaged in pursuing them, the men of each nation endeavouring to secure the chargers of the opposite one as legal spoil. While engaged in this chase we frequently became intermixed, when much laughter was indulged in by both parties at the different accidents that occurred in our pursuit.

I had secured a very splendid charger, when chancing to turn my head, I perceived that the French were playing a deep game. They had succeeded in removing a regiment of infantry, with some cavalry, through the wood in our rear. The alarm, however, was immediately given, and our company, as foremost, had to run for their lives into a square formed by the 52nd, who were close to the foot guards. During this sudden movement I was obliged to part with my horse; the cavalry did not pursue us, but their artillery opened up on the 52nd's square, and did some execution.

These incidents, though fearfully strange to some of my readers, were very enlivening to us. Ours indeed was a noble enemy; they never permitted us to flag, for want of stimuli, but kept us ever on the *qui vive*. We anticipated little terror from capture, and though we ever found them to be our roughest antagonists, yet we always experienced a most generous opposition; indeed, there was, on the whole, such a chivalrous spirit carried on between us, that our men had a kind of respect even for a wound inflicted by a Frenchman.

Our next attempt was upon the left of Fuentes, where one company was detached, while the remainder of the regiment was ordered to take possession of the town. The section to which I belonged were posted near the banks of the River Dos Casas. The 79th Highlanders had suffered very severely here, as the place was strewn about with their bodies. Poor fellows! they had not been used to skirmishing, and instead of occupying the houses in the neighbourhood, and firing from the windows, they had, as I heard, exposed themselves, by firing in sections. The French, who still occupied part of the town, had not escaped a rough handling, as their dead also evinced.

During the latter part of the day the enemy had made some prisoners, which they exhibited to us as they marched them along their lines. One man we saw make a determined attempt to obtain his liberty. He had loitered in the rear as the party were going over a small bridge that crossed the Dos Casas by a mill, when, turning suddenly upon a Frenchman behind him, he threw him into the water, and immediately made a dash for our position, but owing to several of the French being between him and us, we had the mortification of seeing the poor fellow recaptured, without being enabled to render him any assistance; we could see by his kilt that he belonged to the 79th regiment.

That same evening, the enemy evacuated the town, and a flag of truce was sent us to bury the dead. While occupied in this at all times melancholy duty, some idea may be formed of the loss sustained by the 79th alone, when a man of our company brought in his two arms full of the sable plumes which he had taken from their bonnets, strewn about the town.

The opposing lines of sentries were very close to each other: the French being divided from us only by a narrow plank thrown across the mill-dam, which was occupied on one side by our company, who were now on picquet.

A blacksmith of ours of the name of Tidy, who had erected his forge in the old mill, was at work close by, shoeing the officers' horses. The French sentry had crossed the plank to light his pipe, and was standing carelessly chatting with me, when who should I see approaching but General Craufurd, inquiring if Tidy had shod his horse. The Frenchman's red wings [*epaulets*] soon attracted the General's notice, and he suddenly with his well-known stern glance, inquired,

'Who the devil's that you're talking with, rifleman?'

I informed him the French sentry, who had come over for a light for his pipe.

'Indeed,' replied Craufurd, 'let him go about his business, he has no right here, nor we either,' said he, in a low whisper to his aide-de-camp, and away he walked.

Our battalion remained in the suburbs of Fuentes a few days, and the enemy, who had desisted from their attempt to relieve Almeida, retired; we followed them and took up our quarters at Gallegos. . . .

XII

At this period Almeida was closely invested by the 5th division, while we in front watched the main army. Early on the morning of the 10th of May we were ordered to get under arms and march towards Barba del Puerco, the scene of one of our former skirmishes the year before. On arriving near the town we heard some smart firing, and we halted. We now were informed, for the first time, that the French garrison at Almeida, after blowing up the walls at night, evacuated the town, and had cut their way through the blockading force.

The brigades of the 5th division, I believe, did duty by turns. That in which were the 2nd and 4th regiments happened to be on picquet when the French made their way through the investing force, which gave rise to a verse that became very common amongst the troops.

But I must remark that the badge of the 2nd regiment was a lamb, and that of the 4th a lion. The lines were as follows:

> The lion went to sleep,
> And the lambs were at play;
> The eagle spread her wings,
> And from Almeida flew away.

Although these regiments were rendered somewhat unpopular from this circumstance, it is generally admitted, by those capable of judging, that there were not two finer in the service. Our battalion had been particularly fond of the 4th, while they were quartered at Colchester, where they had christened us in a friendly feeling 'The young 4th'. The melancholy death of their Colonel [*Bevan*], who, from an over-sensitive feeling of honour, shot himself shortly after the foregoing unlucky affair, was generally regretted.

The evacuation of the fortress of Almeida having rendered the presence of our division thereabouts no longer necessary, another movement was made to the southward to General Hill, who commanded the 2nd division, at this time menaced by a very superior force of the French.

On the first day's march we passed through Sabugal, crossed the Coa, and encamped in a chestnut wood, close to our former scene of action.

Here a very strange panic occurred, that might have been attended with most disastrous effects. About twelve at night I was stretched on my back under the boughs of a tree, admiring the comet that at that period created some sensation in Europe, from its nearness to the earth, when a general alarm and outcry was raised in the division that 'The French were upon us'. In a moment I started up, and seized my rifle. The different regiments were assembling in the greatest disorder, while the general cries of alarm on all sides induced many to feel a terror that was, perhaps, never felt in battle. Among others I plainly observed General Craufurd, desiring all whom he met to fall in and load. After a short while the panic ceased: we all looked foolish enough at the great ado about nothing, though some attributed the cause to French spies having got among us, others to some bullocks grazing by, that had knocked down several stands of arms; others again accused the comet, and among the latter in our battalion was that worthy, Tom Crawley, who stoutly contended the comet was a sign we ought to leave the country, as it would shortly drop down and burn up that part of Europe. Tom himself at this period, it was shrewdly suspected, had a great desire to turn his steps homewards.

We continued our march through Castello Branco, Portalegre, and encamped on a low ground called Monte Reguengo, on the right of the road leading to Campo Mayor. There we remained about six weeks, during which we suffered dreadfully for want of rations as well as from the oppressive heat of the weather; we called it the furnace camp. Tom, while we remained at Reguengo, imagined himself poisoned. He had eaten rather ravenously of some pork and caravanças (a sort of pulse), and was suddenly seized with violent paroxysms of pain through his overgorging. Old Doctor Burke being sent for, found Crawley on the ground groaning most piteously, and swelled to an enormous size, while two of his comrades were busy rubbing the lower part of his belly. The Doctor, who fancied Spain during the last two years had brought Tom's stomach to suit the convenience of the commissary, commenced a volley of abuse—'You cannibal, what garbage have you been swallowing,' he cried, 'to leave you in this condition?' 'Oh, murther, do you hear him, boys,' roared the sufferer, as he turned up his eyes towards his tormentor. 'By the mother of God, Sir, this infernal country will kill the whole of us—may a curse fall on it; arrah, Doctor dear, when I came into it I had a stomach like any other Christian; but now, oh God, have mercy on me poor stomach, that for want of Christian food is turned into a scavenger's cart, obliged to take in every rubbage.' The Doctor, who seldom did anything by halves, gave him an emetic sufficient to physic a dromedary. Crawley, however, who never feared death on the field, now seemed to hesitate to meet him in quarters, and between the groans he uttered, made the most vehement promises of mending his sinful life if spared. Never was an intended pious scene made more truly ludicrous; our men were in convulsions of laughter.

In July we returned to assist in the blockade of Ciudad Rodrigo, and took up a position at a village called Atalaya, at the base of the Sierra de Gata, a range of mountains. Here Lord Wellington's staff frequently went out hunting. On these occasions they generally had five or six men of the Rifles to assist. The place abounded in wolves and wild boars, so that a great deal of amusement was experienced in this sport. I generally had the good fortune to be selected, with others of our battalion, to attend his Lordship's staff in these excursions. The chase was very exciting, particularly from the ferocious nature of the game we sought. I well remember the first wild boar I saw in one of these hunts: he was a huge fellow, with tusks of a most alarming size, but although we fired several shots, and the hounds pursued him, he escaped. One day we came upon three young wolf cubs, the old ones having abandoned them on our approach. These animals, which we presented to one of our officers, remained in his possession for a long time, and became as docile and playful as kittens.

Here we were joined [21 August] by our 3rd battalion, under the command of Colonel Barnard, Colonel Beckwith having retired through ill health, a gallant and very distinguished officer, now known as General Sir Andrew Barnard; at the same time, also, we were reinforced by a batch of recruits from England, and by one Tommy Searchfield, a character well known to all the Light Brigade. This gentleman, a squat, square little fellow, had formerly been a 'middy' in the Royal Navy, and now come over to us as a cadet, and sub-sequently obtained a lieutenancy.

'Tommy's' first feat was something after the lessons he had received under the immortal Nelson. He had been accustomed hitherto to meet his enemies 'muzzle to muzzle', and, consequently, whenever the least intimation was given of the presence of the French, would imagine them almost passing through the loopholes, or as he termed them, our 'ports'. On one occasion he bawled aloud, 'to quarters', and seizing hold of a rope, suspended outside the church of the village, to one of the bells in the belfry; to our surprise, and that of the inhabitants also, ran up it like a cat, to keep the 'look-out' for the enemy. We, however, were some distance from them. The officers, for want of better employment, occupied their own and our time erecting sham fortifications in the woods, &c., and thus turned 'Tom's' peculiarities to their amusement. Searchfield, however, got 'awake' to them, and his original good-natured simplicity giving way to ex-perience, he gently informed his tormentors that he kept 'a clean brace of pistols' about him, 'at any time at their sarvice'. This un-expected show of pluck made his 'teasers' less gibing, and 'Tommy' took his proper position; and, I believe, became as respectable as any of them.

At Atalaya we were very much in the advance of the main army: the distance made it difficult for the commissariat to forward our rations regularly, and we, consequently, suffered dreadfully through want; and, I may say, underwent more privations than at any other place in Spain, excepting at Dough Boy Hill. The deficiency of bread we had been obliged to make up with roasted or boiled chestnuts, of which we were always allowed a quart a day each. At length we found it necessary to make an incursion into the mountains, to press the Alcaldes of the different villages to supply us.

On one of these expeditions, under charge of a quartermaster, we observed two persons mounted on mules, riding towards us. On their approach we remarked to one another the light-haired appearance of one, and the singularity of a 'fair-complexioned Spaniard', when the fellow suddenly stopped his mule, and jumping toward us exclaimed, 'Oh, by the merciful God, are ye English?' He was immediately answered from a dozen voices in the affirmative, and we discovered him to be one of our cavalry men, who having been made a prisoner by the French at Talavera, had since escaped. His short stay among the Spaniards had not spoilt his 'brogue', and he gave us in the real Irish accent, a full account of his adventures.

When the enemy took him, dragoon-like, together with a slight wound, he could not keep up with his captors, who, having no mules, were in the practice of pressing the strongest and most robust of the inhabitants and making them carry the English prisoners on their backs, now and then keeping up their stamina by pricking their hind-quarters with the bayonets. Our cavalier consequently found himself mounted in like manner; the close contact, however, that this brought him in with the ears of his bearers was followed by whispers, and the Spaniards no doubt as tired of their burthen as the burthen of the French, slipped him into a house on the way-side, whence, having quickly shaved the top of his sconce, they passed him as a priest, and he escaped with them into the mountains. He there got amongst the guerillas, under Don Julian Sanchez, of whom he gave us many amusing anecdotes, and who passed him on till he reached us. As soon as we turned to the village he reported himself to General Craufurd, who laughed heartily at the details he gave of himself, and ordered his servant to give him a coat to supply his almost naked condition until he rejoined his regiment. Meanwhile he was ordered to stop with our company, and took up his quarters in the house with me.

Among other amusements before detailed, we used to get up jumping, wrestling, and cuffing-matches with the peasantry, who generally joined most heartily in the fun. One day, however, a Spaniard of theirs, being overmatched, became exceedingly nettled, and commenced quarrelling with one of our sergeants, named Kitchen; the result was they came to blows, when after two or three slight cuffs the peasant fell suddenly and expired. The village, of course, became a scene of uproar, and we were obliged, to satisfy the inhabitants, to hold a kind of inquest upon him. However, the barber, or 'Sangrado'[1] of the place, together with our own surgeon to their extreme mortification declared, that the man had injured the spleen of his stomach, and actually had died through spite.

I must not forget to mention the sagacity of the pigs, which, in great numbers were kept by the farmers of the village. Though belonging to different owners they all obeyed one master, who, it may be said, with the Alcalde, held absolute sway over 'man and beast'. Early in the morning the animals were assembled, by the sounding of a horn, and taken by him into the wood to feed on acorns, and at night were driven home again in like manner, the swine-herd's only deputies being a short iron on the end of a stick, somewhat like that used by our shepherds. The anxiety of the animals, immediately they heard the tones of his instrument, was remarkable, and if they chanced to be confined at the time, their screams and grunts grew most vociferous, and might be heard a mile off. Indeed it was only for the herdsman to tune up at any time of the day they would come to him instantly, and seldom even one was missing, save and except now and then when they chanced to fall into the clutches of our riflemen.

About this period General [*Marshal*] Marmont, who had succeeded Massena in command of the French army, having concentrated his force, was enabled to relieve Rodrigo. Making a forward movement after this, it was found high time for our regiment to retire. This we did at an hour's notice, as we heard the enemy were stirring to beat up our quarters. We fell in at dead of night, and after making a semi-circular march, for there were some fears of the enemy cutting us off, we arrived at El Bodon. There we found the greater part of the army assembled under Lord Wellington, together with the remainder of our light division, who loudly cheered us as we made our appearance, a report having arisen amongst the rest of the troops that one battalion had been all taken prisoners.

On our arrival, most of us were occupied gleaning accounts of the battle of El Bodon, which had been fought the day before, in which the 5th and 77th regiments, as we then heard, had much distinguished themselves, resisting the desperate charges made upon them by the Polish Lancers in the French service.

From El Bodon, where we remained some time, we retreated to Soito, and shortly afterwards returned to Guinaldo, a town still closer

[1] Doctor Sangrado of Valladolid, an imaginary character in Lesage's *Gil Blas*, illustrates the ignorance of doctors of his day.

to the city of Ciudad Rodrigo. In the beginning of January 1812 our division commenced investing Ciudad. The first day, our brigade crossed the Agueda, about three miles up the river from the city, round which we marched, keeping always at a most respectful distance on account of their round-shot. From the idea this survey gave us of Rodrigo there were few of our men not aware of the great strength of the fortress and outworks, but it afforded only a subject for jest; as I believe at that time, such was the confidence that filled the ranks of our division, it would have been difficult to persuade the men that they could not beat the French, under any odds.

The same evening, Colonel Colborne, with less than two hundred men, of the 43rd, 52nd, and Rifles, carried in the most gallant manner a strong fort of the enemy. Prior to its being stormed a number of Caçadores had been ordered to take blankets to convey away the wounded French as well as the British. But most of those employed in this duty took advantage of it to strip the prisoners, whom to the number of fifty they left almost as naked as they were born, and exposed to all the rigours of the inclement month of January. I was present near the tent of General Craufurd, when a talkative, smart little Frenchman, whom I guessed to be an officer, was brought before him; the poor fellow had nothing on but his trousers, and bled profusely from the nose and mouth, through the blows he had received.

The General was very chagrined at the sight, and lamented his inability to give him clothes, his own baggage being so distant. Tom Crawley, however, who had been actively employed hunting the Portuguese from them, immediately stepped forward, and touching his hat after his own inimitable manner, 'Yer honner,' said Tom, his eyes sparkling at being able to assist, 'I'll lend him my great coat, if ye'll allow me.'

Craufurd, much pleased at his frank offer, instantly answered, 'You are very good, rifleman; let him have it,' and Tom proceeded to strip. Meanwhile more of the Frenchmen were marched in, many worse off than their officer. One of them, a sergeant, and a smart-looking fellow, as soon as he perceived the officer, ran to embrace him, and leaning his head on his shoulder, burst into tears over their mutual misery. Captain Smith, now Sir Harry, the General's aide-de-camp, being present, generously pulled forth his pocket-handkerchief and wrapped it round the sergeant's totally naked person, till further covering could be obtained.

The night of this occurrence came on remarkably cold, and when expecting to be marched back to our quarters at El Bodon, we were suddenly ordered to break ground by commencing to throw up intrenchments in the face of the city. In executing this task, being unsheltered from the enemy's shot, their grape and canister occasionally played in among us, so that although it was freezing hard at the time, we had no reason to complain of not having *a good fire*.

Now was the time to cure a skulker, or teach a man to work for his 'life'. There we were, in twos, each provided with a pick-axe and shovel; now digging with a vengeance into the frozen mould, and then watching the glances of the shot and shell; and again sticking to work like devils, or perhaps pitching ourselves on our bellies to avoid their being 'purged' with grape or canister.

XIII

The following day we were relieved by the 3rd division, and marched back to our quarters, cold, hungry, and fatigued enough. One great annoyance we experienced at this time, was having to cross the Agueda in going to and returning from the trenches. Pieces of ice that were constantly carried down this rapid stream bruised our men so much, that, to obviate it, the cavalry at length were ordered to form four deep across the ford, under the lee of whom we crossed comparatively unharmed, although by the time we reached our quarters, our clothes were frozen into a mass of ice.

Our divisions continued relieving each other in the trenches for some days, until two breaches were considered practicable for an assault. On the 18th, at night, an order came that we were to proceed to the works the next morning. As this took us out of our turn of duty, we all naturally supposed that something unusual was to be done. At daylight we joined the 3rd division in the works, and then heard that the city was to be stormed. Volunteers were immediately required from the different regiments of our division. Many of our men came forward with alacrity for this deadly service. With three others I had, as I then considered, the good fortune to be chosen from our company.[1] This was an occasion, as may be believed, momentous and interesting enough in the life of a soldier, and so we seemed to consider it. We shook hands with a feeling of friendly sincerity, while we speculated as to the chances of outliving the assault. We were at this time in the trenches in front of the city, from whence proceeded a very smart fire of shot and shell, probably to give us an idea of the warm reception we might expect on our visit at night, and here the entire company gathered round our little party, each pressing to have a sup from his canteen. I gave my father's address to my comrade before starting, in case of accident.

Darkness had no sooner closed over the devoted city, and our imaginations awakened to the horrors of the coming scene, than the 'stormers' were immediately ordered to 'fall in' and 'form'. We were four or five from each company, and in all about a hundred and twenty men. The volunteers of our regiment were led by Captain Mitchell and Lieutenants Johnston and Kincaid; the whole of the storming division being commanded by Major George Napier of the 52nd regiment. The forlorn-hope, or stormers, moved to a convent, occupied by the 40th, the walls of which protected us from the enemy's shot. General Craufurd, who led us in person, while we stood formed under the wall, addressed us upon the nature of the duty assigned us. It was the last enterprise his gallant spirit was ever destined to direct. On this memorable occasion his voice was more than ordinarily clear and distinct. His words sunk deep in my memory, and although the shock of many a battle has rolled over my grey locks since that period, I remember some of his language as follows:

'Soldiers! the eyes of your country are upon you. Be steady—be cool,—be firm in the assault. The town must be yours this night. Once masters of the wall, let your first duty be to clear the ramparts, and in doing this keep together.'

1   As some of my readers may not be acquainted with the duty and the character of a 'Forlorn-Hope', I will proceed to explain it. On the eve of the storming of a fortress, the breaches, etc., being all ready, captains of companies, on their private parade, give the men to understand that such and such a place is to be taken by storm. Every man then, who wishes to volunteer to head the stormers, steps forward to the front, and his name is immediately taken down by the officer; if none offer themselves the first men for duty are selected. With our regiment this latter alternative was never required, as a sufficient number were always ready.

This service, or 'Forlorn-Hope', is designated by the French in the not less appropriate term of 'Les Enfants perdus', or 'Lost Children', and has always to lead or make the first attack. [E.C.]

We were now waiting only for the signal, while our division was formed immediately in our rear, ready to second the effort. I could not help remarking at this awful crisis, when all most probably were on the brink of being dashed into eternity, a solemnity and silence among the men deeper than I had ever witnessed before. With hearts beating, each was eagerly watching the expected signal of the rocket, when up it went from one of our batteries.

General Craufurd, calling out, 'Now, lads, for the breach!' led the way. We started off in double time, and got under fire, in turning the left corner of the wall. As we neared the breach, canister, grape, round-shot and shell, with fire-balls to show our ground, came pouring on and around us, with a regular hail-storm of bullets. General Craufurd fell almost immediately, mortally wounded. Without a pause, however, we dashed onwards to the town, and precipitated ourselves into the ditch before the walls, never waiting for the ladders, which were carried by Portuguese, who ran away and never made their appearance until their use had been superseded by a series of jumps made by our men into a trench some sixteen feet deep; at length, one or two ladders having been procured, they were instantly placed against the scarp of the trench, and up we mounted to attack the breach. The fire kept up there was most deadly, and our men for some minutes, as they appeared in small bodies, were swept away; however they still persevered, and gradually formed a lodgment. At this time on our right, where the third division were storming the second breach, we could hear a loud cheering which had a magical effect. Regardless of the enemy's fire and every other impediment, the men dashed in over the breach, carrying everything before them. I had got up among the first, and was struggling with a crowd of our fellows to push over the splintered and broken wall that formed the breach, when Major Napier, who was by my side encouraging on the men, received a shot, and, staggering back, would in all probability have fallen into the trench, had I not caught him. To my brief inquiry if he were badly hurt, he squeezed my hand, whilst his other arm hung shattered by his side, saying, 'Never mind me—push on, my lads, the town is ours!' And so indeed it was, our men entering it pell-mell.

Although dark, among the first I saw on mounting the ramparts was my own Captain, Uniacke, rushing along with a few men to the right of the breach. Though not on the forlorn-hope, this gallant soldier was determined to be first in the town. This was the last time he was doomed to be at our head. A few moments afterwards the French sprung a mine, by which the whole party were killed or maimed.[1] With a few others I had taken a direction to the left. The French as they retired kept up an occasional fire along the ramparts; while running forward I came against a howitzer, and with such force that it actually tumbled me over, and I found myself prostrate across the body of a wounded French officer; beside him was a cannonier of his own in the act of assisting him. The latter instantly seized me, and a fearful struggle ensued, till bent almost double by the height and heavy person of the Frenchman, I began to think that after all my escapes my game was over; at this crisis a few of our men came rushing up, one of which was my old 'chum' Wilkie. The cannonier in his turn was fastened on, and tripped instantaneously by the side of his master. But poor Wilkie the next minute, himself staggered against the howitzer mortally wounded! I flew to his support. But seizing me hastily by the hand, and giving it a deadly squeeze, 'Ned,' he articulated, 'it's all up with me' and relaxing his grasp, he fell back and expired.[2] The officer, perceiving my agitation, and fearful of my retaliating on him, handed me over his gold watch.

Finding I could be of little use to my comrade, and as our division was fast entering the breach, I proceeded with the stormers, clearing the walls of the enemy as we went. Turning to the right we entered a large square or plaza, where we were in a short time joined by some of every regiment in the two divisions, all like ourselves helter-skelter, subject to everything but order. However in a short time one regiment of the 3rd division entered the square, commanded by their officers; something like order then prevailed; while planting the British colours in the centre, three cheers were then given by the whole, proclaiming the town to be taken: when this was over they commenced firing in the air, as well as at windows where any light appeared. Seeing the confusion, a number broke into squads, and went in different directions and entered different streets according to the fancy of their leaders. Myself and about a score others took a large street to the right. The night being dark and the city not being lighted,

[1] Harry Smith says: 'I and Uniacke were much scorched, but some splinters of an ammunition chest lacerated him and caused his death three days after the storm.'

[2] There is no doubt, but Wilkie, Major Napier, and indeed several others in advance fell by the fire of the Portuguese; who being panic-struck by the first volley they received from the town, instantly lay down on the glacis, and commenced firing on the breach. A random shot through the embrasure deprived my friend of life. [E.C.]

we were obliged to grope our way, but had not proceeded far before we got mixed amongst a quantity of French muskets thrown on the ground with their bayonets fixed. One or two of the men getting pricked in the leg by one of the bayonets, swore they had come to a *chevaux-de-frise*,[1] and groping about came across the body of a wounded French soldier, who told us in Spanish that we were close to the barracks.

Knowing the French would not resign their liberty without a struggle, I fully expected a volley to be sent amongst us every minute from the barracks, and began to retrace my steps towards the square, and had only got a short distance when I saw another party with a lighted candle advancing towards me. On hearing the noise of the first party in their front, they commenced firing as they advanced. Squeezing myself edgeways against a door, I waited their arrival and begged them to desist, there being some of their own men lower down. I then went with them and joined the first party. The French wounded soldier pointing to a large gateway, told us there were the barracks. Still having a light we entered, and mounting a large stone staircase, found ourselves in the midst of a French hospital full of sick and wounded; those who were able sitting up in bed supplicating mercy, but they had no occasion to do so, as our fellows not only kindly tapped them on the shoulder but wrapped the bed-clothes round them; but this kindness was of short duration, for a third party coming down seeing a light in our window commenced firing, and the poor fellow who held the candle was shot through the head, and one or two others wounded; one more daring than the rest flew to the window, crying out that they were firing on their own men, the rest lying down while the firing continued. This panic being over, I came downstairs, being anxious to meet some of my own company to know how things were. I found a few outside, and we started in another direction. The next place was a large white house that had been used as a commissary's store by the French: here a crowd had assembled to break it open, when they were warned off by a sentinel, a German, who was posted to guard the premises. Not heeding his threat, the throng rushed at the door. The poor sentry, true to his trust, attempted to oppose their entrance, and the following minute was run through the body by a bayonet.

The house contained several puncheons of spirits, which the men

---

[1] Large beams studded with long spikes and placed in front of and across the breaches to impede an enemy's advance.

present immediately tapped, by striking in the heads. A number soon became madly drunk; and several wretches, especially those mounting the steps that had been placed against the butts, to enable them to obtain the rum, fell into the liquor head-foremost and perished, un-noticed by the crowd. Several fights took place, in which drunkenness of the parties alone prevented mischief; and to crown the whole, a light falling into one of the barrels of spirits, the place was set on fire, and many poor wretches, who from the quantity of liquor they had swallowed were incapable of moving, were consumed in the flames.

Turning from this scene of horrors, hardened as I then was, I went with a comrade to look for a house where we might obtain refresh-ment and take up our quarters for the night. This, after some search, we found in the domicile of a doctor, whom we took from under a bed clasped in the arms of a very pretty girl whom he called his niece, like himself, almost

Distill'd to jelly with th' effect of fear![1]

This, however, we soon dispelled, and were rewarded for our pains with a good supper crowned by a bowl of excellent punch that at the time, in our own minds, compensated for all the sufferings we had endured in the trenches during the siege.

The next morning I was anxious to visit the left breach, to look for the body of Wilkie. I found him, at length, cold and stiff, the bullet having entered his breast close under the left shoulder. He was stripped! But I easily distinguished him by the likeness he bore to his sister; old times then burst vividly over my recollection, and as I stood over his prostrate remains, a few moments brought to mind all the scenes in which he had been so active a coadjutor, my quondam recruit, bed-fellow, press-man, and pot companion, lay stretched before me clotted and besmeared with his blood, a single drop of which, at one time, was even more valued by me than the whole of my own more lucky current. The remembrance of his sister, much as my profession had tended to wipe her off my mind, now resumed its almost pristine freshness; my eyes dimmed for a second, and perchance one solitary proof of my weakness might have left its scalding course behind it, but I felt only as a soldier, a momentary sorrow, for I held my own life as it were in my hand, ready to part with it, at even a moment's notice, and I presumed as much of all belonging to me.

[1] 'Distill'd almost to jelly with the act of fear.'—Shakespeare's *Hamlet*, ii, 204.

The proceeds of the storming 'business' had enabled me to gain over a few half-drunken soldiers, who had been staggering near me stupidly staring at my anxiety. We buried poor Wilkie in the glacis, near the breach, the whole wreck around us displaying the veriest monument ever reared to the memory of a soldier!

I now proceeded to the right breach, which had been carried by the 3rd division, where the mine had been sprung. The sight exhibited was heart-rendering in the extreme. The dead lay in heaps, numbers of them stripped, and displaying the most ghastly wounds. Here and there, half-buried under the blackened fragments of the wall, or reeking on the surface of the ruin, lay those who had been blown up in the explosion, their remains dreadfully mangled and discoloured, and strewed about amongst dissevered arms and legs.

The 88th, or Connaught Rangers, had suffered most severely at this spot, and I observed a number of poor Irish women hopelessly endeavouring to distinguish the burnt features of their husbands.

Though heartily sick of the morning's mournful perambulation, I yet felt anxious to see Captain Uniacke; his remains lay on the suburbs, in a house next to that where those of our brave old General were stretched out. Several of the men of his company crowded about his person, hoping—for he was still living, and sensible—that he might yet return amongst us. But his arm had been torn from the socket, and he died some few days afterwards.

Here let me pay a brief though sincere tribute to his memory; though young in years, he was gallant, daring, and just to all whom he commanded.

During the Peninsular war our men had divided the officers into two classes; the 'come on' and the 'go on'; for as Tom Plunkett in action once observed to an officer, 'The words "go on" don't befit a leader, Sir.'—To the honour of the service, the latter, with us Rifles, were exceedingly few in numbers. But amongst the former, none were seen so often in the van as Uniacke; his affability and personal courage had rendered him the idol of the men of his company.

A very small portion only of the troops that had taken Rodrigo were allowed to remain in the city, and our battalion, among others, were ordered back to their former quarters. The next morning as we marched over the bridge, dressed in all the varieties imaginable, some with jack-boots on, others with frock-coats, epaulettes, &c., and some with even monkeys on their shoulders, we met the 5th division on their way to repair the breach; they immediately formed up on the left of the road, presented arms, and cheered us as we went along.

I was afterwards told by several of our men that the Duke of Wellington, who saw us on our march, inquired of his staff, 'Who the devil are those fellows?'

We entered El Bodon, with songs: and welcomed by the 'vivas' of the inhabitants.

XIV

The second day after the storming of Rodrigo our brave General Craufurd died of his wound, and the chief part of the officers of the Rifles went to pay the last tribute to his remains. He was borne to the grave by four Sergeant-Majors of his own division, and was buried in the breach where he fell. The Duke of Wellington attended the funeral of the gallant veteran; who, though most strict in discipline, was averse to punishment, and was beloved by the men for his justice and care for them, as well as for his bravery. The following incident, of which I was an eyewitness, will serve to show his character.

I happened to be on guard one day, when General Craufurd came riding in from the front with his orderly dragoon, as was his usual custom, when two of our men, one of them a corporal, came running out of a house with some bread which they had stolen from the Spaniards; they were pursued by a Spanish woman crying lustily, 'Ladrone! Ladrone!'—thief! thief! They were immediately pursued by the General and his orderly; the bread was given back to the woman, and the men were placed in the guard-house. The next day they were tried by a brigade court-martial, and brought out to a wood near the town for punishment. When the brigade was formed, and the Brigade-Major had finished reading the proceedings of the court-martial, General Craufurd commenced lecturing both men and officers on the nature of their cruelty to the harmless inhabitants, as he called the Spaniards. He laid particular stress on our regiment, who, he said, committed more crimes than the whole of the British Army. 'Besides, you think,' said he, 'because you are riflemen, and more exposed to the enemy's fire than other regiments, that you are to rob the inhabitants with impunity; but, while I command you, you shall not': then turning round to the corporal, who stood in the centre of the square, he said, with a stern voice, 'Strip, Sir.'

The corporal, whose name was Miles, never said a word until tied up to a tree, when turning his head round as far as his situation would allow, and seeing the General pacing up and down the square, he said, 'General Craufurd, I hope you will forgive me.' The General replied, 'No, Sir, your crime is too great.' The poor corporal, whose sentence was to be reduced to the pay and rank of a private soldier, and to receive a punishment of one hundred and fifty lashes, and the other man two hundred, then addressed the General to the following effect:

'Do you recollect, Sir, when you and I were taken prisoners, when under the command of General Whitelocke, in Buenos Aires? We were marched prisoners, with a number of others, to a sort of pound surrounded with a wall.—There was a well in the centre, out of which I drew water with my mess-tin, by means of canteen straps I collected from the men, who were prisoners like myself.—You sat on my knapsack; I parted my last biscuit with you. You then told me you would never forget my kindness to you. It is now in your power, Sir. You know how short we have been of rations for some time.'

These words were spoken by the corporal in a mild and respectful accent, which not only affected the General, but the whole square. The bugler, who stood waiting to commence the punishment close to the corporal, received the usual nod from the Bugle-Major to begin. At the first lash the corporal received the General started, and turned hurriedly round, said, 'What's that, what's that; who taught that bugler to flog? Send him to drill—send him to drill! He cannot flog—he cannot flog! Stop! stop! Take him down! take him down! I remember it well—I remember it well!' while he paced up and down the square, muttering to himself words that I could not catch; at the same time blowing his nose, and wiping his face with his handkerchief, trying to hide the emotion that was so evident to the whole square.

While untying the corporal a dead silence prevailed for some time, until our gallant General recovered a little his noble feeling, when he uttered, with a broken accent, 'Why does a brave soldier like you commit these crimes?' Then beckoning to his orderly to bring his horse, he mounted and rode off. It is needless to say that the other man also was pardoned, and in a few days the corporal was restored to his rank. On the death of Captain Uniacke, Captain Smith, now the celebrated Sir Harry Smith,[1] was appointed Captain of my company. He being on the staff, his brother, Lieutenant Thomas Smith, now Barrack Master at Chatham, took command.

On the fourth day after we had taken the town, the company received orders to pay the last tribute to our Captain, Uniacke. We marched under the command of Lieutenant Smith, and arrived at Gallegos about twelve o'clock. The men having plenty of money, which they had obtained at Rodrigo, got drinking, and actually while conveying the body to the grave, stumbled under the weight of the coffin, and the lid not having been nailed down, out rolled the mangled remains of our brave Captain, to the consternation of a number of French officers, en parole (prisoners from Rodrigo). One more careless than the rest viewed the occurrence with a kind of malicious sneer, which so enraged our men that one of them, taking the little tawny-looking Italian by the nape of the neck, kicked his hind-quarters soundly for it.

I could not, at the time, help remarking the very undersized appearance of the Frenchmen. They were the ugliest set I ever saw, and seemed to be the refuse of their army, and looked more like Italians than Frenchmen.

On our return to El Bodon, one of the men, overpowered with liquor, laid himself down to sleep in the wood that separates the road from Gallegos. Poor fellow, it was his last sleep, for on the roll being called, a party was sent in search of him, and discovered his body under a tree, torn to pieces by the wolves, which greatly infested that part of Spain.

I now have to relate one of those melancholy incidents peculiar to a soldier's life, that occurred while we remained at El Bodon. On taking Rodrigo we had captured, among others, ten men who had deserted from our division. These were condemned to be shot. The place of execution was on a plain near Ituera, where our division was drawn up, forming three sides of a square; the culprits, as usual, being placed in front of a trench, dug for a grave, on the vacant side.

Two of the deserters, the one a man of the same company as myself, named Hudson, and a very handsome fellow who had been persuaded into the rash step, were pardoned on the ground. The other, a corporal, named Cummins, of the 52nd regiment, and who

---

1 Smith was Brigade-Major to the 2nd Light Brigade. Sir Harry lived until 1860.

had been mainly instrumental, I believe, in getting the others to desert with him, was placed on the fatal ground in a wounded state. He had been particularly noticed at Rodrigo in one of the breaches, most actively employed, opposing our entrance, and cheering on the besieged to resist us. This man was pardoned also. Why he was pardoned I cannot say.

As this was the first military execution I had ever witnessed, I felt not a little curiosity to see the forms pursued. A large trench had been dug as a grave for the wretched men who were to suffer. Along the summit of the little heap of mould that had been thrown up from the pit, the deserters were placed in a row, with their eyes bandaged, so that on receiving the fatal volley they should fall forward into the trench. Some of the poor fellows, from debility, were unable to kneel, and lay at their length, or crouched up into an attitude of despair, upon the loose earth.

The signal to the firing party was given by a motion of the provost's cane, when the culprits were all hurried together into eternity, with the exception of one man of the 52nd, who, strange to say, remained standing and untouched. His countenance, that before had been deadly pale, now exhibited a bright flush. Perhaps he might have imagined himself pardoned; if so, however, he was doomed to be miserably deceived, as the following minute two men of the reserve came up and fired their pieces into his bosom, when giving a loud scream, that had a very horrible effect upon those near, he sprang forward into his grave. To prevent unnecessary suffering, a reserve firing party was brought up, who continued to fire wherever the slightest sign of life exhibited itself in the bodies, the provost himself winding up the tragedy by discharging a pistol-shot through the head of each corpse.

After this very solemn and impressive scene, we were marched in column of companies round the dead, so that the spectacle might be witnessed by every man in the division.

On the 26th of February we broke up our cantonments in the environs of Ciudad Rodrigo, and crossing the Tagus, marched southward for six or seven days, at the expiration of which our division took up their quarters in and about the town of Castello de Vide. The country around the town was the most fruitful and luxuriant I had ever beheld. It was bounded with the most delightful hills and valleys, that produced in abundance the finest fruits, such as grapes, pomegranates, oranges, and lemons. As may be supposed, the men were delighted with such a paradise. The wine was so plentiful that our fellows, while they remained here, made it an invariable custom to boil their meat in it.

Another unhappy criminal was here doomed to pay the forfeit of the crime of desertion. When we took Rodrigo, he made his escape from the town, and on his way to join the French at Salamanca was captured by some of the Spanish troops, and brought back to the regiment a prisoner. The fate of this man (Arnal by name), who had been a corporal in our battalion, excited much commiseration. I knew him well: he was an exceedingly fine-looking fellow, and, up to the period of his unhappy departure from duty, noted for possessing the best qualities of a soldier. Some harshness on the part of an officer was the cause of Arnal's desertion; but from the circumstance of his previous good character, and the fact of his having been marched as a prisoner for many days together during our march from Rodrigo, it was commonly thought he would be pardoned.

I happened to be on guard over him the night prior to his execution. In the evening the prisoner was playing at cards with some of the men, when the provost of the division entered the guard-room, and gave him the intelligence that he was doomed to suffer at ten o'clock the next morning.

Sudden and utterly unexpected as the announcement was, Arnal's face was the only one that showed scarcely any emotion.

'Well,' he remarked to those around him, 'I am quite ready.'

A short time afterwards he sent for the pay-sergeant of the company he belonged to, from whom he received the arrears of pay that were due to him. This he spent on wine, which he distributed among the men of the guard. Noticing one man with very bad shoes, Arnal observed his own were better, and taking them off he exchanged them for the bad pair, saying, 'They will last me as long as I shall require them.'

The morning turned out showery, the division formed in three sides of a square, and the guard, headed by the band with Arnal in front, slowly marched round; the muffled drum beat in dull time the 'Dead March', and the swell of its solemn harmony, though it filled the eyes of every man present, only seemed to strengthen the glance of the doomed. He led the van of his funeral procession, like one who was to live for ever: his step was as firm and more correct than any, and I thought at the time, a finer soldier never stepped. Poor Arnal, I shall never forget when we halted at his own grave, the heavy rains had filled it half with water, which he noticed with a faint smile, and observed:

'Although a watery one, I shall sleep sound enough in it.' He then stood upright in a fine military position, while the Brigade-Major read aloud the proceedings of the court-martial. The provost came to tie the handkerchief round his eyes, when he coolly remarked, 'There is no occasion—I shall not flinch.' Being told it was customary, he said, 'Very well, do your duty.' Before this last office was performed, he turned round, and calling most of the guard by name bade them farewell. As I nodded to him in return, I fancied it was to a dead man, for in two minutes he was no more. The intrepid and cool manner in which he met his fate drew forth a general feeling of admiration.

A few days after the execution we marched for Badajoz, in the environs of which we arrived on the 17th of March. This celebrated city, of which so much has been said and written, stands on an extended plain equidistant three leagues from Elvas and Campo Mayor. The Guadiana, which hereabouts forms the boundary between Spain and Portugal, flows on one side of the fortification, and connects with them by a bridge over its surface one or two forts on the opposite banks. The fortress on all sides is surrounded by strong bastions to the number of thirteen or fourteen, which with trenches and other forts and outworks rendered it almost impregnable. In addition to these the Rivillas, a tributary stream to the Guadiana, flowed round and through the trenches in our front.

Our battalion on its arrival took up its encampment on the Spanish side of the river, where we occupied a small hill and for the first time during our campaigns made use of small square tents, belonging to the Portuguese.

The first night of our arrival we commenced laying siege, by breaking ground within three or four hundred yards of the town, Fort San Roche and Fort Picurina rather on our left; we lost a man named Brooks, whose death was connected with a very singular circumstance.

Brooks, several days before his death, dreamt he saw the body of a rifleman without a head: this apparition appeared three or four nights successively in his dreams. Some days after we had taken one of the forts from the enemy, our battalion was relieved in the trenches. On this occasion, as was very customary with some of us, Brooks, another man named Tracey, and myself jumped out of the trench, exposing ourselves to a fire from the walls of the town while we ran to the next parallel. In executing this feat I was a little ahead of my comrades, when I heard the rush of a cannon-ball, and feeling my jacket splashed by something, as soon as I had jumped into the next parallel, or trench, I turned round and beheld the headless body of Brooks which actually stood quivering with life for a few seconds before it fell. His dream, poor fellow! had singularly augured the conclusion of his own career. The shot had smashed and carried away the whole of his head, bespattering my jacket with the brains, while Tracey was materially injured by having a splinter of the skull driven deep through the skin behind his ear. This circumstance is well known to several now living in London.

About the 22nd of March, a party was ordered to proceed to Elvas for the purpose of conducting some heavy artillery from that strong fortress for our own use against the walls of Badajoz; after placing six or eight large guns on things resembling sledges, the weather being exceedingly wet, it took twelve bullocks to draw each gun. On arriving at the pontoon bridge that crosses the Guadiana River, which separates Badajoz from Elvas, a distance of about three leagues, the bridge was so damaged that the guns could not pass over, so we were obliged to bivouac for the night amongst a party of sappers, stationed there for the purpose of repairing the pontoons.

After the bullocks were unharnessed, they began jumping and frisking about, to the no small amusement of our men, but to their danger, as it afterwards proved. The French seeing the bullocks grazing, commenced firing on them, as well as occasionally sending a twenty-four-pounder at our little party then stationed on a rising ground, amusing ourselves at the random twenty-four-pound shots as they hopped about. At night, placing our advanced picquet near the town, the remainder of the party turned into the tents of the sappers for the night, but their slumbers were not so sound as they anticipated, for at the dead but not silent hour of night, a round-shot came whirling through one of the tents, striking the pole, and brought it down on those within. Their cries having awoke those of the adjoining tent, they immediately flew to their assistance, and having relieved them from this newfashioned man-trap, rats never flew with more agility than did the poor sappers from their lair. I could not forbear laughing at the scene, although attended with bad consequences, as one man had his thigh broke, and another his leg taken off at the calf. While helping to raise the tents every eye was intent, looking about for another French visitor in the shape of a twenty-four-pounder, but the drollery of a countryman of mine gave some zest to their serenity; instead of bolting like the rest, he coolly said, 'Where the devil are you all scampering to? Sure you don't think the French took aim? I wished they did, for if they had, by Jasus they wouldn't hit our tent in a week! You may be easy then, for they never hit twice in the same place.' The two poor fellows thus dangerously wounded were comrades, and natives of Coventry, one named Green, and the other Gea. The next morning, the sappers having put the pontoons to rights, the guns passed over, and we arrived safe at our own camp.

The greatest annoyance we experienced during the siege arose from the shells thrown at us from the town. Our works effectually screened us from the round-shot; but these dangerous missiles, falling into the trenches where we worked, and exploding, frequently did great mischief. Immediately a shell fell, every man threw himself flat upon the ground until it had burst. Tom Crawley, I remember, though tolerably fearless with reference to other shot, had a most inveterate dislike to those deadly visitors. His fears made him believe that more of them were thrown where he chanced to be than in any other part of the trenches. At night, in particular, Tom was always on the *qui vive*: as soon as he beheld a shell coming he would call out, 'Here's another brute—look out!' and instantly fall on his face. This, however, did not always protect us, for the head was no sooner on the ground, than its presence was again required, to watch the falling splinters. These, from their composing large portions of the metal of the missile, descended with great violence, and were sometimes of themselves sufficient to crush a man into the earth.

Lord Wellington used occasionally to pay us a visit during the work, to make observations, and to examine the trenches, &c.

One day when Crawley and myself were working near each other in the trenches, a shell fell inconveniently close to us. Tom was instantly half buried in mud, awaiting the explosion. Perceiving it had sunk itself deep into the earth, the fuse being too long, I intended availing myself of the opportunity to play a trick upon Crawley by throwing a large lump of clay on his head directly the shell exploded, and so make him believe himself wounded. To obtain the clod I sprang at the other side of the trench, but exposed myself to a shot from the walls of the town, which immediately came in the form of grape, splashing me with mud from head to foot, and forcing me to throw myself back into the trench upon Crawley, who, in his fears, made sure that a shell had fixed itself upon his rear, and roared like a bull; in an instant, however, the sunken missile really burst; on the smoke dispersing, who should I behold but the Duke himself, crouched down, his head half averted, dryly smiling at Crawley and me. Shot and shell pay no respect to persons, but the enemy did, as they seemed awake to the near vicinity of his Grace, and poured in shells, grape, and canister, with other delicacies of the kind, with unusual liberality, whenever he came amongst us; which they always appeared alive to. But the fact is, the Duke, like his renowned contemporary [*presumably Napoleon*], had a remarkable cast of feature, which made him ever distinguishable, at an almost incredible distance.

Before I go further into my narrative I must detail an anecdote of Major O'Hare, my old Captain, who was noted for his excellent soldierly qualities.

We were on private parade one morning, when a party of convalescents from hospital came up. Among others was a sergeant of the name of Jackson, who had been absent from our company for the two previous years, during which period it would seem he had been chiefly employed as hospital-sergeant at Belem, near Lisbon.

The Major's aversion to absentees from the regiment was very well known among us, and we anticipated a scene—nor were we deceived.

'Is that you, Mr Sergeant Jackson?' exclaimed the Major, as soon as the party came up. 'And pray where, in God's name, have you been for the last two years? The company have seen a little fighting during that period.'

'The doctors would not allow me to leave the hospital, Sir' replied Jackson.

'I am sorry for that,' dryly observed the Major. 'All that I can do for you is, to give you your choice of a court-martial for absenting yourself from duty without leave, or to have yours stripes taken off.'

The sergeant, after a little hesitation, preferred surrendering quietly his non-commissioned dignity to standing an inquiry into his conduct.

Turning round to the men, the Major remarked aloud, 'By God, I will not have these brave fellows commanded by skulkers.' Then taking the sash and stripes that were cut off by the Sergeant-Major, he handed them to Corporal Ballard, observing at the same time, 'You will not disgrace them.'

A very disagreeable duty, that usually fell upon a few of the best shots of the battalion, consisted in being obliged to run out, in independent files, to occupy a number of holes, that had been dug at night between our batteries and the walls of the town. From these pits, of which each man had one to himself, our particular business was to pick off any of the enemy who exposed themselves at their guns, on the walls through the embrasures. Many a Frenchman was thus knocked off by us. But it often occurred also that our men were killed or wounded in their holes, which made it doubly dangerous for the man of the relieving party, who, instead of finding a ready covering, perceived it occupied by a wounded or dead man. Before he could get a shelter therefore or remove the body, there was a great chance of his being shot.

While employed in this duty in front of our batteries, the tremendous noise made by artillery in both front and rear was attended at first by a most unpleasant effect, as it destroyed the sense of hearing for some hours after leaving the trenches. It was amusing, during the siege, to observe the motions of our artillerymen. They were employed almost incessantly, and their duties most arduous, as the batteries were the chief object for the aim of the enemy's shot and shells. An artillery-man was always stationed as a sort of signal-man, to give notice of the appearance of either of these missiles, and it was remarkable to observe the quickness with which the men at the guns, on the word 'shell', would throw themselves on the ground for protection.

It not unfrequently happened that parties of men were sent out in independent files to pick up the dismembered legs, arms, &c., which sometimes might be seen scattered about by the bursting shells. This precaution was thought necessary to prevent any ill-effect their appearance might cause on the courage of the Portuguese, who were quite as likely to put the heels in motion as their heads.

On one of these occasions I remember observing a party of those gentlemen, after leaving the trenches, carrying across the fields to their camp ground the body of a wounded officer of theirs wrapped in a blanket. They had not proceeded many yards before a ball fired from the town came bounding, half spent, along the ground. The Portu-guese, unconscious of its approach, were just crossing the line of its progress, when the shot glanced between them, and entering the blanket, cut the unlucky officer in two. The bearers, terrified, im-mediately took to their heels, leaving the blanket behind them, which one of our fellows observing, 'That it was an ill wind that did nobody good', shaking the body out, instantly possessed himself of.

The effect of our twenty-four-pound shot upon the wall gave notice that the breaches would soon be practicable. On the 5th of April a storming party was selected for the assault on the following night.

XV

I am now about entering into a personal narrative of one of the most sanguinary and awful engagements on the records of any country. For the second time I volunteered on the forlorn-hope. After having received a double allowance of grog, we fell in about eight o'clock in the evening, 6th April 1812. The stormers were composed of men from the different regiments of the light division. I happened to be on the right of the front section when my old Captain, Major O'Hare, who commanded the wing to which my company belonged, came up with Captain Jones of the 52nd regiment, both in command of the storming party. A pair of uglier men never walked together, but a brace of better soldiers never stood before the muzzle of a Frenchman's gun.

'Well, O'Hare,' said the Captain, 'what do you think of tonight's work?'

'I don't know,' replied the Major, who seemed, as I thought, in rather low spirits. 'Tonight, I think, will be my last.'

'Tut, tut, man! I have the same sort of feeling, but I keep it down with a drop of the *cratur*,' answered the Captain, as he handed his calabash to the Major.

A Sergeant Fleming, a brave soldier, before mentioned in these Memoirs [see p. 47], coming up, informed Major O'Hare that a ladder party was wanted. 'Take the right files of the leading sections,' was the prompt order of the Major. No sooner said than done. I and my front-rank men were immediately tapped on the shoulder for the ladder party. I now gave up all hope of ever returning. At Rodrigo, as before stated, we had fatigue parties for the ladders, but now the case was altered; besides which the ladders, now in preparation, were much longer than those employed at that fortress.

I may just mention that whatever were my own forebodings on the occasion, the presentiments of our brave old Major O'Hare and those of Captain Jones were fatally realised, for in less than twenty minutes after the above conversation, both fell riddled with balls.

The word was now given to the ladder party to move forward. We were accompanied at each side by two men with hatchets to cut down any obstacle that might oppose them, such as *chevaux-de-frise*. There were six of us supporting the ladder allotted to me, and I contrived to carry my grass-bag before me.[1] We had proceeded but a short distance when we heard the sound of voices on our right, upon which we halted, and supposing they might be enemies, I disengaged myself from the ladder, and cocking my rifle, prepared for action. Luckily we soon discovered our mistake, as one of our party cried— 'Take care! 'Tis the stormers of the fourth division coming to join us.' This proved to be the case. This brief alarm over, we continued advancing towards the walls, the Rifles, as before, keeping in front. We had to pass Fort San Roche on our left, near to the town, and as we approached it the French sentry challenged. This was instantly followed by a shot from the fort and another from the walls of the town. A moment afterwards, a fire-ball was thrown out, which threw a bright red glare of light around us, and instantly a volley of grape-shot, canister, and small arms poured in among us as we stood on the glacis, at a distance of about thirty yards from the walls.

Three of the men carrying the ladder with me were shot dead in a breath, and its weight falling upon me, I fell backwards with the grass-bag on my breast. The remainder of the stormers rushed up, regardless of my cries, or those of the wounded men around me, for by this time our men were falling fast. Many in passing were shot and fell upon me, so that I was actually drenched in blood. The weight I had to sustain became intolerable, and had it not been for the grass-bag which in some measure protected me, I must have been suffocated. At length, by a strong effort, I managed to extricate myself, in doing which I left my rifle behind me, and drawing my sword, rushed towards the breach. There I found four men putting a ladder down the ditch; and not daring to pause, fresh lights being still thrown out of the town, with a continual discharge of musketry, I slid quickly down the ladder, but before I could recover my footing, was knocked down again by the bodies of men who were shot in attempting the descent. I, however, succeeded in extricating myself from underneath the dead, and rushing forward to the right, to my surprise and fear I found myself immersed to my neck in water. Until then I was tolerably composed, but now all reflection left me, and diving through the water, being a good swimmer, gained the other side, but lost

[1] Grass-bags are long sacks about six feet by three, filled with grass or hay, and so stuffed as to enable a party, in case the ladders should not be fixed in sufficient time, by pitching them into the trenches before them to descend with comparative safety. With us, however, they answered a double purpose, being carried by our men in front of their persons to prevent the effects of the enemy's fire. [*E.C.*]

my sword; I now attempted to make to the breach, which the blaze of musketry from the walls clearly showed me. Without rifle, sword, or any other weapon, I succeeded in clambering up a part of the breach, and came near to a *chevaux-de-frise*, consisting of a piece of heavy timber studded with sword-blades, turning on an axis: but just before reaching it I received a stroke on the breast, whether from a grenade or a stone, or by the butt-end of a musket, I cannot say, but down I rolled senseless, and drenched with water and human gore. I could not have laid long in this plight, for when my senses had in some measure returned, I perceived our gallant fellows still rushing forward, each seeming to share a fate more deadly than my own. The fire continued in one horrible and incessant peal, as if the mouth of the infernal regions had opened to vomit forth destruction upon all around us, and this was rendered still more appalling by the fearful shouts of the combatants and cries of the wounded that mingled in the uproar.

I now, strange to say, began to feel if my arms and legs were entire: for at such moments a man, I believe, is not always aware of his wounds. I had now, indeed, lost all the frenzy of courage that had first possessed me, and actually felt all weakness and prostration of spirit, while I endeavoured, among the dead and wounded bodies around me, to screen myself from the enemy's shot; but while I lay in this position, the fire still continued blazing over me in all its horrors, accompanied by screams, groans, and shouts, and the crashing of stones and falling of timbers. I now, for the first time for many years, uttered something like a prayer.

After the horrible and well-known scene of carnage had lasted some time, the fire gradually slackened from the breach, I heard a cheering which I knew to proceed from within the town, and shortly afterwards a cry of 'Blood and 'ounds! where's the Light Division?—the town's our own—hurrah!' This proceeded, no doubt, from some of the 3rd division. I now attempted to rise, but, from a wound which I had received, but at what time I know not, found myself unable to stand. A musket-ball had passed through the lower part of my right leg—two others had perforated my cap, which I should have lost had I not taken the precaution to secure it with a cord under my chin before starting. At the moment of this discovery I saw two or three men moving towards me, who I was glad to find belonged to the Rifles. One of them, named O'Brien, of the same company as myself, immediately exclaimed, 'What! is that you, Ned?—we thought you ladder-men all done for.' He then assisted me to rise.

In consequence of the *chevaux-de-frise* still remaining above the breach, we could not proceed over it until more men arrived to remove its fastenings. The 3rd division meanwhile had entered the town on our right by the castle where there was no breach. We proceeded onwards, I moving with great difficulty, though partly supported by O'Brien. At the top of the breach we found another trench with a plank of wood lain across, leading into the town. Not until then I felt drops of blood trickling down my face, and found that one of the balls, in passing through my cap, had torn the skin on my head.

In this crippled state, leaning upon my comrade, and using his rifle as a crutch, accompanied by a few of our riflemen, I entered the town that had been so gloriously won. We hurried from the breach as quick as possible, lest the enemy should spring a mine, as they did at Ciudad Rodrigo. We still however heard occasional firing and cheering from one end of the town, and imagined the fire was still raging, although, as we soon afterwards learnt, the chief part of the French had retired to the citadel or fort, where they surrendered on the following morning. Angry and irritated from the pain occasioned by the wound, we had just turned the corner of a street, when we observed some men, and, from the light that shone from a window opposite, we could see from their uniforms they were evidently Frenchmen. The moment they saw us they disappeared, with the exception of one man, who seemed to make a rush at us with his musket. O'Brien sprang forward and wrested the firelock from his grasp. A feeling of revenge, prompted by the suffering I endured from my wounds, actuated my feelings, and I exclaimed, 'O'Brien, let me have the pleasure of shooting this rascal, for he may be the man who has brought me to the state I am now in!' I then presented the rifle close to his breast, with the full intention of shooting him through the body, but as my finger was about to press the trigger he fell upon his knees and implored mercy. The next moment the rifle dropped from my hand, and I felt a degree of shame that a feeling of irritation should have nearly betrayed me into the commission of a crime for which I could never have forgiven myself.

As soon as the Frenchman perceived me desist, he immediately started from his knees, and, by way of showing his gratitude, threw his arms round my neck, and kissed my cheek. He instantly followed me, and I for the time took him under my protection.

We now looked anxiously around for a house where we could obtain refreshment, and, if truth must be told, a little money. For even wounded as I was, I had made up my mind to be a gainer by our victory. At the first house we knocked at, no notice being taken of the summons, we fired a rifle-ball at the key-hole, which sent the door flying open. This, indeed, was our usual method of forcing locks. As soon as we entered the house we found a young Spanish woman crying bitterly, and praying for mercy. She informed us that she was the wife of a French officer; and to the demand of my companion, O'Brien, for refreshment, replied there was nothing but her poor self in the house. She, however, produced some spirits and chocolate, both of which, being very hungry and faint, I partook of with much relish.

As the house looked poor we soon quitted it in quest of a better. Supported by O'Brien and the Frenchman, we proceeded in the direction of the market-place. It was a dark night, and the confusion and uproar that prevailed in the town may be better imagined than described. The shouts and oaths of drunken soldiers in quest of more liquor, the reports of fire-arms and crashing in of doors, together with the appalling shrieks of hapless women, might have induced anyone to have believed himself in the regions of the damned. When we arrived at the market-place we found a number of Spanish prisoners rushing out of a gaol: they appeared like a set of savages suddenly let loose, many still bearing the chains they had not time to free themselves from, and among these were men of the 5th and 88th regiments holding lighted candles. We then turned down a street opposite to the foregoing scene, and entered a house which was occupied by a number of men of the 3rd division. One of them immediately, on perceiving me wounded, struck off the neck of a bottle of wine with his bayonet, and presented it to me, which relieved me for a time from the faintness I had previously felt. The scenes of wickedness that soldiers are guilty of on capturing a town are oftentimes truly diabolical, and I now, in the reflections this subject gives rise to, shudder at the past. I had not long been seated at the fire which was blazing up the chimney, fed by mahogany chairs broken up for the purpose, when I heard screams for mercy from an adjoining room. On hobbling in, I found an old man, the proprietor of the house, on his knees, imploring mercy of a soldier who had levelled his musket at him. I with difficulty prevented the man from shooting him, as he complained that the Spaniard would not give up his money. I immediately informed the wretched landlord in Spanish, as well as I was able, that he could only save his life by surrendering his cash. Upon this he brought out with trembling hands a large bag of dollars from under the mattress of the bed. These by common consent were immediately divided among us. The whole treasure, to the amount of about one hundred or one hundred and fifty dollars, enveloped in an old night-cap, was instantly emptied and divided into small heaps on the table, according to the number of men present, and called out the same as messes in a barrack-room. I must confess that I participated in the plunder, and received about twenty-six dollars for my own share.

As soon as I had resumed my seat at the fire, a number of Portuguese soldiers entered, one of whom, taking me for a Frenchman, for I had the French soldier's jacket on, my own being wet, snapped his piece at me, which luckily hung fire. Forgetful of my wounds, I instantly rushed at him, and a regular scuffle ensued between our men and the Portuguese, until one of the latter being stabbed by a bayonet, the rest retired, dragging the wounded man with them. After thus ejecting the Portuguese, the victors, who had by this time got tolerably drunk, proceeded to ransack the house. Unhappily they discovered the two daughters of the old patrone, who had concealed themselves upstairs. They both were young and very pretty. The mother, too, was shortly afterwards dragged from her hiding-place.

Without dwelling on the frightful scene that followed, it may be sufficient to add, that our men, more infuriated by drink than before, again seized upon the old man, and insisted upon a fresh supply of liquor. And his protestations that he possessed no more were as vain as were all attempts to restrain them from ill-using him.

It is to be lamented that the memory of an old soldier should be disturbed by such painful reflections as the foregoing scenes must give rise to: but it is to be considered that the men who besiege a town in the face of such dangers generally become desperate from their own privations and sufferings; and when once they get a footing within its walls—flushed by victory, hurried on by the desire of liquor, and maddened by drink, they stop at nothing: they are literally mad, and hardly conscious of what they do in such a state of excitement. I do not state this in justification; I only remark what I have observed human nature to be on these occasions.

Sick of the scene of horrors that had been enacted, and attended by my French prisoner, I left the house for one on the other side of the street. This was found occupied by men of the 3rd division, who were drinking chocolate, not made with water, but wine. They seemed rather more sober and peaceable than those we had just left; but here, also, as in most of the houses in Badajoz, the greatest outrages were being committed.

Having passed a wretched night, the next morning I determined to rejoin what remained of my regiment—for at this time I did not know what number we had lost. I left the house, and proceeded to trace my road through the crowds, accompanied by my Frenchman, who rendered me every assistance in his power. The town was still in great confusion and uproar, although every available means had been taken to suppress it. In one of the streets I saw the Duke of Wellington, surrounded by a number of British soldiers, who, holding up bottles with the heads knocked off, containing wine and spirits, cried out to him, a phrase then familiarly applied to him by the men of the army, 'Old boy! will you drink? The town's our own—hurrah!' In another street I observed a sort of gallows erected, with three nooses hanging from them, ready for service. Johnny Castles, a man of our company, and as quiet and inoffensive a little fellow as could be, but rather fond of a drop, but not that distilled by Jack Ketch[1] & Co., had a near escape. He was actually brought under the gallows in a cart, and the rope placed round his neck, but his life was spared. Whether this was done to frighten him or not I cannot say; but the circumstance had such an effect on him, that he took ill, and was a little deranged for some time after. I am not aware that a single execution took place, notwithstanding the known severity of the Duke in matters of plunder and outrage. I feel bound to say, that a prejudice existed on the part of our men against the inhabitants of Badajoz, owing to their having submitted so tamely to the French. It was different at Ciudad Rodrigo, where the Spaniards had defended themselves gallantly.

Feeling fatigued on my way to join the camp, I sat down with my prisoner on a bench, opposite the bridge which leads to Fort St Christobal. We not had been long seated when I was amused by a large baboon, surrounded by a number of soldiers, who were tormenting him. The poor animal had been wounded in the foot, probably by one of our men, and by his chattering, grinning, and droll gesticulations, he showed as much aversion to the red coats as any of the French could possibly have done. While the men continued teasing the animal, a servant, stating that it belonged to a Colonel of the 4th regiment, who he said was wounded, attempted to take the beast away, whereupon the party being divided in their sentiments, a scuffle ensued, in which several men were wounded with bayonets.

As we got up to proceed, we saw a number of Frenchmen guarded

---

[1] The office of executioner became identified with John Ketch (d. 1686), who executed the Duke of Monmouth and was known for his barbarity.

by our soldiers, coming over the bridge. They were the prisoners taken in Fort St Christobal, which but an hour or two previously had surrendered. These were soon surrounded by our men, who began examining their knapsacks, from whence a number of watches, dollars, &c., were quickly extracted. A short distance further on we came up with a mule, tied to a door, which, in my crippled state, and wishing to relieve my poor prisoner, I immediately appropriated for my own use, but I afterwards sold it to Lieutenant Jackson, of the 83rd regiment. Mounted on the animal, led by the Frenchman, we pursued our way until near the gates that led to the camp, when rather an affecting scene came under my eye. A little fellow, a drummer-boy, belonging to the 88th regiment, was lying wounded and crying bitterly, his leg being broken by a shot. On telling him I would get him carried by the Frenchman if he wished, 'Oh no!—oh no!' said the boy; 'I don't care for myself. Look at my poor father, where he lies!' pointing to a man shot through the head, lying weltering in a gore of blood. Poor little fellow! I gave him a couple of dollars, and called some men to his assistance, when I was compelled to leave him. We soon arrived at the camp ground of the 3rd division. I dismounted, and while sitting on one of the men's knapsacks, a soldier of the 83rd regiment was engaged in cleaning his firelock, when the piece went off and shot a corporal through the head, wounding also the hand of another man. The Frenchman seemed dreadfully frightened: he turned pale as marble, perhaps thinking the shot was aimed at him, as the corporal fell dead at his side. This accident struck me as a forcible instance of the casualties that attend a soldier's life. I could not, indeed, help feeling for the poor corporal, who after surviving the dangers of the preceding night, had lost his life by a clumsy hand cleaning a firelock.

It may appear strange that I did not wish to remain in Badajoz, but I was suffering from my wound, and preferred the quiet of the camp. We had no sooner arrived there than I was obliged to part with my faithful Frenchman, who was sent to join the other prisoners. I gave him a few dollars, which most likely he was deprived of before he got many yards. He left me with many expressions of gratitude for the protection I had afforded him.

I have been in many actions, but I never witnessed such a complication of horrors as surrounded me on the forlorn-hope at Badajoz.

I remained three days in camp before there was a possibility of my being conveyed into the hospital at Badajoz, during which I had an opportunity of hearing of the casualties that occurred. The number of men killed, wounded, and absent was such that the company could not muster a dozen men on parade for three days afterwards. Parties were sent to the breaches to bury the dead, which now began to smell most dreadfully; but we could not collect men enough to perform that duty. My poor old Captain, Major O'Hare, was amongst the slain, and had received not less than ten or a dozen balls through his body.

While in hospital, here as in other places, we were intermingled with the French prisoners who, sick and wounded, were placed indiscriminately in the wards with the British. In that in which I myself lay, and in the next bed, there was a smart young fellow, a Frenchman, with whom I became intimately acquainted. Indeed, he could speak a little English, which he had acquired during a short stay as prisoner in England, whence he had been exchanged to be again captured. He was recovering fast from a gunshot wound he had received in his shoulder. . . .

XVI

Having recovered from my wounds, I left the hospital and rejoined my regiment at Ituero, near Ciudad Rodrigo. An unfortunate accident here occurred to one of our men. He was playing at a game called 'nine holes' with several comrades, and was bowling along the ground a grenade, used instead of a wooden ball, believing it to have been filled with earth only, when a spark from his pipe fell into the hole, and instantly exploded, wounding him dreadfully. The poor fellow never recovered from the injuries he received.

A short time after I had rejoined, our division marched for Salamanca.

On our first day's march we encamped in a wood, on the right side of the road, leading to that city. The evening was beautiful, and the sun having lost its meridian heat, imparted a refreshing warmth to the wearied soldiers. The camp was all astir for some time—everyone being busily engaged cooking and preparing for the night's comfort; which being completed, the eve found us mostly seated and scattered about in small groups, earnestly intent on enjoyment of some sort. I am particular in my recollection of the time, for reasons which the following occurrence will sufficiently account for.

I had finished my evening's meal, and was sitting drinking a tot of wine with a sergeant of ours named Battersby, who a few days previously had rejoined us from Belem, where he had been some time appointed hospital-sergeant. He brought with him a very pretty-looking Englishwoman, that passed for his wife, and who was present with us, and assisted much to keep up the spirit of our conversation. We had been seated for some time under the branches of a clump of cork trees, of which, indeed, the wood was principally composed, when we were interrupted by some of the men calling for Sergeant Battersby, and in a second or so up marched a tall, fine-looking grenadier of the 61st Regiment of Foot, then belonging to the 6th division, which lay encamped some two or three miles in our rear; as he approached, however, he did not notice us, but casting sundry determined glances about him, more in anguish than ferocity, he drew near the woman, and seated himself on a knapsack near her. The latter, from the moment he had first made his appearance, I had perceived, seemed wondrously confused, and changed colour several times.

'Nelly,' said he, fixing a firm and deliberate look on her, his voice at first scarcely articulate with emotion, 'Nelly, why do you treat me so? how can you stoop,' and here he cast an almost contemptuous glance of recognition on Battersby, 'how can you stoop to such a disgraceful, so dishonourable a protection?'

'I am with those,' said she, rather snappishly, 'who know better how to treat me than you.'

'That,' rejoined the grenadier, 'may be your opinion; but why leave the child; it is but three years old, and what can I do with it?'

To this she made no answer.

'Do not think,' he again continued, 'that I wish you to return me, that is impossible. But I cannot help my feelings!'

This was only replied to by reproaches; which I did not listen to, for as it was no business of mine I turned to converse with my companions.

The grenadier, at last, made a move to take his departure, and his wife, for such she evidently was, had agreed to accompany him a little of the way, and they walked together. I did not know how to account for it, but there was a certain uneasiness attended me, which had kept me, as it were, on their trail all the evening; and Battersby and myself followed in their rear. They had proceeded a few hundred yards, and were some distance in advance, when she turned to wish him good night. The poor fellow paused again, as if in deep thought, fixing on her the same cool, deliberate look that he had exhibited all the evening.

'So you are determined, Nelly,' said he at length, 'to continue this way of living?'

'Yes,' said she.

'Well, then,' he exclaimed, holding her firmly by the left hand, which she had extended for him to shake, while he drew his bayonet with his right, 'take that', and he drove it right through her body. The blow was given with such force that it actually tripped him over her, and both fell, the bayonet still sticking in her side. The poor woman gave a convulsive scream, and in a moment expired. The grenadier bounded instantly on his feet again, and stamping one foot on the body of his victim, jerked forth the bayonet reeking with her blood. Wheeling himself round on his heel, the fatal weapon tightly clutched in his right hand, his eyes instantaneously caught the direction Battersby had taken, and he flew after him with the speed and countenance of a fiend, to wreak a second vengeance.

The sergeant fortunately arrived in the camp in time enough to call out the rear-guard, who, of course, were instantly on the alarm to meet him. The grenadier no sooner beheld him in safety than he stopped, and casting a half-contemptuous smile towards the body of his dead wife, wiped the bayonet through his fingers, returned it to the scabbard, and drawing himself to his full height, calmly awaited the approach of the guard. When brought before the Colonel, he said in a rough and manly tone of voice, while he extended his arm towards his wife, 'I have done the deed, but sorry her seducer has escaped.'

He was afterwards brought to a court-martial, and sentenced to three months' solitary confinement. But he suffered for one month only, when, as I suppose, in consideration of his case, he was ordered to return to his regiment. I have since been informed that he was shot in one of the actions on the Pyrenees. He certainly was a fine-looking fellow, and by name Bryen.

As for Nelly, we buried her that very night near the spot where she fell, having dug her grave with the same kind of weapon as that by which she had been deprived of life.

It was rather strange that Battersby was not noticed, but still held his rank. It is also as curious, that he was the second man I saw fall at the battle of Quatre Bras, on the 16th June, 1815, being shot by a musket-ball through the head.

On our arrival at Salamanca [17 June], we took up our position to the right of that city, near the River Tormes.

Here we remained for some days, our chief having completely out-manœuvred Marmont. On the evening of the 4th of July stormers were required from our division, to lead in the assault on Fort St Vincent, the strongest of the three forts that the enemy had constructed in the city, and which commanded the other two; two men from each company of our regiment were selected, the first for duty. After marching the men down close to the fort, waiting the signal for attack, they were countermanded. A few days afterwards this fort was set on fire by red-hot shot from our artillery, when it immediately surrendered, along with the two others.

The enemy, baffled in their views on Salamanca, slowly retreated, our army following until we arrived near Rueda [2 July]. Here our light troops had a smart brush with their rearguard, which ended in the capture of some few French prisoners. I remember seeing on this occasion a party of the Rifles bringing in a very fine-looking man, a French sergeant, who seemed inconsolable at his capture. He actually shed tears as he lamented the circumstance. The following day, how-ever, to his infinite joy, he was exchanged for a sergeant of our cavalry, who had been made prisoner a few days before.

After this skirmish, our regiment advanced to the neighbourhood of Rueda, where we occupied a hill, completely covered with vines, and close to the town. The country thereabouts abounded in grapes, from which an immense quantity of wine was annually made. The places used for the making of wine in this part of Spain are of a very singular description. They are all subterranean, and of immense extent, sometimes undermining many acres of ground. Over these are chimneys constructed to admit the air and light. The vats, into which the juice of the grape is pressed, are in proportion to the size of the vaults, and would entirely put to shame the same description of receptacle used for beer by Barclay and Perkins.

Our fellows, ever alive to the value of good liquor, notwithstanding the French had well ransacked the 'wine-houses', used frequently to find something to reward them for their search in these cellars. Our way of proceeding was to let one or two of our men down the above-mentioned chimneys by means of a rope. I shall never forget the terror I experienced in one of these adventures. Three or four comrades and myself one evening assembled over the chimney of one of these wine-vaults, and it was proposed that one of us should descend to bring up some wine. This was no comfortable task, as the proprietors frequently watched below, and would scarcely hesitate to greet an intruder with his cuchillo or long knife. After some deliberation, and plenty of peeping, it was at last decided that I should take the first chance; a rope accordingly was obtained from one of the muleteers, and being secured round my waist with a number of canteens, which clinked enough to awake almost the dead, I was gradually lowered.

The vaults were generally as deep as a three-storied house, and before I got half way down, I was left dangling in the air, the canteens chinkling as if with the intention of hailing a knife the moment I arrived into the lower region; at last I touched the ground. The place was so dark that I could scarcely see a couple of yards before me, and was obliged to grope my way for the vats; at length one of the tins, that formed a kind of breast-work for my approach, came in contact with something, and putting my hand forward, I placed it upon the cold clammy face of a corpse. My whole blood tingled, the canteens responded, and at a glance I perceived, from the red wings [*epaulets*] (for whether or not, I could see now) that it was a French soldier, exhibiting most frightful gashes, evidently inflicted by the same kind of weapon, which I at every turn was expecting.

The canteens clattered awfully, for I confess I shook with terror, having no weapon to defend myself, and every instant looking for the arm of some concealed assassins, who probably were watching my movements. Afraid to call out, I instantly tugged at the rope (the signal to pull up), an answer from above expressed a doubt of the canteens being filled so soon, and damned my eyes and limbs for me, but this only made me shake the rope more violently, until, to my great satisfaction, I found myself again dangling, and ascending. My comrades seeing me really come forth with hollow tins, and blowing with agitation, burst into roars of laughter.

I related my adventure, but this only increased it, until their mirth rallying us all, one, however, more daring than the rest, loaded his rifle, and with an oath, suffered himself to be lowered, and shortly returned, bringing up the canteens filled with excellent wine.

After remaining here for some time, we left Rueda at twelve o'clock at night on the 16th, the enemy, who had concentrated their forces at Tordesillas, being on the advance. The following morning the sun rose unclouded, presenting distinctly to the view the two armies moving in parallel lines along a ridge of low hills, separated only by the intervening valley and a river fordable in most places. The French columns appeared in such beautiful order, as to call forth the plaudits of even our own men. Skirmishing, however, was soon commenced between some of the cavalry and light troops.

One or two companies of our Rifles, seconded by a troop of the 14th Dragoons, were soon partially engaged with about a corresponding number of the enemy, who would occasionally dash through the little river, and attempt to take up a position to annoy our skirmishers. Our riflemen, in particular, were highly delighted with several little cavalry brushes that occurred this day between our dragoons and the French. One instance of gallantry on the part of a French dragoon, which fell under the eyes of most of us, was particularly exciting: in a kind of half charge that had been made by about a section of French and English cavalry, one of the Frenchmen had dashed alone through some of our dragoons. His own party having retired, there seemed every prospect of his being instantly killed or taken prisoner, and, indeed, most of us thought, as there were at least a dozen of our 14th Dragoons between him and his section, that he would surrender. Not so, however, thought the gallant Frenchman, but wheeling round, he gently trotted his horse for about twenty yards, when he gave spurs to his steed, and after several hand-to-hand conflicts with our dragoons in passing, he actually succeeded in reaching his party, I believe unhurt, and attended by the cheers of our own men, who were not insensible, at any time, to the intrepidity even of an enemy.

Another incident occurred also, which, as an appropriate companion to the foregoing, I will relate. Indeed, in gratitude, perhaps, I ought to do so, as I was a gainer on the occasion by a new pair of trousers. A man of the 14th Dragoons, named Pratt, a fine strapping young fellow, and a townsman of my own, brought in a French dragoon on his horse prisoner. The Frenchman had lost his helmet, and displayed a severe cut on his cheek. Poor fellow! he seemed exceedingly chop-fallen, and declared with much vehemence to Lieutenant Gardiner of our company, who spoke excellent French, that the Englishman could not have taken him had he possessed a better horse. This Mr Gardiner repeated to Pratt, who answered, 'Then by Jasus, Sir, tell him if he had the best horse in France, I would bring him prisoner, if he stood to fight me.' The words caused roars of laughter from all but the prisoner, who affectionately patting the goaded and smoking steed, exclaimed, 'My poor beast has not had his saddle off for the last week.' And such, indeed, appeared to have been the case, as, on the saddle being removed, prior to the sale of the poor horse, a part of the flesh that had become a sore came away with the saddle-cloth. The animal in this condition was sold to Lieutenant Gardiner for five dollars. Pratt, on opening the valise of the unfortunate prisoner (who with folded arms looked on with a mournful eye), came upon a pair of trousers which he threw to me as a gift that was exceedingly welcome, as my own were worn to rags.

The following day, after some slight skirmishes with the advance of the enemy, we retreated upon Salamanca. As few occurrences of any interest took place after this, for some days, beyond the manœuvring of the two armies, interesting only to the tactician, and which so many professional men have done ample justice to, I will at once proceed to the battle; in which, however, I must remark, the Rifles were less engaged than in any other action fought during the war: for which reason I shall have but little to state upon the subject.

XVII

The night previous to the morn that ushered in the day of battle, viz. the 22nd of July 1812, was the most stormy, I think, I ever witnessed. The thunder, lightning, and rain seemed striving which should excel, while their united effect was terrible. We lay, without covering, in an open field close to the River Tormes. It is needless to say, not a man that night had on a dry shred. It has, I believe, been previously remarked, by military and other writers, that rain has been the forerunner of almost all our general battles. From my own recollection, the truth of this assertion is singularly supported by facts.

The battle of Salamanca commenced about ten or twelve o'clock, upon our right, on a rising ground. Our position was first disturbed by some cannon-shot of the enemy that fell very near, but fortunately without doing any harm.

Although every moment expecting to be sent into the thick of it, we kept undisturbed possession of our ground, from whence we could see the column of the enemy on the heights engaged in attempting to repel the advance of our troops. When the 'glad sounds of victory' reached us, a general feeling of pleasure pervaded our ranks, mixed perhaps with some regret that we had not taken a more active share in the battle. But all we could do we did, which was to pepper the French well in their hurried retreat from the field. In fact, it seemed to me as if the whole French army might have been cut off by a little promptitude.

We halted at Huerta. The following morning our division crossed the River Tormes in pursuit of the enemy. We came up with their rear strongly posted on the side of a hill on the left of the road. Here we beheld one of those few charges that so seldom succeeded against well-trained infantry: this was the celebrated charge of Major-General Bock, who, at the head of his heavy German cavalry, broke the French squares, taking them prisoners almost to a man. It was the most gallant dash of cavalry that ever was witnessed.

This day I began to feel the ill effects of the wound I had received at Badajoz, which the fatigue of marching and the warmth of the weather had again caused to break out. On inspecting the sore, our surgeon immediately recommended me to go into hospital at Sala-manca, for a few days of medical treatment and rest. Accordingly I set out for Salamanca with the guard appointed to escort the prisoners taken in the recent cavalry affair by our Germans. I never before saw such severe-looking sabre-cuts as many of them had received; several with both eyes cut out, and numbers had lost both ears. Their wounded, who were carried in waggons, were extremely numerous, and it was painful, even to an old soldier, to hear their groans and incessant cries for water. The escort consisted chiefly of the Germans that had taken them prisoners, and it was pleasing to behold these gallant fellows, in the true spirit of glory, paying the greatest attention to the wants of the wounded. Water, as I have remarked, from the loss of blood that had taken place among the wounded, was in particular request. One of the prisoners, who had his arm hanging, probably in endeavouring to defend his head from a sword-cut—for, indeed, there were very few gun-shot wounds among them—was in particular very frequent in his demands for 'eau' (water), when none could be obtained. Perhaps imagining himself neglected, we were not a little surprised to hear him suddenly change his language, and call out in English, 'For the love of Jesus, give me something to quench my thirst; I am a fellow countryman of your own.' On entering into conversation with him I found he formerly belonged to the 9th Regiment of Foot, and had been taken prisoner with a number of others of his regiment, while on board a ship some time previous, since which occurrence he had been prevailed upon to enter the French service in preference to being kept in close confinement. At Salamanca a sentry was placed over him; what became of him I know not.

On arriving at Salamanca our wounded prisoners, some other invalids, and myself were immediately taken into hospital. There we were, French and English, laid up together; and there, I must say, I saw sufficient practice daily in the use of the surgeon's knife to become perfectly familiar with every form attendant upon amputation. While lying in hospital, at all times a wretched place, from the groans of the numerous sufferers, I was here placed under the immediate attendance of Sergeant Michael Connelly, in charge of our ward, who being sufficiently recovered from a slight wound, was appointed sergeant to the hospital. He was one of the most singular characters I ever met with, and if an awkward person and uncouth face had gained him the preferment, his match certainly could not be found elsewhere. Mike was exceedingly attentive to the sick, and particularly anxious that the British soldier, when dying, should hold out a pattern of firmness to the Frenchmen, who lay intermixed with us in the same wards.

'Hould your tongue, ye blathering devil,' he would say, in a low tone, 'and don't be after disgracing your country in the teeth of these ere furriners, by dying hard. Ye'll have the company at your burial, won't you? Ye'll have the drums beating and the guns firing over ye, won't you? Marciful God! what more do you want? ye are not at Elvas, to be thrown into a hole like a dog—ye'll be buried in a shroud and coffin, won't you? For God's sake, die like a man before these ere Frenchers.'

Mike, however, had one great failing, he drank like a whale, and did not scruple to adopt as gifts or legacies the wine rations of both the dying and the dead, until he drank himself out of the world, and as his patients remarked, after all, he died 'like a beast'.

The news of Mike's death spread like wildfire, and all his old friends and the convalescents crowded to do honour to his remains.

The funeral of the Duke himself could not have made a greater stir, for cavalier and foot soldier, from the drumboy to the trumpeter, and all the women, children and camp-followers in the locality, flocked to follow his remains, the town became unusually alive, and the variegated throng, headed by the deceased sergeant, borne by four bearers, and the usual complement of soldiers with their arms reversed, slowly wound their way through the city of Salamanca. Many a jest made the streets ring with laughter, as the crowd followed the coffin, till they reached the burial-ground (near the French battery taken by us some time previously.) The bearers here proceeded to enter the gateway, when they were suddenly aroused by a slight cry from within the coffin, with a kind of scraping noise, like an effort to open it. They suddenly halted, paused, and listened. It was surely Mike scraping. On they moved again doubtfully. A second time the voice broke upon their ears. 'Whist!' ejaculated the bearers, their caps moving almost off their heads. 'Oh blood and ouns! where am I? Oh bad luck to yer souls, let me out, won't you? oh, merciful Jasus, I'm smoothered.' In a twinkling out bolted the bearers from under the coffin, and a dozen bayonets in an instant were sunk under and lifted the lid. The crowd crushed dreadfully to take a look. But there lay Sergeant Michael Connelly, sure enough as stiff as a fugleman but something colder, and my old friend, the blackguard Josh Hethering-ton, the cockney ventriloquist, who had been one of the bearers, as 'innocent' as you please, joining in the astonishment of the rest of us.

Josh winked at me and I at Josh. 'Ned,' said he, 'I'm blessed if I think he's dead. Why don't some of them chaps go for a doctor.' 'To be sure,' cried the crowd, 'send for the doctor.' Meanwhile a regular rush was made to press him to swallow some of his favourite liquor, but his teeth as obstinately opposed the draught, so that poor Mike was already pronounced 'not himself', when the doctor arrived.

While here, I got acquainted with a pleasant and intelligent man who belonged to the 13th Light Dragoons, and was fast recovering from a wound he had received in the shoulder. We used frequently to alleviate as much as we could the unpleasantness of our situation by a little conversation. His history both amused and interested me.

He had been taken prisoner by the French near Badajoz while serving in General Hill's division, but managed shortly afterwards to make his escape between Vittoria and Pampeluna. The following morning he fell in with a party of General Mina's Guerillas,[1] who, as soon as they found him to be an Englishman, wished him to enlist in their band until he could regain his regiment. This offer he was glad to accept. After giving me a very amusing account of the manners of the Guerillas, their rich picturesque dresses and arms, and their wild

---

[1] In 1810 the Spanish Regency conferred on Mina the title 'Colonel and Com-mandant General of all the Guerrilleros of Navarre', and by 1813 he had the rank of general and commanded about 14,000 men near Pamplona.

military life in the mountains, he proceeded to detail several anecdotes of their cruelty and ferocity, among which I can well remember the following, from the impression it then left upon my mind, and the simple manner in which he related it:

Uniting suddenly several of his Guerilla bands in the neighbourhood of Vittoria, Mina, whose information of the movements of the French seemed unerring, one morning surprised and captured a number of waggons filled with stores. They had been sent from Madrid for the army at Vittoria, and were escorted by gendarmes, who were all either killed or taken. The prisoners, about twenty in number, were immediately marched into the mountains, but not before they had time to draw a dark augury of their own fate by seeing all their wounded comrades brutally stabbed to death on the ground where the skirmish had taken place. The prisoners, after having been stripped of nearly every article of wearing apparel, even to their boots, were confined in a space of ground encircled by pens or hurdles, and used for keeping cattle, round which were planted many sentries. In the evening the ferocious mountaineers, elated with their day's success, being joined by a number of females, their sweethearts and wives, made merry with drinking wine and dancing to the music of several guitars. During this merriment both men and women frequently taunted their wretched prisoners, recapitulated the wrongs the Spaniards had suffered at the hands of the French, until they gradually had excited their passions to a partial state of frenzy. In this state, the signal having been given by one of their number, they rushed in among their hapless prisoners, and commenced a general massacre, drowning the cries and supplications for mercy of their victims, as they gave each blow, by enumerating the different losses each had sustained in his family during the war. 'Take that for my father you shot'—'that for my son'—'this for my brother', &c., until the work of death was complete. The most inhuman, and perhaps most revolting trait in this general murder was some of the women having actively assisted in the slaughter.

A short time after I had heard the preceding sketch, I had an opportunity of observing that sanguinary feeling of revenge that so peculiarly characterised the Guerillas during the war. I rejoined my regiment at a little village about three leagues from Madrid, called Getafe. In the farm-house, where the greater part of our company were quartered, was a very pretty Spanish girl who had a brother serving with the Guerillas. One hot summer evening, when several comrades and myself were sitting on a bench outside the door, joking with the girl, a swarthy, savage-looking Spaniard came up, and was welcomed with much joy by the girl and her parents. The new-comer was armed to the teeth with pistols, daggers, and a long gun, which, together with his crimson sash and free bearing, at once proclaimed him the Guerilla. At first we imagined him the girl's brother, but soon perceived another, though equally dear tie, cemented their affection: he was her lover or suitor. While engaged in conversation with his sweetheart and her parents, we observed him take rather ostentatiously from his side a long heavy-looking silk purse, the contents of which he emptied into the lap of his mistress. The Spaniard's eyes sparkled with pleasure; but, for the honour of a British soldier, a general disgust pervaded the minds of my comrades and myself, when we beheld a number of human ears and fingers, which glistened with the golden ornaments they still retained. He then told us, with an air of bravado, that he had cut them from off the bodies of the French whom he himself had slain in battle, each ear and finger having on a golden ring.

'Napoleon,' he observed, in his native dialect, with a grim smile— 'Napoleon loves his soldiers, and so do the ravens'; as he pointed to several of those carrion birds perched on the walls of an old convent covered with ivy. 'We find them plenty of food; they shall never want, so long as a Frenchman remains in Spain.' Such are the men who were considered the greatest patriots attached to the Spanish army during the war.

The chief business of the British at this time was laying siege to Burgos. The enemy having also assembled in great numbers betwixt it and Vittoria, Lord Wellington, thinking he was not able to oppose their force, ordered the whole of the divisions to retire on Salamanca. We of the light division received orders to the same effect.

On the 22nd of October we left Madrid: the contempt with which the inhabitants treated us for leaving them once more to the mercy of the French cannot easily be forgotten.

For what the men said gave us little concern; but to be taxed and taunted for cowardice by the Spanish ladies was most galling. Even my handsome dark-eyed Clementeria, sister to the Guerilla lover, who seemed so much attached to me, and with whom I spent many a moonlight night serenading to the Spanish guitar, and who first taught me to use the castanets in the Spanish dance—even she, with all her pretended love, refused me a buss at our last moment of parting, though I used all my eloquence, welding the Spanish, French, and English together in pleading my cause. All had no effect on the hard-hearted *Moza* [*girl*]. Her last words were: 'Begone, you cowardly English, you have not the courage to fight the enemy of our country: those who have butchered my dear father and brother.'

After a harassing march through a mountainous country we joined the remainder of our army at Salamanca. There we took up our quarters for a few days in a convent, which exhibited such a loathsome picture of filth as to be almost unendurable. In consequence of our men having torn up a part of the balustrades for firing, a young officer of the third battalion fell down a height of fifty feet, and was killed on the spot.

On the second morning after our arrival we again proceeded towards Rodrigo. The rain fell in torrents, and from the heaviness of the roads, which were in many places a foot deep in mud, most of our men lost their shoes, and were obliged to march barefooted. Among this number I was unfortunately included. When we had reached our halting-ground for the night, our prospect was most desolate. Wet to the skin—without fire or shelter—and at the same time possessed of a ravenous appetite, with nothing to satisfy it, formed one of the *disagreeables* so often attendant upon our life in the Peninsula—to say nothing of incessant duty and fatigue. It was these sufferings, in fact, I am convinced, that oftentimes rendered our men so callous about death, at different periods during the war, as some men, from the privations they endured, wished to be shot, and exposed themselves in action purposely.

On our halt on the above night, the first thing I did was to take off my jacket and shirt, and after ringing about half a gallon of water out of them, I replaced them upon my back to dry as they might. Most of our men had employed themselves in cutting down boughs of trees to keep themselves out of the mud; but it was some hours before we could obtain that greatest of luxuries, under our present circumstances, a good fire. Still we had not a morsel to eat after the day's fatigue—no rations having been issued—and our men suffered from all the pangs of cold and hunger. Fortune, however, during the evening favoured a few of us. Towards the middle of the night one or two of our men brought intelligence that several cars laden with spirits and biscuit for the Spanish army were stuck fast in the road, and could not proceed onwards. The temptation to our hungry maws could not be resisted; leaving our fires, and getting up to the cars, screened by the darkness of the night, we managed to get a portion both of biscuit and aguardiente; but the Spanish guard, discovering our fellows, commenced firing on them: this was quickly returned, and several, I believe, were shot; indeed, the firing continued all night, which alarmed the chief part of our army. Had the offenders been discovered, it would not have been difficult to have foretold their fate, as the Duke's orders were particularly strict against plunder, (if such this might be called, for after all, the whole fell into the hands of the French next morning, as the carts were then able to be moved). For my own part, such were my feelings this night, that I believe I should have expired, but for the liquor I had drank.

With all their hunger, however, there existed among the men a sympathy for the officers, which, considering their distance, was rather remarkable; several of the most haughty of the latter gladly received little kindnesses from the soldiers; and if the noble lord be now living, he may chance to recollect an instance connected with it. Lord Charles Spencer, then a youth about eighteen years of age, suffered dreadfully from the hunger and fatigue of this retreat; trembling with cold and weakness, he stood perched upon some branches, that had been cut down for fuel, the tears silently starting from his eyes through the pain he experienced, while thus sharing in the common lot, anxiously watching a few acorns, which to stay the pangs of hunger he had placed in the embers to roast. I dare say his Lordship had never known till then the joys of poverty—a good appetite! Nor will he, I expect, forget how willingly the rough soldiers flew to offer him biscuits, which their own sufferings could not withhold from one so tenderly and delicately reared; but his Lordship was very much liked amongst us, and, no doubt, it did many a veteran's heart good to hear his thanks, and see the eagerness with which he devoured the offering. These are times when Lords find that they are men—and men, that they are comrades.

Before daylight we pursued our route, the rain continuing to fall in torrents, while the state of our regiment was pitiable. To add to our comfort, the enemy were close upon our heels: this night we spent something like the last—wet, cold, and hungry. On the following morning we were obliged to continue our retreat rather precipitately, as the shots of the French, who were in great force, came rattling in among us. During the morning the enemy's cavalry succeeded in getting through a wood, and managed to cut off the baggage of the 7th division, then in front of ours. Among some captives the enemy made on this occasion were several children in panniers carried by donkeys. One Irishwoman, in particular, I remember seeing, whose grief seemed inconsolable for the loss she had sustained in that of her child. In a few days, however, the French, desiring to be as little encumbered as ourselves with children, sent them back with a flag of truce. This was followed by a most interesting scene, as the different mothers rushed forward to clasp their darlings in their arms.

This day we were hard pressed by the enemy's advanced-guard, and two of our companies, the one in which I served being one, were ordered to cover the retreat of our division. The French, confident in their numbers, pressed us vigorously, and it was with difficulty we could check their advance. While hotly engaged skirmishing, I was about taking possession of a tree, when I beheld a poor woman at the foot of it, who, being unable to keep up with the regiment, had sunk down exhausted. Poor soul! she seized my hands, and begged of me to assist her; at the same moment the enemy's balls came rapping into the tree that only partially screened us. I was obliged, however, to leave her, as there seemed every prospect of most of us being cut off; the 'assembly' sounded, and away we dashed, 'devil take the hind-most', in upon the battalion. Here our illustrious chief, who was generally to be found where danger was most apparent, seeing us come puffing and blowing up to our column, called out to us, in a cheering voice: 'Be cool, my lads; don't be in a hurry!' But, in faith, with all possible respect for his Lordship, we were not in greater haste than the occasion demanded, as the French were upon us, and we were obliged to dash down the sides of the hill, where we halted for a moment, and his Lordship also, and then ford a river. While engaged in crossing the stream, that was much swollen by the late rains, a round-shot from the enemy, who were now peppering away at us, took off the head of a Sergeant Fotheringham, of our battalion, and smashed the thigh of another man. On gaining the other side of the stream we turned to give a salute in return, but owing to the wet our rifles were unserviceable.

We remained that night stationary on the banks of the river, exposed to all the delights of cold, hunger, and fatigue. These feelings were not improved by a course of shelling that the enemy did us the honour to indulge in at our expense. But, as I have remarked, the sufferings of our men were such at this period that many of them con-sidered death a happy relief. The morning at length dawned upon our half-famished persons, but brought no alleviation to our miseries. The rain still continued to come down in torrents. Pursuing our route, we arrived at Ciudad Rodrigo, and took shelter under its walls, where we found some sheds used as stables for the Spanish cavalry. The moment I entered, the first thing that caught my eye was some Indian corn-leaves, which I considered a lucky chance, and instantly throwing myself on them, wet as I was, soon fell into a sound sleep, the only rest I had had since we left Salamanca. However, in the morning when I awoke I found myself in a glow of heat, and covered with perspiration, and on attempting to rise found myself as if paralysed, and could not move. Calling some of the men to assist, they were astonished at the steam that emitted from under me like smoke. I then found my bed had been hot horse-dung, slightly covered by the Indian corn-leaves. The doctor being sent for ordered me instantly to be carried into the town, where with hot baths and a salivation in a few weeks I was able to join my regiment.

XVIII

Towards the end of November our battalion again became stationed at its old quarters, in the little village of Alameda. We obtained here fresh clothing, certainly not before it was wanted; green having become by far the least conspicuous colour in the regiment, while so various had been the expedients resorted to for obtaining a substitute for shoes that the fresh supply from England was welcomed with no common joy. It was quite amusing to see how our fellows enjoyed their clothing, strutting about as proud as peacocks among the Spanish peasant girls, in whose estimation they doubtless conceived they should be considerably advanced.

Headquarters were at Guinaldo, some miles distant from where we lay, and a company of our regiment occasionally did duty over the Duke whose quarters were in the house of the Alcalde. We had strict orders to admit no one inside the gates leading to the house, unless some particular dispatch from the front, or from Don Julian Sanchez, the Guerilla chieftain. Indeed, a report had arisen among us, at the time, that his Grace was not altogether right in his head; but this was mere fiction. I used to observe him walking through the market-place, leading by the hand a little Spanish girl, some five or six years old, and humming a short tune or dry whistle, and occasionally purchasing little sweets, at the child's request, from the paysannes of the stalls.

Here, for the first time, I saw Don Julian Sanchez, the noted Guerilla leader, linked arm in arm with the Duke—an instance peculiar to the time, of obscure merit rising of its own impulse to an equality with the greatest man of the age.

My readers may well suppose I did not slightly notice the square well-set figure, dark scowl, and flashing eyes of the Guerilla, whose humble birth-place I afterwards visited, in a small village between Rodrigo and Salamanca. I had been informed that he first began his career as a pig-boy, but owing to some cruelties exercised on a branch of his family by the French, he took an inveterate hatred to them, which he exemplified by surprising and slaughtering two or three of their soldiers, whom he found asleep in a wood. Accompanied by one or two others, he continued and increased his sanguinary feats, and gradually collected a small band, then a body, and eventually commanded upwards of twenty thousand Guerillas, well armed, and equipped with British arms and accoutrements, and who rendered more assistance to the cause of the British than all the Spanish troops beside.

Our regiments, by constant collision with the French, were getting exceedingly thinned, and recruits from England came but very slowly, until we found it necessary at last to incorporate some of the Spaniards; for this purpose several non-commissioned officers and men were sent into the adjacent villages recruiting. In the course of a short time, and to our surprise, we were joined by a sufficient number of Spaniards to give ten or twelve men to each company in the battalion. But the mystery was soon unravelled, and by the recruits themselves, who, on joining, gave us to understand, by a significant twist of the neck, and a 'Carajo'[1] (much like the very breaking of one), that they had but three alternatives to choose from, to enter either the British, or Don Julian's service, or be hanged! The despotic sway of Sanchez, and his threat in the bargain, so disjointed their inclination for the Guerillas that they hastily fled their native 'woods' and 'threshold', for fear of really finding themselves noosed up to them, and gladly joined the British regiments. Many of them were even made corporals, and, indeed, proved themselves worthy of their new comrades, whom they rivalled in every undertaking of courage and determination.[2]

---

[1] 'The devil!' 'Damn it!'

[2] The gallantry of the Spaniards of our regiment make me believe, had those countrymen during the war been properly commanded, they would have made excellent soldiers. [E.C.]

While lying here I will give a short description of our regiment's opinion of flogging, not indeed by words, but by signs, as the following anecdote will show, although the sound of cats was seldom heard in our battalion; for I can safely say that for the six years I served in Spain not more than six men, to my recollection, were punished in our battalion, and yet withal I cannot brag of our fellows being the honestest branch in the British army. At the time I speak of we had a man in our regiment of the name of Stratton, who, after robbing several of his comrades of trifling articles, took it into his head to desert to the enemy, and was detected in the act, in a wood that leads from Rodrigo to Salamanca, by the vigilant Guerillas, and brought back prisoner to our cantonments. He was tried by a regimental court-martial, and sentenced to receive four hundred lashes.

After the proceedings of the court-martial were read by the adjutant, in a wood near the village where the regiment was formed for punishment, Major Cameron, who commanded us at the time, devised the following plan to find out the true character of the prisoner, for the Major was not only a brave and gallant soldier, but a shrewd man, and knew well that the men were better judges of the good or bad qualities of each other than the officers could possibly be. He addressed the prisoner as follows: 'Stratton, I ought to have had you tried by a general court-martial; in that case you would have been shot; but the high character the regiment has borne in the army prevents me from having it mentioned in general orders that a man of the Rifles could be guilty of the heinous crime of desertion to the enemy. I am yet willing to show you kindness. Now, Sir, if the men of the battalion will be answerable for your future good conduct, I shall pardon you.' Turning round at the same time, Major Cameron looked the men in the face while he stood in the square, as if waiting for an answer.

A pause took place, no answer being given. The Major said: 'Strip, Sir.' He was tied to a tree, and received twenty-five lashes; the second bugler was preparing to commence, when the Major again said, 'Will you not be answerable, men, for Stratton's conduct? Well, then, if his own company will be answerable for his good behaviour I shall forgive him.' The prisoner, at these words, looked round with an imploring eye, as far as his position would allow him, looking towards his own company, saying, 'Do men, speak for me. I will not act so in future.' I recollect it well, each man leaning on the muzzle of his rifle with his left hand, while his right covered his face, and all silent; not a man spoke. 'Go on,' said the Major; the culprit received twenty-five lashes more, when the Major again said, 'Now, Sir, if only one man in the regiment will speak in your behalf, I shall take you down.' Still silent, while the third bugler commenced: when the prisoner had received about sixteen lashes, a voice from the square called out, 'Forgive him, Sir!'—'Stop, bugler, stop!' said the Major; 'who was the man that spoke?' 'I did, Sir!' was the answer. 'Step into the square'; when a man of the prisoner's own company came forward. 'Oh! is it you, Robinson?' said Major Cameron; 'I thought as much; as little-good-for-nothing a fellow as himself; but take him down.'

When the prisoner was conducted out of the square, the Major addressed the men, saying: 'Your conduct in the field is well known by the British army; but,' added the Major, 'your moral worth I have not known before; not a man would speak in that fellow's behalf, except the man who did, whom you know as well as I do.' This may serve to show that however soldiers dislike this mode of punishment they still like to see a rascal punished; and nothing tends to destroy all feeling of pity for his sufferings more than his having been guilty of an act of cowardice, or robbing his comrade.

Some months before our sojourn at Alameda, Napoleon had made his disastrous campaign in Russia, when Moscow was burnt. The circumstance was now brought to our notice by the general order, soliciting a day's pay from the officers and men of the army towards defraying the losses sustained by the Russians. This was most cheerfully bestowed by every man in our battalion except two, the above-mentioned Stratton and another man of the name of Frost; and to crown the occurrence the day was made one of jollity and fun. Country dances were struck up by the band, and it was most laughable to behold, one and all, officers as well as private soldiers kicking about their heels to the tune of 'The Downfall of Paris'.

Our division had been cantoned in and about Alameda during the winter, when, soldier-like, ever sighing after a change of scene, the men of our battalion generally began to grow tired of their mono-tonous and inactive life: however, we received orders for marching. This occurred about the middle of May [*21st*], when we commenced the campaign of 1813, and a spirit of enterprise, notwithstanding past sufferings, extended itself throughout the light division. We left Alameda in high spirits. On the third day's march our battalion en-camped near Salamanca, in a wood, where we were joined by the Life Guards and Oxford Blues,[1] that had just come out from England,

---

[1]   The Royal Horse Guards. Formed in 1661, the regiment was known as the

and whom we beheld drawn up at the side of the road. Their fresh and well-fed appearance gave rise to many jests at the expense of the 'householders'. They, in fact, as I learnt, took us at first, from our dark clothing and embrowned visages, for a foreign regiment.

The first peep we got of the enemy was at a place called Toro, on the road towards Burgos. There our hussars had a sharp skirmish, in which they took some prisoners. Continuing our advance, we overtook their rear-guard the following day. After a little skirmishing and cannonading they continued their retreat to Burgos. The next morning [13 June] we were startled by a tremendous explosion, that at first induced many of our men to think it an earthquake, until we ascertained the fact that it arose from the explosion of a mine, with which the French had destroyed the castle and some of the works of the town of Burgos.

On the 16th of June we passed through the pretty little town of Medina del Pomar, and encamped on the other side of it close to the banks of a large river [Trueba]. On this march we suffered much from a deficiency of supplies from the commissariat, as anything like rations we seldom received. Myself and one or two others, having some few pence, determined to start off on the sly, as we were not allowed to move from our camp ground, and purchase bread at a little village we beheld at the other side of the river, which we forded unobserved and entered the village. There, however, the alarm of the people became very great upon our appearance, and not wishing apparently to have any dealings with us, they asked an immense price for the bread. Irritated at this conduct, and urged by hunger, every man seized a loaf and threw down the usual price in the country. Seeing that we were all totally unarmed, for we had not even our side-arms, an immediate outcry was raised against us by the people, and we had to run for safety. This we did, carrying the loaves with us, until we were overtaken by some of the swift-footed peasantry, who came up to us with knives and clubs. Our lives being thus in jeopardy for the dearly obtained bread, our party instantly had recourse to stones for defence. 'Muerte a los perros Ingleses.' 'Kill the English dogs,' was the general cry of the Spaniards, as they brandished their long knives. They were evidently about to make a rush in among us, by which

---

Oxford Blues after its blue uniform and its first colonel, Aubrey de Vere, Earl of Oxford. Colonel Leach says the two regiments 'looked as fair and beautiful as lilies, when contrasted with the sunburnt visages and battered appointments of the cavalry regiments which had been many years in the country'.

my own personal adventures, and those of my comrades, would, in all probability, have been finished on the spot, when several men of the 43rd and 52nd regiments, belonging to our division, came running up, like ourselves, foraging. It was the turn of the Spaniards now to retreat—which they did in a hurry.

We had scarcely escaped the attack of the Spaniards and arrived at the bank of the river, when General Sir Lowry Cole came galloping up to us with some of the mounted staff, which indeed might be termed the police of the army. 'Hallo! you plundering rascals of the light division—halt!' was the General's command, as he pulled up his temple spectacles, which he generally wore. One only resource was left us, and that was to plunge into the river, which at that part was very deep, and swim across, holding the bread in our teeth. This we immediately adopted, when Sir Lowry, in an agitated tone, that did honour to his heart, called out—'Come back, men, for God's sake— you'll be drowned! Come back, and I'll not punish you.' But the General's fears were needless; we soon landed on the other side.

On arriving at our camp we found that the roll had been called over several times, and that we had been set down 'absent without leave'; but we were lucky enough to escape with a slight reprimand.

I cannot here forbear making a few remarks with reference to the men who composed our battalion in the Peninsula. The reader will be apt to imagine that those men who were in the habit of foraging after a day's march were but indifferent soldiers. Allow me, with some pretensions to the name of a veteran, to correct this error, and inform the reader that these were the very men whose bravery and daring in the field far exceeded the merits of their more quiet comrades in quarters.

Our men, during the war, might be said to have been composed of three classes. One was zealous and brave to absolute devotion, but who, apart from their 'fighting duties', considered some little indulgence as a right; the other class barely did their duty when under the eye of their superior; while the third, and I am happy to say, by far the smallest in number, were skulkers and poltroons—their excuse was weakness from want of rations; they would crawl to the rear, and were seldom seen until after a battle had been fought, when they might be observed in the ranks until the Commissary again placed them on short allowance, when off they started; in this manner they swelled the muster-rolls.

But the first of these were the men who placed the Duke on his present pinnacle as one of the great captains of the age. During the

whole of our advance from the frontiers of Portugal, until we entered
the Pyrenees, not more (on the average) than one biscuit per day was
served out to each man—and it consequently could not be expected
that a soldier, weighed down by a heavy knapsack, and from sixty to
eighty rounds of ammunition (such as we Riflemen carried at the
time), could march from twenty to thirty miles a day on so short an
allowance.

It was not unfrequent, therefore, after a day's march to observe
groups of our regiment, and, indeed, of the division, rooting up the
fields with their swords and bayonets, in search of potatoes, &c., and
these were the men who were able to undergo the fatigue of the next
day.

The French, also, in their hurried retreat stocked themselves with
several days' provisions in advance; these were hung very temptingly
from their knapsacks,[1] and as it were, in defiance of our hungry jaws;
as a consequence, this gave rise to the well-known remark, or alternatives of the Light Division: 'Damme, boys, if the Commissary don't
show his front we must either find a potato field or have a killing day!'

Indeed, but for these rescources, so dependent on our individual
energies, his Grace, from our being always in front, might have
occasionally found half his Light Division 'stiff', and the other half
tucked under the blankets as 'Belem Rangers'.

On the 18th of June (a very memorable day to our army afterwards)[2] we passed along the banks of a fine river. Our company,
along with but half a troop of German Hussars, formed the advance.
On turning a winding of the road, we suddenly came within sight of
a party of the enemy's cavalry who formed the tail of their rear-
guard. Our Germans, who were commanded by a very smart young
fellow, immediately charged them. The French, perceiving the number of our cavalry only equal to their own, instantly wheeled about
and calmly awaited the attack. A very smart combat soon took place,
and was supported by great resolution for some time on both sides,
but terminated in the flight or capture of the enemy. Several prisoners
were brought in, all of whom were badly wounded; and scarcely
one of our gallant Germans had escaped without some sabre-wound.
Another singular circumstance occurred at this skirmish. One of the
German cavalry, as he came in with a prisoner and his horse, exclaimed in broken English, as he came up to us—'Mein Gott! Mein

[1] As before stated, the French carry no haversacks. [E.C.]
[2] The battle of Waterloo was fought on 18 June 1815.

Gott! he is mine own broder!' It appeared he had brought in his own brother prisoner, wounded, who was in the French service. The officers of both parties had been killed in the preceding charge; and Lord Wellington, who came up at the time, was so pleased with our cavalry, that he promised the sergeant a commission, which a few days after, I was told, he obtained.

The whole of our battalion, which soon came up, was ordered to push forward. We found the French rear-guard in possession of a little town called San Milan, in front of which they had drawn themselves up, apparently with the intention of defending. As we continued to advance in extended order, they changed their minds and turned tail. This day I noticed a novel system many of the enemy had adopted, of firing their muskets over their shoulders in their retreat, without turning round to face us. This resulted, in all probability, from the excessive heat and fatigue they had endured.

XIX

On the 20th we remained encamped near Puebla, a town within ten or twelve miles of Vittoria. On the following morning we fell in rather earlier than usual, when a general rumour among the ranks augured we should have a busy day. We were, indeed, on the eve of the memorable battle of Vittoria. We marched along the left of the high road towards the previously mentioned city, leaving Puebla [*de Arganzón*] a little to the right. Our battalion, as the advanced-guard, preceded the remainder of the division until we came in sight of the enemy on the other side of the River Zadora. We commenced a smart brush with their voltigeurs, who slowly retreated, and took up a position in the rear of some rocks, from whence their fire swept a bridge in our immediate front. While thus occupied in skirmishing, we heard a loud cheering on our left, where we beheld the 3rd division charge over a bridge much lower down the stream. Fired by the sight, we instantly dashed over the bridge before us in the face of a galling discharge from the enemy. We then drove them from the rocks, and in our turn had to sustain a heavy fire from several guns mounted upon a hill that commanded our position. The rocks were splintered round us in every direction from this fire, and many of our men were killed or wounded by shot or fragments of stone.

We were soon joined by the remainder of our division, and pushed forward up a hill, from the summit of which we could clearly discern the city of Vittoria. By this time the action had become pretty hot and general with the other divisions, as well as our own. The chief scene of conflict was on an extended plain within a mile or two of the city on the left. Continuing to advance, we arrived near a small village on the main road, from which we were annoyed by a furious fire, until, rushing in, we drove them out, and captured a howitzer in the market-place, the first that was taken. We were doomed, however, to have it but a short time in our possession, as a whole regiment of the enemy came charging upon us, and our force, consisting of only two companies, had to retreat with precipitation, when turning round, however, we beheld our favourite 3rd division coming double quick down the main road to our assistance—with Picton, who was never absent in time of need, at their head.

After retiring for about a hundred yards, this sight encouraged us, and we were at them again. While thus engaged, a grape or round-shot struck my pouch with such violence that I was hurled by the force a distance of several yards. From the sudden shock I thus experienced, I imagined myself mortally wounded; but, on being picked up, I found the only damage I had sustained was the partial destruction of my pouch, which was nearly torn off.

A man of the name of Hudson, who was one of the pardoned deserters at Rodrigo, while running to my assistance, as I afterwards learned, was struck by a bullet in his mouth, which knocked out several of his teeth, and came out at the back of the ear. From this wound, severe as it was, he however recovered.

Placing some of the ammunition in my haversack and the remainder in my cap, we were at them again, and recaptured the howitzer in the village, by the assistance of part of the 3rd division.

Still pursuing them, the chief part of my company kept on the right of the main road. In all my military life, this sight surpassed anything I ever saw: the two armies hammering at each other, yet apparently with all the coolness of field-day exercise—so beautifully were they brought into action.

At this moment I noticed a regiment, which by its yellow facings

I think [*correct*] was the 88th or Connaught Rangers, marching in close column of companies to attack a French regiment which was drawn up in line on the verge of a hill with a small village in its rear.

The 88th, although at the time under a heavy cannonade from the enemy's artillery, continued advancing gallantly onwards, which, we skirmishers perceiving, took ground to the left close to the road, in order to enable them to oppose this line in front.

Though hotly engaged at the time, I determined to watch their movements. The 88th next deployed into line, advancing all the time towards their opponents, who seemed to wait very coolly for them. When they had approached to within three or four hundred yards, the French poured in a volley or I should say a running fire from right to left. As soon as the British regiment had recovered the first shock, and closed their files on the gap it had made, they commenced advancing at double time until within fifty yards nearer to the enemy, when they halted and in turn gave a running fire from their whole line, and without a moment's pause cheered and charged up the hill against them. The French meanwhile were attempting to reload. But being hard pressed by the British, who allowed them no time to give a second volley, came immediately to the right about, making the best of their way to the village.[1]

As I have before observed, we had several Spaniards in our regiment. These men were generally brave; but one in particular, named

[1] As of late, much has been said concerning the use or non-use of the bayonet in action, I shall here take the liberty, supported by the above fact, of intruding my own opinions in the matter; an opinion, which falling from the mouth of an old soldier only, might otherwise be thought worthless, if not presumptuous.

It is generally known of course that riflemen, when in action, are at all times extended, and have always better opportunities of watching the movements of two armies, than those troops who are compelled to march in compact and closely wedged masses.

Both parties, it will be observed by the above, were with their fire-locks unloaded, the British having fired and charged before the French could reload, and both consequently had no resource left but their bayonets. Now I would ask the no-bayonet gentlemen, if the French, who well knew their mutual position, had seen the British advance with bare muzzles or with no bayonets, would they have given way with their own bayonets fixed to oppose them. If they did, they ought to be hanged, from the colonel downwards. On the other hand, if the English had attempted to charge with bare muzzles against fixed bayonets, each man from the commanding officer down should be sent to a madhouse.

Upon this then I should say, if my opinion be acceptable, that the bayonets had better remain in present use until such time as we can bargain with the French or other enemies to disuse them. [*E.C.*]

Blanco, was one of the most skiful and daring skirmishers we had in the battalion. His great courage, however, was sullied by a love of cruelty towards the French, whom he detested, and never named but with the most ferocious expressions. In every affair we had since the advance from Portugal he was always in the front; and the only wonder is how he managed to escape the enemy's shot, but his singular activity and intelligence frequently saved him. His hatred to the French was, I believe, occasioned by his father and brother, who were peasants, having been murdered by a French foraging party. On this day he gave many awful proofs of this feeling by mercilessly stabbing and mangling the wounded French he came up to. In this massacre he was, however, stopped by a veteran of our regiment, who, although suffering from a severe wound in the face, was so exasperated at the Spaniard's cruelty that he knocked him down with a blow from the butt of his rifle. It was only by force we could prevent the Spaniard from stabbing him on the spot.

I now observed the Duke come riding up with some of his staff; and, seeing the confusion the enemy were in, cried out to one of his aides-de-camp, 'Send up a few of Ross's guns; here is work for them': saying to us at the same time, 'That's right, my lads; keep up a good fire', as he galloped in our rear to the right. In an instant up came Ross's guns, and commenced peppering them at the distance of not more than three hundred yards. Here the whole seemed blocked together in a mass, while we stuck to them like leeches.

When we arrived close to the barriers of Vittoria, we found them blocked up by a great portion of the French waggons, bearing the *matériel* of their army. After passing the gates, we were still engaged through the town skirmishing with their rear-guard; but, notwith-standing the street-firing, many of the inhabitants threw open their windows, and, appearing at their balconies, welcomed us with *vivas*, while the ladies, according to the established mode, threw flowers into the streets on us as we passed along.

In following up the enemy, a few other men and myself had left the company a little in the rear. While going through the square I was fortunate enough to save the life of a French soldier who had been wounded. He was endeavouring, poor fellow! to follow in the route of the French when, observing me coming up, he dropped his musket, with which he had been assisting himself, and intimated that he sur-rendered; a Spanish vagabond, however, observing him, brandished a club, evidently intending to give the Frenchman the *coup de grâce*, when he was knocked down. The poor Frenchman expressed his gratitude, but we were obliged to leave him, probably after all to the same fate he had just been rescued from, unless he fell into the hands of our troops who were coming up at the time.

A few minutes after this, some of the 10th Hussars and a party of the Life Guards came dashing through the town, sword in hand, shouting as if they had taken it by storm.

When I had passed the gates and forced my way through the immense quantity of baggage that blocked up the further end of the town, and through which the cavalry could scarcely pass, I beheld a French mounted officer, sword in hand, escorting a carriage and four out of the town. My comrade and myself immediately fired, when the officer fell. At the same moment the carriage stopped. On rushing up to the vehicle we perceived it contained two ladies, evidently of high rank. They seemed much alarmed as the balls kept whisking round them from both sides. We desired them not to entertain any fears for their safety, as we would not harm them. While thus engaged an officer of the 10th Hussars came galloping up, flourishing his sword over his head. Not knowing his uniform at first, I cocked my rifle, upon which he exclaimed, 'I am an English officer, Sir.' Hearing this, I stepped on one side of the carriage, but in withdrawing I observed a small but exceedingly heavy portmanteau that was carried by a Spanish muleteer in the French service. He was in the act of conveying it towards the town, and as I thought I contributed more towards its capture, I made him lay it down—not, indeed, before I was compelled to give him a few whacks of my rifle in the ribs. My comrades had gone in another direction, so that I had no one to claim a portion of my booty, which on inspection I found to consist of several small bags filled with gold and silver in doubloons and dollars.[1] Although I never knew exactly the amount, I should think it not less than £1,000. I afterwards learnt that the lady in the carriage was no other than the Queen of Spain, the wife of Joseph Bonaparte.[2] The officer of Hussars, I also heard, obtained possession of the *bâton* of Joseph[3] himself from the same carriage.

My chief anxiety now was how to secure my prize; and, when all who had an opportunity were employed in reaping some personal

[1] Sixteen dollars equalled one doubloon, the equivalent then of about £4.

[2] Costello is in error. The lady was the wife of General Gazan. She came to Wellington's headquarters in search of one of her children who had been lost in the confusion of the French retreat.

[3] The baton belonged to Marshal Jourdan.

advantages from our victory, I determined not to be backward, but this was a difficult thing to accomplish. As I could not well carry the portmanteau from its weight, I soon found means, taking one of the many mules that were blocking up the road, to bear the valuable load; but being at a loss how to fasten the portmanteau, I resorted for aid to a sergeant and two men of the 10th Hussars, who were passing. For this service I, perhaps incautiously, rewarded them too liberally, by giving them several handfuls of dollars. In doing this they got a glimpse of the gold, half of which they demanded. Perceiving the probability of being thus deprived of the only prize I had made after years of hardship and suffering—and particularly by those new-comers, as this regiment had newly joined from England, made it still worse—I inwardly resolved to forfeit it but with my life. So catching up my loaded rifle, which I had leant against a gun-carriage, I instantly cocked and, retiring three or four paces, brought it to my shoulder, swearing I would shoot the first man dead that placed his hands upon my treasure. My determined air, and the ferocity of my appearance—my face being completely covered with perspiration and gunpowder—induced them to pause, and finally to desist. Taking the sergeant's word not to attempt molesting me, with his assistance I completed the strapping of my treasure, and departed for the camp.[1]

I had not proceeded far with the intention of gaining the battalion when I observed the Duke of Wellington forcing his way, with some of his staff, through guncarriages and waggons into Vittoria. To my great relief, however, he took no notice of myself and mule. In fact, his Grace was too much occupied in securing the brilliant results of our victory in the capture of the entire *matériel* of the French army which fell into our hands.

Almost all our men at this time, I must remark, to use a phrase much in vogue among us, were endeavouring to see what they could *make*—in other words *take*. I reached our camp, however, in safety.

This night we encamped amidst the wreck of the French army, every man bringing into his camp ground whatever he fancied—for the unfortunate enemy were compelled to leave everything behind

[1] Strange to say, this very sergeant, whose name was Lee, and who had the fame of being the best boxer in his regiment, after the battle of Waterloo, lay wounded in the bed next to mine in the hospital at Antwerp. 'Holloa, Rifleman!' said he, when he first perceived me near him, 'don't you recollect me!' At first I did not. 'By God,' said he, again, 'you frightened me more than a bit at Vittoria, when guarding your money-bags.' This soon settled the recognition; but, poor fellow! he died after the amputation of his arm. [E.C.]

them, even to their women and children—so that, if our fellows were inclined to be honest, their good fortune would not allow them. The ground occupied by our regiment was near a small village, a little off the main road that leads to Pampeluna.

As soon as our fires were lighted, the men, who had been under arms from three o'clock in the morning until eleven at night, and consequently had not tasted food for the whole of the day, began to fill their hungry maws from the luxuries of the French camp. Roast fowls, hams, mutton, &c., were in abundance, and at midnight the wine and brandy went round in horn tots which we generally carried about us. The men mostly lay stretched on the ground, their feet towards the fires, and elbows resting on their knapsacks; as soon as the grog began to rouse up their spirits from the effects of the day's fatigue each one commenced inquiries about their absent comrades, for riflemen in action, being always extended, seldom know who falls until the affray is over. . . .

The next morning the sale of the spoils which fell into our hands took place in the village, near the camp ground, where our battalion lay. The Spaniards were in general the purchasers, and property late belonging to the French, such as uniforms, horses, camp-equipage, &c., was sold in abundance at about one-tenth of its value. Mules worth thirty or forty dollars brought on an average three. As I had no means of conveyance for the spoil I had obtained, I set about depositing it where I thought it would be safe: three hundred pounds I intrusted to our quartermaster, and several sums to other officers of the battalion, distributing nearly the remainder of the silver, to the amount, I suppose, of about one hundred pounds, among the men of my own squad, who undertook to carry it for me; very little of the latter, however, I ever received back. But after all money, as may be imagined, was of very little use during some of the hardships we afterwards endured, when I state that I frequently offered a doubloon for a single glass of rum, and was not always able to obtain it.

About twelve o'clock we marched in pursuit of the enemy through the town of Salvatierra, many of our men gibing me for my wealth, saying, among other agreeable things, that if I fell they would take care of my knapsack for me. To tell the truth, I was not now over-anxious to go much to the front, as I began to look upon my life as of some value.

On our second day's march we came up with the rear-guard of the enemy, who made a stand in the road, assisted by the only gun they had carried from Vittoria. The first shot fired from this piece took off the arm of one of our corporals at the socket. But on our dashing at them they soon abandoned their gun, which we took, making the first and last piece of ordnance we had captured from them on this retreat.

We halted a couple of days in a small village opposite Pampeluna; and as I considered that our fellows had contributed towards my greatness in money matters, I could do no less than treat them to a dinner; but unfortunately, the place afforded no other luxuries than bacon, eggs, and wine, for which the inhabitants took care to charge treble: I paid ten doubloons for three flitches of bacon, and three pig-skins of wine. This we enjoyed within the walls of a house that the French had burnt the roof off on their retreat. There were some excellent toasts given, such as—'May we have another brush with them before they get to Paris', &c. &c.

As nothing of any interest to the reader occurred for some time, I shall merely say that we continued in pursuit of one division of the French army night and day. During this period the fatigue we under-went was almost incredible, nor could we have supported it but for the excellent wine with which that part of the country then abounded, and which we all had plenty of money to purchase. After continuing these harassing marches for several days, we at length chased them into France. We next retraced our steps in some degree to Pampeluna, in the suburbs of which city we remained a few days, and from thence we again advanced in the direction of the Pyrenees, and took up our quarters at the pretty little town of San Estevan; here we halted some days also. Our next march was to Lesaca. The enemy had possession of the heights of Santa Barbara, from whence we dislodged them after some hard fighting. We remained upon these mountains for several days, but the enemy making an endeavour to relieve Pampeluna which some of our troops were then besieging, a part of our division were ordered to cross the Bidassoa to frustrate this attempt. This could only be done by a forced march at night. We were obliged to have torches and lighted straw to enable us to find our way over the mountains, which were in most places rugged and precipitous, and even without the semblance of a path. The fatigue incident to that night-march, I think I may say, was greater than any of the men of our battalions had before endured; and after all, you could fire a rifle-ball to where we started from.

Accidents were numerous, many of our men had severe falls, and numbers of rifles were broken. But all our hurry was of no avail, as the enemy had been already frustrated in throwing supplies into

Pampeluna. We had again the agreeable task of retracing our steps, with the same hurry we had advanced. By this addition to the fatigue we had previously endured, we lost many of our men who were unable to endure it. There was a sort of rivalry between the regiments of our division who should hold out the longest; urged by this feeling many continued marching until they fell and expired by the road-side. I myself on the second day fainted; but, on having my stock taken off, recovered sufficiently to stagger on and finish the march.

Descending from the mountains, we pursued our march till we came to the bridge that crosses the Bidassoa, where we beheld the French moving along on the other side of the river. The poor fellows, like ourselves, seemed dreadfully harassed. Part of our battalion commenced firing upon them across the river, every shot telling as they retreated. To the honour of the British soldiers, however, I am happy to say, that many of our men, knowing the sufferings of the French from what they had themselves endured, declined firing, while they called out to the others to spare them, as it was little better than murder. We remained encamped here this night, and the next morning marched back to the heights of Santa Barbara.

As soon as we had arrived on the hill, and were anticipating a little rest, the assembly sounded, and we were ordered to drive the enemy from a high mountain which they occupied on our right. This was a heavy task at the time; but to it we went, and in extended order mounted the hill, on the summit of which the enemy were clustered as thick as bees on a hive. After some very hard fighting we carried their position, but not before we had lost many men. While engaged I lost a friend to whom I was much attached, a sergeant named Kelly. He had just invited me to take a draught of wine out of his canteen, and was in the act of handing it to me, when he received a shot through the right temple that came out at the eye. I never before saw a man die so hard. He writhed about, poor fellow, in the greatest agony, without it being in my power to afford him the slightest relief. Some of our men raising a shout that the enemy were flying, I was obliged to leave him for a time. On my return I found him quite dead. This was a bad day's work. Another regiment was left in charge of the hill, and we returned to our camp ground by the river-side.

On the 25th August, it being the anniversary on which the regiment was raised, called among us 'The Regiment's Birth-day',[1] a

---

[1] The Regiment first saw service in an attack on Ferrol, northern Spain, on 25 August 1800. It was formed earlier in the same year. Kincaid writes: 'Two

general jollity was kept up throughout the regiment. On this occasion I have often reflected with pleasure on having assisted in saving a gallant soldier from the consequences of a pecuniary loss he had sustained, and which might have embittered the remainder of his life. I allude to a pay-sergeant of one of the companies of our battalion, who, getting rather tipsy, was robbed while in that state of £31 belonging to his company—the first money, indeed, that had ever been intrusted to his hands, having only just been appointed pay-sergeant. The circumstance had so strong an effect upon him that on waking me up the following morning and acquainting me with his loss, he stated to me his determination of deserting, as his credit would be for ever destroyed in the regiment, and he could not endure remaining with the battalion afterwards. Having money by me, I felt much pleasure in arresting the despair that seemed to take possession of the mind of a gallant soldier, and one whom I much esteemed: I enabled him to make up his losses. Some time after, this very sergeant obtained a commission in the 2nd battalion of our regiment: this was the late Quartermaster Robert Fairfoot.[1]

Having by me still a very considerable sum, the remnant of my prize at Vittoria, I was naturally apprehensive respecting its safety, particularly as I had no place to keep it but in my knapsack, which I could not always carry about with me.

I was consequently obliged to intrust my treasure to the care of a comrade of the name of Bandle, who, true to his charge, never gave me reason to repent my confidence. Many were the stratagems resorted to, to persuade Bandle to relinquish his guard. Sometimes he would be suddenly warned for duty by the non-commissioned officers, as these last assured me 'for fun' only, in hopes he would leave it behind him; but Bandle was always awake, and on these occasions would take my knapsack on his back and leave his own. He was wakeful as

---

trenches, calculated to accommodate seventy gentlemen's legs, were dug in the green sward; the earth between them stood for a table, and behind was our seat.' Colonel Leach adds some details: 'Seventy-three officers sat down to such a dinner as we could scrape together, under a large hut made of branches of trees, and within a short distance of the most advanced French sentinels. They looked down on us from the heights of Vera, but were too civil and well-behaved to disturb the harmony of so jovial a set of fellows. Neither vocal nor instrumental music was wanting after the feast; and with the aid of cigars and black strap, we enjoyed the most extraordinary *fête champêtre* I ever witnessed.'

[1] Fairfoot died in Galway in 1838.

a weasel, and faithful as the dog, for both of which qualities I took good care not to be ungrateful.

San Sebastian was now closely invested by the British, and eventually, the breaches being considered practicable, preparations were made for the assault. Volunteers accordingly were required from our regiment. The duty was so 'attractive' that although two only were to be selected out of each company, six stepped forward from ours. This brought on a controversy, and lots were drawn according to regulation, and decided in favour of two, named Royston and Ryan.

The reader may judge of the value attached to this service, when I tell him that the offer of £20 was made and refused for the exchange, thus illustrating the truth of the great dramatist,

> He that is truly dedicate to war
> Hath no self-love; nor he, that loves himself,
> Hath not essentially, but by circumstance,
> The name of valour.[1]

The next day the town was to be attacked. Our men were all on the fidget to know the result, and every tree and hillock within sight or hearing of the scene was taken possession of.

At about twelve o'clock, A.M., the breaches were assaulted, and the place carried after a severe contest.

Three or four hundred French, unable from the great rains to ford the Bidassoa, charged fiercely upon one of our companies, and another of the 2nd battalion, then posted at the bridge of Vera. After a sanguinary struggle they effected their purpose, and escaped. They were the remnant of the French troops that had forded the river in the morning, and whom our Spanish force distinguished themselves in repulsing. After this we remained quiet for several days in our camp ground.

It was about this time that those men of the 52nd, who were fortunate enough to have survived the 'forlorn-hope' of Rodrigo and Badajoz, were distinguished with a badge of laurel on the right arm. It was given by their commanding officer as a testimonial of their gallant conduct, which was expressed by the two letters V.S. or 'valiant stormer' placed beneath the wreath. Why the men of our battalion and those of the 43rd, who had equally distinguished themselves on those occasions, were not similarly honoured, I know not.

[1] Shakespeare's, *Henry VI* (Second Part), V. ii. 37–40.

For my own part, all I ever received in the way of reward, for my services as a stormer, was the sum of six dollars. This was after the taking of Badajoz. In the French service, those men who volunteered in the ranks of 'Les enfants perdus' were always first in the list for commissions, and were distinguished also by a cross of the Legion of Honour, which was so respected among their countrymen that even their comrades were always obliged to salute him who wore it. How must the heart of those thus distinguished beat at the possession of such a mark. How different is the case of the British soldier! This 'hope' in his country remains unnoticed, and he quits its service 'equally forlorn' for obscurity without distinction, save that which points him out with his empty sleeves or wooden stump limping his way to Chelsea. Some, perhaps, may argue that an improvement took place at Waterloo. That may be, if we allude to those who on that occasion performed their first and last military feat, and came away unscathed. How 'pleasant' then must it be to the old Peninsulars, whose battles fought and won outnumber perhaps the men of their company, to see whole squads of Waterloos strutting about with medals dangling on jackets which, as their first and last, had scarcely been on long enough to collect the dust of a 'donkey's trot'.

In this camp an order also arrived from the Horse Guards for the appointment of a colour-sergeant in each company, to be considered as a senior or sergeant-major with an extra sixpence per day. As no badges (the cross swords) had arrived from England, the deficiency was supplied by our master-tailor, who formed an imitation with coloured silks worked on the arms of the men appointed.

XX

We remained encamped, for several weeks, close to the River Bidassoa, Lesaca in our rear and Vera in our front. We used to amuse ourselves while here, bathing. This river, which divides the French and Spanish territories, we were on the eve of crossing to go into France. It was heart-stirring to witness our men, as it were, unconsciously exposing to liberated Spain the evidence of the dangers they had endured for her liberation, stripped on its banks, and prepared to dash into the clear water; the perforated and wounded exteriors of the Rifles proved what they had seen and suffered. But the veterans, not thinking thus, generally amused themselves on these occasions by remarking and jesting to each other on the peculiar situation of the different bullet-holes, and the direction the shot had taken in passing through them.

One day I remember nearly losing my life by my own folly. It was as follows: We had a very handsome little Spanish girl attached to one of our sergeants, named Dillon: she by some means got to the other side of the river, which was generally occupied by the enemy, crying bitterly, and begging of the men, that were on our side, to get her over, as she was afraid to go to a bridge lower down lest she should be taken by the French. Having a respect for her, I instantly stripped off all except my trousers, and swam across—for here the river was not wide but deep—and, without a moment's hesitation, placed pretty Louisa, for so she was called, on my back, with the intention, as I thought, of bring her to our side. Placing her arms round my neck, I waded as far as I was able, and then commenced swimming; but I no sooner got into the deep water than she squeezed me so tight round the neck that I lost all power, although a good swimmer, and down I went. At first our fellows thought I was playing tricks; but on rising and bellowing out for assistance, they became alarmed, for she stuck to me all the time like a leech. Several of the men upon seeing me go down a second time, stripped and jumped in to my assistance; one of the name of Kelly, of my own company, diving down, for the place was twelve feet deep, seized her by her long hair, and brought both to the surface of the water; and, by the assistance of the rest, dragged us to land insensible. When I came to myself, I found our head surgeon, Dr Burke, with some of our fellows, rubbing me to life again; and, with the assistance of a little brandy they had poured down our throats, both recovered. For myself, I was able to walk to my tent in the course of some time: but not so with the pretty Louisa, as she was kept wrapped in blankets the whole day. Poor thing! she remained with the regiment while in Spain, and afterwards followed us to England; but what ultimately became of her, I know not.

Here my old friend, Tom Crawley, got the whole of our regiment out of a precious scrape. It was as follows: Our division was served out with linen bags, made exactly to fit across our knapsacks, and, at the same time, three days' biscuit (3 lb.) in each bag. This biscuit was to be kept strapped on the top of each man's knapsack, well tied, with brigade orders for no man to taste a morsel of it, unless given out in written orders to that effect, as our brigadier [*Kempt*] expected we should be on short commons while on the Pyrenees, and this was to be, in case of scarcity, our last resource. These bags were examined regularly every morning by officers commanding companies, but, while seen strapped snugly on the knapsacks, were considered by them all right. However, our fellows, who were never at a loss for a subterfuge, devised the following plan to evade the officers' vigilance: they ate their biscuits except one whole one, which they kept at top to be seen, and in their place substituted chips. This passed on very well for some time, as the sight of the top biscuits satisfied the officers, until one day Captain Johnston of our regiment took it into his head to see his company's biscuit shaken out, and whilst on private parade ordered them to untie their bags to see their biscuit. The first man on the right of his company was the unfortunate Tom Crawley.

'Untie your bag, Crawley,' says the Captain. Tom instantly did as he was ordered, and showed the Captain a very good-looking biscuit a-top.

'Shake the whole out,' said the Captain, 'until I see if they are getting mouldy.'

'Oh, faith, there is no fear of that,' said the astonished Crawley, looking the Captain hard in the face, at the same time casting a woeful eye on his bag. However, the Captain was not to be baulked, and taking the bag by both ends, emptied out its contents, which turned out to be nothing more nor less than a few dry chips. Poor Tom, as upright as a dart, stood scratching his head, with a countenance that would make a saint laugh.

'What have you done with your biscuit? have you eaten it, Sir?' said the Captain. Tom, motionless, made no answer. 'Do you know it is against orders?'

'To be sure I do,' says Tom; 'but, for God's sake, Sir, do you take me for a South American jackass, that carries gold and eats straw?'[1] This answer not only set the Captain, but the whole company, in roars of laughter. On further inspection, the Captain found his whole company, indeed the regiment, had adopted the same plan. Through this our bags were taken away and we relieved from carrying chips.

[1] Tom served under General Whitelocke in South America. [*E.C.*]

About the beginning of October we had an opportunity of witnessing the gallantry of our 3rd battalion. Although they had not seen our service in the country, yet on this occasion they showed themselves 'old hands', and worthy of their green jackets. They had to dislodge the enemy, then holding possession of a high hill behind Vera. This they did in most excellent style, in the sight of our division and the 4th. Our battalion was not suffered to remain idle, and we soon joined in pursuit of the enemy, who took refuge in the valleys of France. On taking possession of their camp ground we found a whole range of huts, constructed in the most ingenious manner of turf and stone. One of our men came in for rather a novel prize: this was a large monkey, which we kept in the regiment for some time. One strange antipathy this animal was remarkable for was his utter dislike to the sight of a woman.

On the morning of the 9th, the day after the preceding skirmish of Vera heights, we took ground considerably to the right, marching along the summit of the Pyrenees until we came to a very high hill, on the top of which stood the remains of an ancient castle. Our men styled the hill the 'father of the Pyrenees', as it was by far the highest mountain we had ever seen, and was called La Rhune by the French, who had possession of it. On our arrival we had the satisfaction of compelling them, after a smart skirmish, to evacuate their lofty tenement. Of the difficulty of this enterprise some notion may be entertained when it is known that our men had, in most instances, to crawl up the mountain on their hands and knees, in consequence of its steepness. The French, fortunately for them, had a less precipitous side to retreat down, or they must all have been destroyed.

My curiosity, after this, led me to explore the old building, in company with one or two comrades. It was originally the ruin of a very strong fortress or castle, in which, I subsequently heard, the Spaniards used formerly to keep state prisoners. After searching about for some time we discovered a narrow pathway that conducted us to a cellar or cavern, which, to our surprise, we found tenanted by an old gentleman with a venerable beard, and who received us very courteously. He seemed a hermit from his appearance, but how he managed to maintain his residence against the dominion of eagles, vultures, and owls, as well as the occasional jar of contending parties, was a wonder he did not condescend to explain. The only gift we could obtain was a little spring water, which, after our scramble, was refreshing. The splendid view from our elevated position, however, made ample amends for our work.

Our battalion at this time was stationed about a mile below La Rhune, and greatly exposed to the storms of wind and rain that we experienced at this period, together with scarcity of provisions. Few of the country people visited us, so that even those in possession of money found little or no benefit from it. Meanwhile the French army, who were encamped about three-quarters of a mile in our front, we had reason to believe, were more fortunate, as they were plentifully supplied with provisions. Occasionally, too, some of our officers were visited by a supply that was smuggled past the French lines.

A general attack upon the enemy was now daily expected, as Lord Wellington with his staff had been observed inspecting the enemy's position with more than ordinary care for the last two or three mornings. On the 9th of November every disposition having been made for attack, the following morning ushered in the battle of the Nivelle. The company I belonged to being this night on picquet, we had orders on the first dawn of light to attack and drive in the enemy's picquet opposed to us; and as we were preparing for the task, to our surprise we beheld the whole of our division about a hundred yards in our rear waiting to support us. As soon as our attack commenced we could hear the alarm given by at least a hundred drums and bugles; and as the light dawned more clearly, we could see the French columns all in motion. The remainder of our battalion and division coming up, we were soon hotly engaged, a valley only partially separating us from the main body of the enemy.

After we had routed them from their first line, and were getting close to their second, an incident occurred that fell under my observation, and I may say, of the greater part of our company. There was a man of the name of Mauley, a shoemaker, who fell shot through the head. This man, nearly the whole time we had been in Spain, lived with a Spanish woman, who was tenderly attached to him. She always got as near to her lover as possible during action, generally on a donkey. On this occasion some of our wounded men passing informed her Mauley was killed. The poor girl was almost distracted; leaving her donkey and stores behind her (for she acted in some degree as one of the sutlers to our regiment), she rushed down to the spot where Mauley had fallen. We were then in the thick of the fight, and our only safety was cover, as the balls came as thick as hail, so that every moment I expected to see the poor woman shot. She, however, seemed callous to every danger: throwing herself on the blood-stained body of her lover, she commenced giving way to the most appalling ebullition of grief, tearing her hair and wringing her hands.

The gallantry of Blanco, the revengeful Spaniard, whom I have previously mentioned at Vittoria, was conspicuous on this occasion. He had been an intimate friend of Mauley. Seeing the danger his countrywoman was exposed to, he rushed boldly from his cover, and placing himself in front of her, continued loading and firing at the enemy, loudly swearing all the time such oaths as only a Spaniard can do justice to. Notwithstanding the real horrors of the scene, it was impossible to resist the impulse of laughter at the fierce grimaces and oaths of Blanco, who escaped as it were almost by a miracle.

A part of our division at this time were endeavouring to enter the French lines on our right. But the enemy seemed determined to defend their huts, which they had doubtless been at considerable trouble to construct, and the action there was close and sanguinary; part of our battalion taking them on the right flank, they were eventually obliged to yield. As soon as we had arrived at the huts, which they had arranged in most excellent order, and from which they had reluctantly been compelled to retreat, in passing along a row of them I heard a scuffle going on in one, and on entering it I beheld a huge French grenadier, with red wings, and my old acquaintance Tom Crawley struggling together on the ground. The Frenchman had been surprised, but was getting the better of Tom, when my appearance at once determined the matter, and the grenadier surrendered.

It appeared from what I could make out that the Frenchman in his hasty retreat from the hut had forgotten some of his needfuls, and on his return for them, was met at the doorway by Tom, who, according to his old custom, was preparing to explore its interior. Crawley was immediately attacked by the grenadier with fixed bayonet. Poor Tom, in his attempt to parry off a thrust, received the blade through his right hand, and bled profusely. We did not kill the Frenchman, but left him to the mercy of the Caçadores, who were following close behind us. Tom went to the rear, and I never saw him afterwards, nor can I say I have since heard of him. Many an anxious inquiry was made, many an old scene was revived, and passed current amongst us, and Tom Crawley will live in our recollections as long as we can enjoy the good company of a comrade.

The enemy, although retreating, did so in an orderly manner, keeping up a tolerably brisk fire. I had no sooner regained the line of skirmishers than I received a severe hit just about the centre of my waist, that nearly knocked me down, and for the moment I imagined myself mortally wounded through the body; however, on my examining, I found myself only slightly bruised. A ball had actually stuck in the serpent[1] of my waistbelt, from whence it was afterwards taken out with difficulty.

After I had recovered from the shock, I joined in the pursuit of the enemy, who once or twice attempted to make a stand, but we were close at their heels, so they thought it better to pursue their way at an accelerated pace, covered, however, by some battalions of light troops, who displayed considerable coolness. The French descended the heights at the foot of which stands the pretty little town of St Jean de Luz, with its white houses. Our battalion was hotly following, engaged in sharp skirmishing, when our gallant Colonel, Sir Andrew Barnard, who was very conspicuous during the day, on a brown long-tailed horse, received a shot in the breast. On running up to him, which I did with several other men, we perceived him spit blood, but he would not dismount. One of our buglers supported him on his horse, while another led it to the rear.

Immediately after this occurrence, my attention was attracted by seeing the 52nd regiment charge up the side of a hill on our right, and take a fort. Shots are very strange things, and fly fast: a Sergeant Watts, of the Rifles, at this moment received a ball in the head; being next to him, he laid hold of me with both hands, at the same time calling out—'Am I dead? Am I dead?' Poor fellow! he was mortally wounded, and it was with difficulty I could extricate myself from his deadly grasp.

The French, after a severe loss, made good their retreat across the river that leads to St Jean de Luz. With our usual luck we took up our camp on the side of a bleak and barren hill for the night. After this we got into better quarters on the other side of the river. This was at a château called Arcangues. We were as usual in the immediate front of the enemy, and our outlying sentinels and theirs were little more than thirty yards apart. While here, such a good feeling reigned among the French and our men, that they frequently went into each other's picquet houses—terms of intimacy which they extended to neither the Spanish nor Portuguese troops, for whom they expressed an unmeasured contempt. But this state of things at our outposts was too subversive of discipline to be tolerated by those in command, and of course was only done upon a reliance of mutual honour on the sly; still it exhibits a pleasing picture of the absence of all revenge and

---

[1] The brass clasp or hook that fastens the belt. [*E.C.*]

prejudice on either side among men of opposing interests. This feeling, however, could not stay the effusion of blood that was still to be shed.

XXI

On the 9th of December they drove in the picquets, which were chiefly furnished from our battalion. The columns of the enemy came briskly forward with the apparent intention of driving us from our position. Our company had been ordered to line some brushwood on the side of a lane that led from the château, where we received them with a fierce and deadly fire, as they came on, which they replied to with spirit, at the same time endeavouring to outflank our position. In assisting to repel this attempt we came in for a shower of shot, and Lieutenant Hopwood and Sergeant Brotherwood, with several more of our party, were killed on the spot.[1] By this time they were getting round us, and our opponents perceiving how few our numbers were, comparatively to their own, at once attempted to close, and fairly obliged us to take to our heels down a field. From thence we sprang into the lane, in doing which I remember dropping my cap, where it remained during the day, until I regained possession of it on the retreat of the enemy.

At this period Lord Wellington and his staff were watching our motions through their glasses from the château, which some one made known. Seeing ourselves under the eye of the Commander-in-Chief, we instantly rallied. Our 3rd battalion meanwhile were hotly engaged on our left. They, however, found themselves unable to make any serious impression, and were not sorry, I dare say, when night closed upon their baffled columns. As to ourselves, we had little respite from the fatigues of the day, as we were busily employed in fortifying the château for the anticipated attack of the morrow.

[1] Simmons says: 'A ball passed through both their heads, happening to be standing a little behind one another.'

On the following morning, however, the enemy retreated within their works, upon which we took possession of our former ground, where we found the bodies of Lieutenant Hopwood and of poor Brotherwood, both of which had been stripped, and covered partially with a little loose earth.

After this we had a succession of fights or skirmishes with the enemy for the five or six days following, which is called the battle of Bayonne, but without eliciting any particular result. We still kept up an excellent private feeling on both sides at the outposts. As an an instance, although I must remark a general order had been pro-mulgated prohibiting all intercourse with the enemy on pain of death, our company was on picquet near a dwelling called Garrett's house, when we clubbed half a dollar each, and sent a man into the French picquet-house to purchase brandy. It was, I recollect, Christmas-night. Grindle, the name of the man who was our messenger, staying longer than was usual, we became alarmed, and imagining something must have happened to him, sent two other men in quest of him. These learnt from the nearest French sentry that Grindle was lying drunk in their picquet-house. Fearful that the circumstances should come to the knowledge of Lieutenant Gardiner, the officer of our picquet, they went and brought Grindle back with them quite drunk; but just as they were emerging from the French lines, who should ride down to the front post but Sir James Kempt, who commanded our division at that time. He instantly ordered Grindle to be confined; he was so fortunate as to escape, however, with only a slight punishment.

About the beginning of January 1814 the enemy were seen advanc-ing, as we understood, to straighten our lines, that were in a half-circle. With three or four others, I was ordered to hold possession of a small farm-house that communicated with some cross-roads, and to keep up a brisk fire until the *assemblée* sounded, in which case we were to retreat upon the company, who occupied a hedge two hundred yards in our rear. On our right was a high stone wall, and on our left, in parallel, was a hedge also that served as a cover for the French, who, by this time, had possession of it. Between was an open field, our only passage. As soon as the *assemblée* was heard, we of course were on the alert to retreat, but this was to be accomplished only at very imminent risk, for the moment we showed our noses, we were saluted with a regular hailstorm of bullets, which put us all in rather moody condition. It was proposed, however, to retire by independent files.

The first to 'run the gauntlet' was a tall, gaunt Irishman, and such a shower whizzed about him as almost unnerved the rest of us. Johnny Castles, who had figured at Badajoz with a rope round his neck, and yet had escaped, was one of the party. He was particularly at a stand-still; since the 'hanging business' he had made up his mind to live for ever, and had grown fat on it; but his corpulency now threatened to mark him out.

'Oh, dom your limbs,' growled Johnny, in the true Caledonian dialect, with an awful grin, 'ye are the rascals to drink and carouse with as yer did yesterday. Eh, look at 'em! dom their eyes, they are sure to hit me!' and away he bolted, ducking his head, his face half averted all the way. Johnny, however, was spherical, and puffed and blowed like a whale, while the French peppered away at him in prime style, the dust rising from the balls in every direction. Johnny, however, escaped with a brace of samples through his knapsack and mess-tin, and rolled over the hedge.

Taking advantage of the welcome given to Castles, Gilbert and I, without allowing them to reload, followed, and as the devil would have it, the pair of us arrived as safely. There now only remained our comrade Jones, a good-looking Welshman, who quickly came after us, but he, poor fellow! was met half-way by a shot.

After all, the enemy never took the house, for by a reinforcement from the 52nd we beat them back again. I often laugh at the recollection of Johnny Castles, though I must say, I funked dreadfully. Like the frogs in the fable, though death to us, it was sport to the French, who kept roaring with laughter as we bolted by.

Castles, after this affair, could never be induced to drink or hold any acquaintance with the enemy.

Having remained some four or five months at Arcangues, on the 21st of February 1814 the army broke up their cantonments and marched for Toulouse. Our battalion, standing in need of new clothing, did not march with the division, but were ordered into St Jean de Luz, where we received them. In the course of some time afterwards we rejoined our division. This was after the battle of Orthez had been fought [27 February], which our battalion felt much chagrined in not being present at.

On the 18th of March a circumstance occurred at Plaisance, near the town of Tarbes, which I cannot help noticing. A French peasant was shot, under circumstances that fixed the crime upon some of the men of our company. Although the greatest endeavours were made to discover the culprit, and the company punished to make them give him up, still it was without avail. The facts of the case were these.

Blanco, the Spaniard, accompanied by one or two of our men, went out this evening in search of wine. They entered the house of a peasant who, resisting the intrusion, struck Blanco, for which the Spaniard instantly shot him on the spot. A very handsome collection was made for the widow and children of the poor peasant, for whose distress a very sincere sympathy was entertained by our battalion. Three months afterwards I was told that Blanco was the perpetrator of this cruel deed.

The morning we left Plaisance we had a long and dreary march over a range of hills, until we came to the village of Tarbes, a short distance beyond which we observed the enemy in possession of a hill both sides of the road to Toulouse. We were immediately ordered to commence an attack upon them. Passing on at the 'double', some of our regiments of cavalry gave us an encouraging huzza as we passed up the road. The French had thrown up strong entrenchments, and were, to use a nautical phrase, 'tier above tier'. I never remember to have been so warmly engaged as on this occasion, except at Badajoz. The enemy were in great numbers, our attacking force few, being only our three battalions of Rifles which their bullets were fast thinning as we struggled up the hill: still, although under every disadvantage, the victors of so many hard fights were not to be repelled, and the French were obliged to retreat. I was very sorry this day for striking a poor Frenchman whom I came up with, as I discovered he was badly wounded; but I made the *amende honorable* by a sup from my canteen, which he received with grace.

We saw but little of the enemy after this, until we came within sight of Toulouse, where they seemed determined on a resolute stand. We took up our cantonments on this side of the Garonne in the beginning of April. The aspect of the country here was very agreeable: it abounded in wine of a rather superior quality to what had hitherto been served out as our rations. Although the inhabitants, from Marshal Soult's orders, had been obliged to fly on our approach, yet I am happy to say that our men were restrained from most of those excesses in the waste and destruction of property, that had taken place in Portugal and Spain. This was greatly occasioned by the very excellent general order of Lord Wellington, published throughout the army at that period,[1] explaining to the troops that although we were

---

[1] Wellington's general order dated 9 July 1813 included the words: 'The officers and soldiers of the army must recollect that their nations are at war with France solely because the Ruler of the French nation will not allow them to be at peace, and is desirous of forcing them to submit to his yoke.'

at war with a usurper and his army, we were not with the inoffensive country-people, who were subjected by fear.

About twelve o'clock on the night of the 9th April we were ordered to fall in. We marched to the side of the Garonne, which we crossed by means of a pontoon bridge, and took up our station behind the walls of a château about a mile from the town. Having had scarcely any rest the preceding night, most of our men were buried in profound sleep, when we were suddenly roused by the most expressive words to the ear of a soldier—'Fall in.' This was done in an instant, and we were ordered to advance in double time.

As we proceeded, we heard a heavy firing as if from the left of the town, and soon after beheld a disorganised mass of Spanish soldiers flying towards us. At first some of our fellows took them for the French, and fired among them, by which some lives were lost. They were a part of the Spanish force who attempted to carry a French fort or redoubt, from which the enemy had sent them to the right-about faster than they had come. We continued to approach the town, which was protected by a long series of fortifications, and that appeared full of men. On our approaching, they opened a running fire from some fieldworks, but with little execution, as we were sheltered by some trees and walls of houses near the place where we halted. We had not remained in this quiescent state long, when the thunder of the conflict was heard going on in full roar on our left: the salvoes of artillery, with the constant cracking of musketry and the rushing sound of shells, together with the occasional wild 'hurra', formed a very pretty concert. The scene was still more electrifying when we found it to be the 6th division engaged in storming batteries, which the Spaniards had just run from; they at length carried them, after a hard tug, in glorious style; General Picton's division was also conspicuously engaged on our right, close to the river. The general attack was crowned with the Duke of Wellington's usual success: the enemy retreating over the bridges of the canal of Languedoc into the town of Toulouse, while we took possession of their outworks.

The French army on the second day evacuated Toulouse, as the town was completely commanded by the batteries we had taken. Our battalion was ordered to take possession of part of the suburbs, near the canal. Although there was a strict order that no man should be allowed to go into the town, my curiosity induced me to take 'French leave' to see a place I had heard so much of; so I managed to elude the vigilance of the sentry. I found almost all the shops open, and business going on apparently as if nothing had taken place. Hearing that the theatre was open, I was induced to pay it a visit: it was very crowded. One box I perceived very magnificently fitted up, and surmounted by laurel, and while I was wondering for whose occupation it was intended, my curiosity was at once allayed by the arrival of the Duke and his staff, who were received with loud acclamations. 'God save the King' was played, and all appeared to testify the greatest pleasure on the occasion but myself. I, indeed, I must fairly confess, feared that my insignificance would not conceal me from the glance of the chief or some of his staff, although wedged into the centre of a dense crowd in the pit. My dark dress, however, effectually screened me.

XXII

A few days after we had to execute our old manœuvre of allowing the French no time to rest, as we were put in motion after them. On the second day, as we halted on the Paris road, our men reposing from the fatigue of the morning's march, we heard several loud huzzas in our front. This was followed by the appearance of a carriage and four horses, which contained a French officer, who we afterwards understood was Marshal Soult. The carriage was attended by a detachment of English and French cavalry; the shouting arose from the tidings that were joyfully repeated, that peace was proclaimed, and that Bonaparte had retired to Elba.

We were immediately on this intelligence ordered to the right-about, and marched back to Toulouse. Before we had proceeded many miles we were overtaken on the road by great numbers of French soldiers who had been disbanded, or had disbanded them-selves, and who now were about returning to their homes, tired enough, no doubt, like ourselves, of the war they had been engaged so long in carrying on. The good feeling testified by many of these really fine-looking fellows to us was general, the Frenchmen in many instances sharing the fatigue in carrying our men's knapsacks, &c.

As for myself, upon my simple word,
I'd rather see a score of friendly fellows shaking hands,
Than all the world in arms.

From Toulouse we marched, in a few days, to Castle Sarazin, situated on the right bank of the Garonne, between the previously mentioned town and Bordeaux. Here we came in for most delightful quarters, being billeted in the houses, where we all had excellent beds. But it was highly amusing to see our rough, hardy fellows spurn this latter luxury—which one would have thought would have been most welcome—with contempt. From having almost constantly been exposed for the previous five or six years to have 'the earth their rude bed, their canopy the sky', with generally a stone for a pillow, our men could obtain no sleep on beds of down; and it was actually a fact that they preferred wrapping a blanket round them, and the hard floor as a place of rest: so much for custom.

At Castle Sarazin we used to be on our usual excellent terms with the French quartered in the neighbourhood, and to while away the time had constant matches with them in running, jumping, and gymnastic exercises. I got acquainted here with a very smart fellow—a French sergeant belonging to the 43rd regiment. A friendship was cemented between us, naturally enough, by our both being Freemasons.

One day we were sitting in a wine-house, when the subject of fencing—a science at which the French prize themselves in excelling—was started. My friend, the sergeant, was observing he was a tolerable hand with the foil, when a short lump of a fellow, who proved to be the fencing-master of the town, overhearing him, immediately challenged him to a trial of skill. This the sergeant in an instant accepted, and the sport, at which he showed himself a perfect adept, at the fencing-master's cost, was carried on with perfect good humour, until a fierce dispute arose about a hit, when it was mutually agreed to determine the controversy with points. A pair of foils with sharpened points, kept for this particular service, were immediately produced, while the bystanders instantly commenced betting upon the combatants with all the sangfroid in the world. Both had taken off their coats and bared their right arms for the strife, when—I am sorry to disappoint the reader, who may expect an account of a duel—our guard, which some good-natured soul had privately summoned, came in and put an end to the affair, greatly to the chagrin of the sergeant, who swore he would have killed the professor on the spot.

That same evening the sergeant, whose name, in the lapse of years, I have forgotten, went to our Colonel and obtained leave for me to visit him at Montauban, where his regiment, the 43rd, was quartered. He had invited a corporal, myself, and another, to a dinner given by the non-commissioned officers of his regiment. On the day appointed away we started, Gilbert, the corporal, and myself. I shall never forget it. It was a fine morning. After crossing the Garonne in open boats, for the bridge had been destroyed previous to the battle of Toulouse, we entered Montauban, and found the 43rd and two other regiments forming a brigade, drawn up on parade in the square of the town, and two splendid bands playing in front.

As we went in search of our friend we had to pass down the front of two of the French regiments, which we did, saluting, soldier-like, their officers. The latter returned our salute in the manner for which they are so justly remarked, and made us feel not a little proud of their courtesy. Our uniforms were almost new, and fitted us well. My two comrades had the advantage of being tall, and exceedingly smart-looking fellows; for myself, I was fat as a butt, and as strong as I looked. We moved along the line, until we fell in with the sergeant. who, starting out of the ranks, gave us a hearty welcome. We waited beside him while the band played some favourite airs, until the regiments were dismissed. But they had scarcely broken their ranks when their officers crowded around us, and severally shook us by the hand, giving us also sundry smacks on the shoulders, with 'Bravo les Anglais, soyez les bienvenus', &c. The sergeant escorted us immediately to his quarters. The dining-room was a splendid one, and fitted up beautifully. The tables groaned under every delicacy of the season, and we did not forget, even here, to do 'justice' to the acknowledged 'merits' of John Bull in all matters of this 'nature'.

Much good feeling and conviviality followed; and encomiums and compliments were passed on the English; all went on very well until singing was introduced with the removal of the cloth. It had been agreed among the French that no song should be sung that reflected upon our country. Several famous songs, so far as we could understand, were introduced. Our sergeant gave us an excellent specimen; and Gilbert and myself joined also in our own rough manner. But a French corporal, under the influence of wine, commenced a 'Chanson de guerre', rather *contre les Anglais*, for which, with a very proper feeling, he was by general consent kicked down stairs. The guests, however, resumed their seats, and all went on as quietly as before; here we remained enjoying ourselves till three the next morning, when we were accompanied to the boats by a number of their band, playing 'Patrick's Day', as they escorted us down to the river-side.

The foregoing anecdote, trivial and uninteresting as it may seem, still serves to show, in a pleasing point of view, the hospitality and kind feelings of the French, who have always claimed our highest respect.

In a few days [31 May] we received an order to proceed to Bordeaux, to embark for England. The delightful emotions of pleasure this generally induced throughout our men, after all their hardships and sufferings, may be better imagined than described. The second day's march we stopped at a village [Bazas, 11 June], the name of which I forget, where we had to part from our allies, the Spanish and Portuguese. Much, and even deep feelings of regret, were particularly felt by the men of our battalion on parting from the Spaniards, who had been for so long a period incorporated in our ranks. They had been distinguished for their gallantry, and although sixteen had been drafted into our company, but five had survived to bid us farewell. Poor fellows, they had grown attached to the battalion, and expressed much grief on leaving! Even Blanco, the sanguinary Blanco, actually shed tears. Notwithstanding the wretched and ineffective state of the Spanish armies during the campaigns in the Peninsula, I am convinced, and have indeed become more so from subsequent experience,[1] that there is right stuff in the men to make excellent soldiers, far superior to the Portuguese.

Many men of our regiment, bound by the charms of the señoritas, who had followed their fortunes throughout the war, took this opportunity to desert their country's cause, to take up that of their Dulcineas.[2] Among others were two of my own company, who, not contented with the 'arms' offered by these 'invincibles', took rifles and all with them, and we never saw or heard of them after.

We embarked [1 July] in high spirits at Bordeaux, for Portsmouth, on board the Ville de Paris, Captain Jones, commander. She was a splendid ship, and astonished us all with the size and regularity of her crew. The sailors, who seldom like a red coat, went hand in hand with us green jackets, and were a jolly set of fellows. . . .

[1] In 1835-6 Costello served with the British Legion in northern Spain.

[2] Dulcinea del Tolosa, the country girl with whom Cervantes' Don Quixote was once in love.

XXIII

Safely returned to England, and quartered in Dover barracks, our men soon forgot the fatigues of the Peninsular campaigns; and being joined by a batch of recruits, and supplied with new clothing, the old soldiers once more panted for fresh exploits; for their souls were strong for war, and peace became irksome to them—nor were they long disappointed.[1] [25 April] In the beginning of May 1815 we received orders to embark at Dover for Ostend, where we arrived safe; from thence we proceeded through Bruges to Ghent in open boats by the canal: here we halted a few days, and then marched to Brussels, where we remained several weeks, not even dreaming an enemy was near us.

On the 15th of June, as I retired to bed, at the hour of eleven o'clock at night, I heard bugles sounding and drums beating through different parts of the city. Equipping myself as quickly as possible, and entering the marketplace, I found the whole of our division assembling. I then belonged to the 5th division, under the command of General Sir Thomas Picton. Being orderly non-commissioned officer of the company at the time, I received orders to draw three days' rations for the men; the chief part of this was left behind, as none but old soldiers knew its value, or felt inclined to take part with them; some of the men, however, cursed their hard fate for not taking away a portion. All things arranged, we passed the gates of Brussels, and descended the wood of Soignies, that leads to the little village of Waterloo. It was the 16th—a beautiful summer morning—the sun slowly rising above the horizon and peeping through the trees, while our men were as merry as crickets, laughing and joking with each other, and at times pondered in their minds what all this fuss, as they called it, could be about; for even the old soldiers could not believe the enemy were so near. We halted at the verge of the wood, on the left of the road, behind the village of Waterloo, where we remained for some hours; the recruits lay down to sleep, while the old soldiers commenced cooking. I could not help noticing, while we remained here, the birds in full chorus straining their little throats as if to arouse

---

[1] Napoleon left Elba on 26 February 1815, landed in the Golfe de Juan on 1 March and reached Paris on the 20th. London heard of his escape on 10 March.

the spirits of the men to fresh vigour for the bloody conflict they were about to engage in. Alas! how many of our brave companions, ere that sun set, were no more! About nine o'clock the Duke of Wellington with his staff came riding from Brussels and passed us to the front; shortly afterwards, orders were given to the Rifles to fall in and form the advanced-guard of our division, and follow. We moved on through the village of Waterloo, and had not proceeded far when, for the first time, we heard distant cannon; it was, I believe, the Prussians engaged on our extreme left [*at Ligny*].

About three o'clock in the afternoon we arrived at four roads; at this time there was a smart firing going on in our front; this, I believe, was caused by some Belgians playing at long shot with the enemy. Here I again saw the Duke of Wellington looking through his glass, as we halted a few moments; this was at Quatre Bras, and immediate orders were given by one of the Duke's staff to occupy a clump of trees a little on our left; our company were ordered to take possession of it. While performing this task I could see the enemy emerging from a wood about a mile on our right, which was rather on a hill, with a clear plain between us. We had scarcely taken possession of the wood, when for the first time, I beheld a French cuirassier or vidette. He was in an instant fired at by our men and his horse shot under him; he disengaged himself from the stirrups as the horse was falling, waving his sword over his head to put us at defiance, but he was immediately dropped by another rifle-shot. I think I can venture to assert that our company was the first of the British army who pulled a trigger at this celebrated battle.

The enemy's light troops I could soon perceive, in extended order and in great force, coming down to oppose us. This caused a corresponding movement on our part, and we were ordered to take ground to our left, passing close to a pond of water, the main road separating us from the enemy. While executing this the French commenced a very brisk fire on us, until we gained possession of a few houses on the main road on a rising ground, which two companies of our Rifles instantly occupied. The remainder of our division was now enveloped in one blaze of fire on the plain before mentioned. But we remained very quietly where we were until the French, bringing up some artillery, began riddling the house with round-shot. Feeling rather thirsty, I had asked a young woman in the place for a little water, which she was handing to me, when a ball passed through the building, knocking the dust about our ears: strange to say, the girl appeared less alarmed than myself.

Fearing that we might be surrounded, we were at length obliged to leave the building, in doing which we were fiercely attacked by a number of French voltigeurs, who forced us to extend along a lane, from whence we as smartly retaliated, and a galling fire was kept up for some time on both sides.

It is remarkable that recruits in action are generally more unfortunate than the old soldiers. We had many fine fellows, who joined us on the eve of our leaving England, who were killed here. The reason of this is that an old rifleman will seek shelter, if there be any near his post, while the inexperienced recruit appears as if petrified to the spot by the whizzing balls, and unnecessarily exposes himself to the enemy's fire.

Being hard pressed by superior numbers, we were at length joined by a number of Belgians, and received orders to advance, which we did, driving the enemy through the skirts of a wood, and passing a field of rye, which obstructed them from our view. As soon, however, as we emerged from the wood, a regiment of French infantry on our right received us with a running fire. I was in the act of taking aim at some of our opposing skirmishers, when a ball struck my trigger finger, tearing it off and turning the trigger aside; while a second shot passed through the mess-tin on my knapsack. Several of our men were killed by this volley, and Lieutenant Gardiner, a worthy little officer of the company, was severely wounded in the lower part of the leg. We wounded men made the best of our way to the rear; and on my return to the house at the corner of the lane, I found the pretty Belgian still in possession, looking out of the window, and seemingly quite unconcerned, although a dozen shots had perforated the house: all our entreaties for her to leave were in vain, as her father, she said, had desired her to take care of the place until he returned from Brussels.

The dusk of the evening soon set in, myself and numbers of others disabled took up our quarters for the night in another farm-house, lower down and some distance from the main road.

The house became soon thronged with the wounded of our division, who were momentarily brought in, until the out-houses, courtlages, &c., were literally crammed. All the straw and hay that could be obtained was procured, of which, fortunately, there was plenty, and strewed everywhere to lay the men on. To sleep was impossible with the anguish of my shattered hand and the groans of my fellow sufferers. The dawn came on before we were aware of it, and ere it was light our advanced sentries were again in continual skirmish along the whole line; indeed, the balls kept patting through the doors and windows as we lay there. Such as were able to walk soon started for Brussels; but several of the severely wounded were obliged to be left behind for want of conveyances.

We had not proceeded far towards the main road along a pathway partially protected by a hedge from the enemy's fire, when one of my companions heard the cries of a child on the other side; on looking over he espied a fine boy, about two or three years of age, by the side of its dead mother, who was still bleeding copiously from a wound in the head, occasioned, most likely, by a random shot from the enemy. We carried the motherless, and perhaps orphan child by turns to Genappe, where we found a number of women of our division, one of whom recognised the little fellow, I think she said, as belonging to a soldier of the First Royals.

Genappe, also, was literally crowded with the wounded, who were conveyed with every possible dispatch to Brussels. Feeling most anxious to know the fate of our regiment, I stood on a hedgerow on the skirts of the village, when I descried the division retreating towards us, the rain at the time coming down in torrents. I remained until some of the regiments entered the village, together with many of our wounded, who gave me information that our regiment, with the cavalry, formed the rear-guard. I now retraced my steps the same road I had advanced, and once more arrived at the little village of Waterloo, which many of our men never saw again, as our battalion lost more on the 16th than on the 18th of June. Here I stopped for the night. The cries of the wounded on their way, in cart-loads, to Brussels, were most distressing, and many carts broke down through being overloaded, and through their haste to get forward.

It is curious to observe the confusion and uproar that generally exists in the rear of an army in battle, while all in front is order and regularity. Many people imagine the reverse. This, however, is generally to be imputed to the soldiers' wives and camp followers of all descriptions, who crowd in great numbers, making inquiries after their husbands, friends, &c., for whom they generally are prepared with liquors and other refreshments. I had no such ties, save my comrades, who now were too busily occupied watching their enemies, and with their own personal considerations, to have either time or opportunity to inquire after mine. The crowds of carts, horses, &c., which thickly thronged the roadway, were greeted on all sides by anxious faces and earnest inquiries. But now and then as one of the vehicles hurried along, a burst of laughter hailed it, and indeed, it seemed to bear a load of a more enlivening nature than that which characterised the others. My sound legs, for my arm only was wounded and hung suspended in a sling, enabled me to approach the cart and scrutinise its contents. My surprise was soon dissipated, and wounds almost forgotten, in the merry features of my old friend, Josh Hetherington, who, having received a flesh wound in the leg, was now being borne to the hospital with other fellow sufferers.

Josh, like myself, had no ties—no one to bring him brandy, &c.; but wider awake, and better acquainted with the world, in the bustle of a dark night, he had laid himself at his length on the inside of a cart, and there awaited the current of fortune.

One or two women in search of their husbands he particularly knew, and knowing also their spouses, he replied to their inquiries in as exact an imitation of their voices as one could reasonably give a man credit for. The result was that the bottle was instantly handed into his hiding-place. Josh took sundry deep gulps, while the duped woman continued anxiously walking by the side of the wheels, wishing to heaven that the daylight, or some other light, would enable her to enjoy the sight of her better half. The denouement of the cheat came with the return of the empty flask, and a sincere hope from Josh that her husband would find enough liquor left—and not be wounded at all—at all.

The disappointment and rage of the woman only gave rise to a burst of merriment, in which the wounded men joined heartily, and the circumstance travelled forward, among her companions, and accompanied the cart the whole of the way to Brussels.

The next morning I proceeded slowly onward, for my wound, as yet, had not been dressed. I could not help remarking, on my way through the woods, droves of Belgians, and even English, with fires lighted, busily cooking, having left their comrades in contest with the enemy, and apparently nothing the matter with them.

On my arrival at Brussels, and going to my quarters, I found it so crowded with Belgian officers and men (some of them quite free from wounds), that I could get no reception. It was about six o'clock in the evening of the 18th. I was entering the large square, and gazing on some hundreds of wounded men who were there stretched out on straw, when an alarm was given that the French were entering the city; in a moment all was in an uproar; the inhabitants running in all directions, closing their doors, and some Belgian troops in the square, in great confusion; loading my rifle, I joined a party of the 81st regiment who remained on duty here during the action. The alarm, however, was occasioned by the appearance of about 1,700 or 1,800 French prisoners, under escort of some of our dragoons.

The panic over, I partook of a little bread and wine, and lay down for the night on some straw in the square; and in spite of the confusion and uproar, occasioned by the continual arrival of waggons loaded with wounded men, I slept soundly. In the morning the scene surpassed all imagination and baffles description: thousands of wounded French, Belgians, Prussians and English; carts, waggons, and every other attainable vehicle were continually arriving heaped with sufferers. The wounded were laid, friends and foes indiscriminately, on straw, with avenues between them, in every part of the city, and nearly destitute of surgical attendance. The humane and indefatigable exertions of the fair ladies of Brussels, however, greatly made up for this deficiency; numbers were busily employed—some strapping and bandaging wounds, others serving out tea, coffee, soups, and other soothing nourishments; while many occupied themselves stripping the sufferers of their gory and saturated garments, and dressing them in clean shirts and other habiliments; indeed, altogether careless of fashionable scruples, many of the fairest and wealthiest of the ladies of that city now ventured to assert their pre-eminence on the occasion. It was enough that their ordained companions were in need, to call forth the sympathies that ever must bind the sexes to mutual dependence.

One lady I noticed particularly; she was attended by a servant bearing on his shoulder a kind of pannier, containing warm and cold refreshments: her age I guessed about eighteen, and the peculiarity of the moment made her appear beyond the common order of humanity. She moved along with an eye of lightning, glancing about for those whom she thought most in need of her assistance. A tall Highlander lay near her as she hurried along and drew her attention with a deep groan, arising from the anguish of a severe wound in the thick part of the thigh. The soldier fixed his eye with surprise on her, as in a twinkling she knelt at his side, and gently moving aside his blood-stained kilt, commenced washing the wounded part; the Scotchman seemed uneasy at her importunity. But with the sweetest voice imaginable, she addressed him in English, with, 'Me no ashamed of you—indeed, I will not hurt you!' and the wounded man, ere he could recover his rough serenity, found his wound bandaged, and at ease, under the operations of his fair attendant. Such acts as these must ever draw forth our admiration.

XXIV

I remained in Brussels three days, and had ample means here, as in several other places, such as Salamanca, &c., for witnessing the cutting off of legs and arms. The French I have ever found to be brave, yet I cannot say they will undergo a surgical operation with the cool, unflinching spirit of a British soldier. An incident which here came under my notice may in some measure show the difference of the two nations. An English soldier belonging to, if I recollect rightly, the 1st Royal Dragoons, evidently an old weather-beaten warfarer, while undergoing the amputation of an arm below the elbow, held the injured limb with his other hand without betraying the slightest emotion, save occasionally helping out his pain by spirting forth the proceeds of a large plug of tobacco, which he chewed most unmercifully while under the operation. Near to him was a Frenchman, bellowing lustily, while a surgeon was probing for a ball near the shoulder. This seemed to annoy the Englishman more than anything else, and so much so, that as soon as his arm was amputated, he struck the Frenchman a smart blow across the breech with the severed limb, holding it at the wrist, saying, 'Here, take that, and stuff it down your throat, and stop your damned bellowing!'

The accommodation at Brussels not being sufficient for the wounded, it was found expedient to have many of them conveyed to Antwerp, myself among the rest; and the entire of the 81st regiment were employed conveying the men on stretchers to the boat on the canal, communicating between the two cities; there I had my wound attended to, and my shattered finger taken off at the socket. A singular case of loss of limb here fell under my notice: a young fellow, a German, one of the drivers to the German artillery, had lost both his legs by a round-shot, which passing through the horse's belly, had carried away both limbs; while on the ground in this mangled state, he received a dreadful gash in one of his arms, from a French cuirassier, and a ball in the other; through these he was also obliged to undergo the amputation of both arms, one below the elbow and the other above; here the unfortunate youth (for he was not more than nineteen) lay a branchless trunk, and up to the moment I left, though numbers died from lesser wounds, survived. At first the latter were so numerous that it became a matter of surprise to even the doctors, who at length discovered that the water, which the patients were in the habit of washing their wounds with, was brought from a spa, which in some instances had the effect of poisoning the flesh.[1] In the course of a few weeks, however, I was sufficiently recovered to rejoin my regiment, at Clichy camp, near Paris.

Shortly after my arrival I was ordered on the Provost Guard, which my readers will better understand is a kind of military police. We were under the command of the Provost Marshal, named Stanway, whose instructions were to take all whom he found marauding about the gardens in the neighbourhood of Paris, and to march them down to his guard-house for punishment.

The Provost was a keen fellow, and sometimes would pounce on as many as eighteen or twenty in the course of a morning; these were immediately flogged, according to the amount of their offence, or the resistance they made, and instantly liberated.

The depredations, however, became so universal that the inhabitants of Paris complained to the generals of divisions, and we, in consequence, received orders to keep a stricter look-out, and take into custody and flog every man we caught in the act of plunder. Our guardhouse consequently was daily filled by soldiers of every uniform; indeed, ours may be said to have been a true Owenite[2] Guard, for we made no objection to 'sect, country, class, or colour', as we served them all 'alike'.

We had a deal of trouble with the Belgians especially. These fellows would go forth in sections, and lay everything waste before them. This was not for want, as they were well supplied with regular rations daily from Paris, which we were aware of. As soon as they perceived the guard hemming them in on all sides, they would invariably salute us with brickbats, stones, and sometimes even make a regular attack. But Stanway seldom let any escape him.

One morning we brought in sixteen of them, and the Provost, as usual, marched them into the little yard where the punishments were generally inflicted. The triangles stared them in the face from the centre of the ground, and the culprits one and all, as soon as they rolled their eyes on it, gave a bellow of horror, fell on their knees, and commenced praying and crossing themselves, and other symptoms of

[1] This being only a report amongst us wounded men, little reliance can be placed on it. [E.C.]

[2] Referring to the theories of Robert Owen (1771–1858), socialist and philanthropist.

repentance; but Stanway was inexorable. Our men had the greatest difficulty in unbreeching them, and getting them tied to the halberts. The first stripped, I recollect, was a short, stumpy, fat, desperate-looking fellow, who by the circumference of his seat of honour, and his struggles for its safety, seemed to bear about it all the honour of his native Belgium. The first whistle of the cat, even before it reached him, appeared to have verified the assumption, for he roared to such a degree, and his fellow culprits sympathised so loudly, and with such a crash of Belgic, that it set the whole vicinity by the ears, and actually aroused their whole regiment quartered in the village, and the place became in an uproar. The Belgians flew to arms and instantly surrounded the guard-house; Stanway nevertheless was determined not to relax his duty, and ordered every man of us to load, and placed us in different parts of the building, barricading the doorways, prepared for every resistance, and during intervals continued the flagellation. The assailants meanwhile became furious, and attempted to scale the walls for a rescue, but they were kept off by the guard with fixed bayonets, until a shower of brickbats, &c., being thrown over the walls, made us gladly retire into the building. Our lives were now in jeopardy; not a man of us dared to stir out, until a signal being given to some English soldiers who were passing, these gave the alarm to the division then encamped outside the village, and our Rifles, followed by the 52nd, came instantly to our assistance.

The two regiments remained under arms the whole night, and the Belgians, out of bravado, retired to a field, a little distance from them, and kept under arms also. The morning after the occurrence they were removed from Clichy, and we saw no more of them.

Going into Paris a day or two after this disturbance to draw rations for the guard, I had to pass the Barrière de Clichy, and before entering the gates I perceived a crowd collected round a doorway in the street adjoining. Naturally anxious to know the cause, I mingled with the throng, and pushing to the centre perceived the dead body of a French gentleman stretched out on some straw, literally saturated in blood, and on inquiry, I was informed that he had been slain by a Cossack or Prussian officer some few minutes before. The deceased (who was a French Count) and the Cossack, it appeared, had quarrelled the night previous, and had decided on settling the matter the next morning by a meeting with pistols. It had been agreed by the seconds that the two principals should be placed back to back, and each measuring six of his own paces, should, as the distance was completed, turn round and fire.

As soon, however, as the Count commenced his first pace, the Cossack turned round, discharged his pistol into the back of his adversary's head, and stretched him lifeless on the ground, exclaiming as he did it, 'I have been shot at enough by your cursed countrymen; now for my turn.'

The assassin and his second, fearful, however, of the consequences, fled instantly and, taking horse, rode off to their camp, but they were never discovered, although I was told that the Duke, when the circumstances were related to him, offered a reward for their apprehension.

The unfortunate Count had been an officer in the French service, and to all appearance was a very smart young fellow.

In the beginning of February 1816 we left Paris and marched to the environs of Cambrai; shortly afterwards we were presented with medals sent out by the British Government, in commemoration of that celebrated battle; every man who was in the field on the 16th, 17th, and 18th of June was distinguished with this honourable badge. I am sorry to say this caused many dissensions among the men, particularly some of the old veterans of the Peninsular campaigns.[1] One named Wheatley, as brave a man as any in the service, was unfortunately in hospital at Brussels during the action, and was not honoured with this mark of bravery; whenever he met with badges on what he termed recruits, he would instantly tear them off, and frequently throw them away. For this too often repeated offence poor Wheatley was tried by a court-martial, and sentenced to three months' solitary confinement. He was sent to Valenciennes, where the 43rd regiment lay, who formerly belonged to our light division during the Spanish war. The men of that regiment, who knew Wheatley, as well as the offence he had committed, not only fed him well during his imprisonment, but at the expiration of his confinement sent him back in all the pomp a hero could wish. He was conveyed in a carriage drawn by four horses, Wheatley's head, as well as those of the postilion and horses, were decorated with blue ribands. On seeing the gay equipage enter the village, we were much surprised, but more so on seeing Wheatley jump from the carriage amidst the loud acclamations of his old companions. Poor Wheatley felt neglected on receiving no medal, and became, from one of the bravest, one of the most

---

[1] Men who had fought in a score of actions between 1794 and 1814 but who missed Quatre Bras and Waterloo had to wait until 1847 for any medal. The Military General Service Medal was issued, but many entitled to it had already died.

dissipated men in the regiment; he was shortly afterwards discharged.

My own company was quartered at Mœuvres, a pretty little village off the main road that leads to Douai, myself and three privates being billeted on the house of a rich old fellow named Bernard Loude; he was the richest man in the village, possessing upwards of three hundred acres of land, his own property, with stables, granary, waggons, and cattle, indeed everything that constitutes a farmer's stock. The house, like all others in that part of the country, was built long, with only a ground floor. On entering it, I observed three pretty girls spinning; the youngest, about sixteen years of age, was named Léocadie; the next, about nineteen, named Augustine; and the oldest, who was not above twenty-four years of age, was named Julie; they were all attractive in appearance.

After living there some weeks, I looked upon myself as one of the household; and, soldier-like, began toying with the girls: the one who attracted my attention most was Augustine; she was a fine young woman, with light hair and fair complexion. Her manners were playful, yet gentle, and there was an air of innocence in her freedom, which showed her thoughts were untainted by that knowledge of the world which restrains the levity of youth. Her disposition corresponded with her manners, frank, generous, and confiding; her sisters used to say she was of a most forgiving temper, yet of a firm and determined spirit, and they loved her with more than the love sisters generally bestow upon each other. I now, day after day, became more intimate with the family, and the fair Augustine, whether serious or jesting, was always my favourite. The courtship of a soldier may be somewhat rough; I used to steal a kiss now and then, which my pretty Augustine would check me for doing; yet so much goodness was there in her manner that her reproof, rather than otherwise, tempted a repetition of the offence. To those who know the inconveniences to which soldiers are subjected in being billeted, it must appear I was now in clover; I certainly never shall forget the happy hours I then enjoyed.

One day, it was, I remember, on a Saturday, I was ordered on duty to the headquarters of our regiment, at a small village called Bourlon, about two miles from Mœuvres. Previously to my departure, the youngest sister Léocadie told me Augustine was soon to be married, being engaged to a young Frenchman who lived our side of Cambrai, and had formerly been a prisoner in England, jokingly adding that he could speak a little English. It was customary for me to dine with the family every Sunday; and on my return off guard next day, as usual, I joined the domestic party. I noticed a stranger at table, who by his manner appeared the favoured suitor of Augustine. We had, however, scarcely been seated, when he gazed intently upon me, and suddenly starting up, seized me by the hand, and nearly bursting into tears, exclaimed, 'Mon brave soldat, est-ce vous?' I immediately recognized in him the faithful Frenchman whose life I had spared in the streets of Badajoz before mentioned [see p. 96]. Returning to his seat, he described to the party the scenes we had gone through at Badajoz, which sometimes called forth fits of laughter, and sometimes tears.

All eyes were fixed on me; I particularly noticed Augustine; she looked more serious than I had ever seen her; she did not shed a tear or yet smile during the whole narrative of her young French lover; but I could plainly perceive by the heaving of her bosom, she was more deeply affected than the rest. He extolled me to the skies, but he knew not the interest he was exciting in favour of an unknown rival. The French I have observed to be a people fond of glory and senti-ment, and a story of la Gloire et l'Amour will always excite their admiration. He then related to me the cruelty he had received from the Portuguese soldiers who conducted him with the remainder of the garrison of Badajoz on their march to Lisbon, where he was put on board a ship and conveyed to England. After Bonaparte had been conducted to Elba, he, with some thousand other prisoners, returned to his native home. He took no part, he said, in the battle of Waterloo. After dinner I and my old companion parted, having both enjoyed mutual good cheer. The attention of Augustine after this accidental interview was redoubled, and what I before suspected I now plainly discovered, I had won her heart. From this time we were more frequently alone; and although her father wished her married to the Frenchman, he being a relation as well as in good circumstances, she had never herself been seriously attached to him. The affection that subsisted between us became no secret in the family, and it was rumoured even about the village; at length it burst out in songs composed by the 'Troubadours' of the neighbourhood. Her father thought it prudent to get my quarters changed: he accordingly applied to the Colonel, and I was sent to another hamlet in charge of tailors making clothing for the regiment; it was at a pretty neat little village called Sains les Marquion, on the main road to Cambrai. At the house of an old widow who lived at Mœuvres I still corres-ponded with Augustine, and enjoyed many stolen interviews. At length, harassed with the remonstrances of her family, who insisted on diverting her affections from me, she determined on leaving her father's roof, and in the dusk one evening met me at the widow's, where we betrothed ourselves to each other. On hearing of her elopement, her father unrelentingly pursued her; he went to Cambrai and applied to the executor to deprive her of her patrimony, but the law prevented him doing so. He then appealed to the military authorities, and one morning, about ten o'clock, four gendarmes, to my surprise, entered my quarters in search of her. I was about to give them a very rough reception, and some of my comrades, who were quartered with me, proposed giving them a threshing; but the corporal who commanded the party warning me I should be held responsible for any ill-usage they might receive, then produced a written order for her return to her father's house, signed by General Sir John Lambert, who commanded our brigade, and countersigned by Colonel Balvaird, our head colonel, Sir Andrew Barnard being at the time Commandant of Cambrai.

I saw all remonstrance was vain, and there was no alternative; so accompanying her myself, she was obliged with a heavy heart to retrace her steps. Her reception by her father was most unkind; he confined her in a room, the windows of which were darkened and secured by crossbars of iron, the handiwork of the village smith, whose services were called in requisition upon the occasion. In this gloomy prison she was not permitted to see her sisters; her meals were sent her at long intervals, and scantily supplied; a priest was sent for, who was paid handsomely for trying to wean her affections from me; but the bars of iron, and the prayers of the priest, were alike in vain. She contrived on the first opportunity to escape from this durance vile to me, as we had been clandestinely married at her first elopement by an excommunicated priest; for I must here mention, the Duke of Wellington had given positive orders that no British soldiers should be allowed to marry French women. Immediately on her return we went together to our colonel, who lived at the château of the village, to request she might be allowed to remain with me. On entering the room, she threw herself in an impassioned manner on her knees, and begged we might not be separated. The Colonel, taking her by the hand, raised her from her humiliating posture, saying it was not in his power to grant the request, but he would speak to General Lambert on the matter, which he did, and she was allowed to remain with me. We now fancied ourselves in a great measure protected, but she was again pursued by her father, who one day very unceremoniously rushed into our cottage, and desired she would return with him. She instantly flew to me for protection, throwing her arms around me, exclaiming, 'Mon Edouard, je ne te quitterai jamais.' Her father, as if seized with a sudden fit of frenzy, laid hold of a hammer that was on the table, and struck himself a blow on the forehead with such force that he fell, and remained some time on the floor insensible. The distress of poor Augustine cannot be imagined, for it was some time ere she recovered, but after this we remained unmolested, and lived happily together.

About the latter end of June 1818 we broke up our cantonments, and encamped on the glacis of Cambrai, where we remained until the latter end of October, when we received orders to proceed to England, after remaining in its environs for the space of three years. The Colonel, who did not know we were married, sent for me, and informed me she must return to her parents, as she would certainly not be permitted to embark with me for England. We now consulted together as to what step would be most advisable to adopt. It was agreed I should go to her uncle, who resided in Cambrai, and request him to intercede with her father to allow her to receive part of her patrimony; for, although he could not deprive her of it after his death, she was not entitled to receive it during his lifetime; and, if he consented to do so, I promised to obtain my discharge from the army, and publicly marry her. Her uncle, after my interview with him, accompanied me to Mœuvres (a distance of about three or four miles), with the intention of discussing the matter with the father; but, on my entering the house, all was uproar; a tumult of voices from all the family assailed me, during which one of the brothers cried, 'Délie le chien! Délie le chien!' Upon which a huge wolf-dog was unchained; but, instead of attacking me, remembering that I had once lived in the house, he came and fawned on me. In the midst of this confusion I expected every moment would be my last, as there were no British soldiers nearer than Cambrai. At this instant Augustine entered. She had heard at her uncle's that I had gone with him to her father's, and, apprehensive of the consequences, had followed me. Not attending to any other person present, she entreated me to leave the house, and return to Cambrai with her. I did so; and early next morning, the regiment being in marching order, I was reluctantly compelled to part from my almost broken-hearted faithful Augustine. It was agreed she should remain with the family of her uncle until I could communicate with her from England, where we hoped happier days awaited us.

Bibliography

COLE, G. W. 'The Romance of a Soldier of Wellington, Sergeant Edward Costello', *Rifle Brigade Chronicle*, 1945.

COPE, SIR WILLIAM. *The History of the Rifle Brigade (The Prince Consort's Own) formerly the 95th.* London, 1877.

FERNYHOUGH. *Military Memoirs of Four Brothers (Natives of Stafford-shire) engaged in the Service of their Country, as well in the New World and Africa as on the Continent of Europe.* By the Survivor. (Lieutenant Robert Fernyhough's journals of service with the Rifle Brigade form most of this volume.) London, 1829.

FITZMAURICE, MRS F. M. *Recollections of a Rifleman's Wife at Home and Abroad.* London, 1851.

GREEN, W. *A Brief Outline of the Travels and Adventures of William Green (late Rifle Brigade) during a period of 10 Years in Denmark, Germany and the Peninsular War.* Leicester, 1857.

HARRIS. *Recollections of Rifleman Harris (Old 95th). With Anecdotes of his Officers and his Comrades.* Edited by Henry Curling. London, 1848.

KINCAID, CAPTAIN J. *Adventures in the Rifle Brigade, in the Peninsula, France, and the Netherlands, from 1809 to 1815.* London, 1830.

—— *Random Shots from a Rifleman.* London, 1835.

LEACH, LIEUTENANT-COLONEL J. *Rough Sketches of the Life of an Old Soldier: During a Service in the West Indies; at the Siege of Copenhagen in 1807; in the Peninsula and the South of France in the Campaigns from 1808 to 1814, with the Light Division; in the Netherlands in 1815; including the Battles of Quatre Bras and Waterloo: &c.* London, 1831.

—— *Rambles on the Banks of Styx.* London, 1847.

SIMMONS, MAJOR G. *A British Rifleman. The Journals and Correspondence of Major George Simmons, Rifle Brigade, during the Peninsular War and the Campaign of Waterloo.* Edited by Lieutenant-Colonel Willoughby Verner. London, 1899.

SMITH, SIR HARRY. *The Autobiography of Lieutenant-General Sir*

Harry Smith, Baronet of Aliwal on the Sutlej, G.C.B. Edited by G. C.
Moore Smith. 2 vols. London, 1901.

SMITH, HENRY STOOKS. *An Alphabetical List of the Officers of the
Rifle Brigade from 1800 to 1850.* London, 1851.

SURTEES, WILLIAM. *Twenty-Five Years in the Rifle Brigade.* Edin-
burgh, 1833.

Index of Persons

Abercromby, Gen. Sir Ralph (1734–1801), 1

Allen, Humphrey, Rifleman, 53, 54 and n.

Arbuthnot, Lt the Hon. Duncan, 63

Arnal, Cpl, 87–8

Ballard, Cpl, 91

Balvaird, Capt. (later Lt-Col.) William, 53, 162

Bandle, Rifleman, 132

Barnard, Col. (later Gen.) Sir Andrew Francis (1773–1855), 72, 140, 162

Battersby, Sgt, 102–4

Beckwith, Col. (later Gen. Sir Thomas Sidney) (1772–1831), 4, 5 and n., 8, 11, 13–15, 19, 26, 54, 58, 62–4, 72

Bevan, Lt-Col. Charles, 70

Blanco, 126, 139, 144, 149

Bock, Major-Gen. Baron Eberhardt Otto Georg von, 108

Boswell, James, 9n.

Brooks, Rifleman, 88–9

Brotherwood, Sgt, 141–2

Bryen, Rifleman, 102–3

Bryen, Nelly, 102–3

Bull, Capt. (later Lt-Col.) Robert (1778–1835), 28

Burke, Dr Joseph, 71, 135

Burke, Rifleman, 64

Cameron, Major John, 118–19

Castles, Rifleman Johnny, 99, 143

Cervantes, Miguel de, 149n.

Charity, Rifleman, 34

Clementeria, 112

Coane, Lt Alexander, 33–4

Colbert, Gen. Auguste-Marie-François, 11 and n.

Colborne, Lt-Col. John (later Field-Marshal Baron Seaton) (1778–1863), 75

Cole, Lt-Gen. Sir Galbraith Lowry (1772–1842), 121

Connelly, Sgt Michael, 109–10

Cope, Sir William, 11n.

Cox, Col. William, 35n.

Craufurd, Major-Gen. Robert (1764–1812), 17 and n., 18–19, 27, 30–1, 47–8, 57, 66, 69, 70, 73, 75, 77–8, 82–4

Crawley, Rifleman Tom, 7, 41–2, 44–6, 55, 70–1, 75, 90, 135–6, 139

Crooks, Sgt, 4

Cuesta, Gen. Don Gregorio García de la (1740–1812), 20, 21 and n.

Cummins, Cpl, 85–6

Demosthenes, 58

Dillon, Sgt, 135

Dundas, Gen. Sir David (1735–1820), 39 and n.

Elder, Lt-Col. George, 28, 45

Erskine, Major-Gen. Sir William (1769–1813), 48

Fairfoot, Sgt (later Quartermaster) Robert, 132 and n.

Fleming, Sgt, 47, 51, 93

Fotheringham, Sgt, 115

Frost, Rifleman, 119

Gardiner, Lt John, 106–7, 142, 152

Gazan de la Peyrière, Gen. Count Honoré-Théodore-Maxime (1765–1845), 127n.

Gazan, Countess, 127 and n.

Gea, Rifleman, 90
Gibbon, Edward, 20
Gilbert, Rifleman, 148
Green, Rifleman, 90
Grindle, Rifleman, 142

Hetherington, Rifleman Josias (Josh), 39, 40, 110, 154
Hill, Lt-Gen. Sir Rowland (later Viscount) (1772–1842), 70, 110
Home, John, 1n.
Hopwood, Lt John, 51, 141–2
Hudson, Rifleman, 85, 124

Jackson, Lt, 100
Jackson, Sgt, 91
Johnson, Dr Samuel, 9 and n.
Johnston, Lt William, 12, 77, 136
Jones, Capt. William, 93
Jones, Capt., 149
Joseph Bonaparte, King of Spain (1768–1844), 127
Jourdan, Jean-Baptiste, Marshal of France (1762–1833), 127n.

Kelly, Sgt, 131
Kempt, Major-Gen. Sir James (1764–1854), 136, 142
Ketch, John, 99 and n.
Kincaid, Capt. (later Sir) John (1787–1862), 11n., 25n., 51n., 62n., 77, 131n.
Kitchen, Sgt, 73

Lambert, Major-Gen. Sir John (1772–1847), 162
Leach, Capt. (later Col.) Jonathan, 27, 46n., 55n., 62n., 120n., 132n.
Lee, Sgt, 128 and n.
Lesage, Alain-René, 74n.
Loude, Augustine, 160–3
Loude, Bernard, 160
Loude, Léocadie, 160
Louisa, 135

Maguire, Private, 24
Mahon, Rifleman Pat, 56
Marie-Louise, Empress of the French, 29
Marmont, Auguste-Frédéric-Louis de, Marshal of France (1774–1852), 74, 104
Massena, André, Marshal of France (1756–1817), 37, 49, 59, 63, 74
Mauley, Shoemaker, 138–9
M'Cullock, Lt John Garlies, 32
Meagher (?Maher), Rifleman, 26–7
Mellish, Major Henry, 50, 64
Miles, Cpl, 84
Mina, Gen. Espoz de, 110 and n., 111
Mitchell, Capt. Samuel, 38, 77
M'Nabb, Rifleman Billy, 38
Monmouth, James Scott, Duke of (1649–85), 99n.
Moore, Lt-Gen. Sir John (1761–1809), 5, 11
Murphy, Rifleman Jack, 45

Napier, Major (later Gen. Sir George Thomas) (1784–1855), 77–8, 79n.
Napier, Col. (later Gen. Sir William Francis Patrick) (1785–1860), 19n., 20
Napoleon I, Emperor of the French (1769–1821), 27, 29, 66, 112, 119, 146, 150n., 161
Nelson, Horatio, Admiral Viscount (1758–1805), 72
Ney, Michel, Marshal of France (1769–1815), 57

O'Brien, Rifleman, 95–6
O'Hara, Capt. (later Major) Peter, 6 and n., 26, 32–4, 41, 43, 45, 48, 52, 55, 58, 91, 93, 101
Owen, Robert, 157 and n.

Paget, Lt-Gen. Sir Edward (1775–1849), 11 and n.

Pakenham, Hon. Capt. (later Major-Gen. Sir Edward Michael) (1778–1815), 23 and n.
Palmer, Rifleman, 50–1
Picton, Lt-Gen. Sir Thomas (1758–1815), 124, 145, 150
Plunket, Rifleman Tom, 8–9, 10, 11 and n., 12–16, 82
Plunket, Mrs, 15, 16 and n.
Pratt, Lt John D., 35, 36 and n.
Pratt, Dragoon, 106–7

Robinson, Rifleman, 119
Ross, Capt. Hew Dalrymple (later Field-Marshal) (1778–1868), 30, 31, 34, 50, 126
Royston, Rifleman, 133
Ryan, Rifleman, 133

Sanchez, Don Julian, 73, 116–17
Searchfield, Rifleman Tommy, 72
Shakespeare, William, 81n., 133
Sharp, Sgt-Major, 65
Simmons, Lt George, 21n., 36n., 141n.
Slade, Major-Gen. (later Gen. Sir John) (1762–1859), 65
Smith, Capt. (later Lt-Gen. Sir Harry George Wakelyn) (1788–1860), 21n., 35n., 75, 79n., 85 and n.
Smith, Lt Tom, 35n., 85
Soult, Nicolas, Marshal of France (1769–1851), 144, 146
Spencer, 2nd/Lt Lord Charles, 114

Stanway, Capt. F., 157–8
Stewart, Lt James, 26, 62 and n.
Stewart, Major the Hon. John, 12, 32, 55 and n.
Stratton, Rifleman, 118–19
Strode, Lt T. Lear, 55–6
Swift, Jonathan, 1

Talbot, Lt-Col. Neil, 31
Tidy, Blacksmith, 69
Tracey, Rifleman, 50

Uniacke, Capt. John, 78, 79n., 82, 85

Victor, Claude-Victor Perrin, called, Marshal of France (1766–1841), 17

Watts, Sgt, 140
Wellesley, see Wellington
Wellington, Arthur, Field-Marshal Duke of (1769–1852), 9, 17, 21 and n., 23n., 29, 35, 37, 46 and n., 58, 61, 71, 74, 83, 90–1, 99, 104, 109, 112, 116–17, 121–3, 126, 128, 138, 141, 144 and n., 145–6, 151, 159, 162
Wheatley, Rifleman, 159–60
Whitelocke, Lt-Gen. John (1757–1833), 10 and n., 84, 186n.
Wilkie, Rifleman, 2–4, 61–2, 79 and n., 81–2

York and Albany, Frederick Augustus, Field-Marshal Duke of (1763–1827), 7 and n.

General Index

This Index contains the names of places, rivers and British and Allied regiments mentioned by Costello.

Abrantes, 65
Agueda, River, 64, 75–6
Alameda, 30, 116, 119
Almeida, 23, 30, 32, 33n., 35, 38, 63, 69, 70
Alva, River, 60
Antwerp, 156
Arcangues, 140, 143
Arruda, 41
Astorga, 11
Atalaya, 71–2

Badajoz, 6n., 34, 47, 51, 64, 88–100, 134, 143–4, 161
Barba del Puerco, 25, 27, 69
Bazas, 149
Belem, 38, 91, 102
Bidassoa, River, 130–1, 133–4
Bordeaux, 147, 149
Bruges, 150
Brussels, 26, 150–6, 159
Buenos Aires, 6n., 10n., 17n., 84
Burgos, 112, 120
Bourlon, 160
Bussaco, 6n.

Cambrai, 159–63
Campo Mayor, 12, 22, 71, 88
Carpio, 28
Casal Nova, 55–6
Castello Branco, 71
Castello de Vide, 86
Castle Sarazin, 147
Ceira, River, 60
Chatham, 85
Chelsea, 14–15, 134
Ciudad Rodrigo, 23, 27–9, 63–5, 71, 74–83, 85–7, 93, 96, 99, 101, 115, 117, 124, 133

Clichy, 157–8
Coa, River, 25, 33, 62, 70
Coimbra, 36
Colchester, 3–5, 16n., 70
Condeixa, 55
Coria, 19
Corunna, 5, 6n., 8, 10–11
Coventry, 90

Dos Casas, River, 68
Douai, 160
Dover, 9, 26, 150
Dublin, 1–3

El Bodon, 74–5, 85
Elvas, 22, 88–9

Ferrol, 131
Figueira, 37
Fort Conception, 30–2, 65–6
Fort Picurina, 88
Fort St Christobal, 99, 100
Fort St Vincent, 104
Fort San Roche, 88, 94
Foz d'Arouce, 58
Freixedas, 28, 62
Fuentes de Oñoro, 6n., 65–6, 68

Gallegos, 27–8, 63, 69, 85
Garonne, River, 144–5, 148
Genappe, 153
Getafe, 111
Ghent, 150
Guadiana, River, 88–9
Guinaldo, 74, 116

Huerta, 108
Hythe, 6, 8

Ituero, 101

Jafra, 39

Kilmainham, 15
Knightsbridge, 54n.

Languedoc, Canal of, 145
La Rhune, 137–8
Lesaca, 130, 134
Liffey, River, 3n.
Ligny, 151
Lisbon, 17, 37–8, 41, 59, 62, 161
London, 4, 38, 89, 150n.
Londonderry, 1

Madrid, 111–12
Malpartida de Placencia, 19
Manchester, 3
Marialva, 28
Mayor, River, 43, 47
Medina del Pomar, 120
Melo, 61
Molina dos Flores, 28
Mondego, River, 35n., 37
Montauban, 148
Monte Reguengo, 71
Moscow, 119
Mount Mellick, 1
Mœuvres, 160–1, 163

Navarre, 110n.
Nave de Haver, 65, 67
Nivelle, River, 138

Orthez, 143
Ostend, 150

Pampeluna, 110, 129–31
Paris, 157–9
Pinhel, 34, 35n.
Plaisance, 143–4
Pombal, 50
Portsmouth, 149

Puebla de Arganzón, 123

Quatre Bras, 15, 64, 104, 151, 159

Redinha, 52
Ringsend, 3
Rivillas, River, 88
Rolica, 6n.
Rueda, 104–5

Sabugal, 70
St Jean de Luz, 140, 143
Sains les Marquion, 161
Salamanca, 87, 101, 104, 107–10,
    112–13, 116–17, 119, 156
Salvatierra, 129
San Estevan, 130
San Milan, 123
San Sebastian, 64, 133
Santa Barbara, 130–1
Santarem, 17, 26, 43, 48–9, 59
Sierra de Gata, 71
Soignies, 150
Soito, 74

Tagus, River, 17, 43, 86
Talavera, 12, 17, 20, 21 and n., 73
Tarbes, 143–4
Tordesillas, 105
Tormes, River, 107–8
Toro, 120
Torres Vedras, 37, 41
Toulouse, 143–8
Trueba, River, 120

Val de Mula, 30
Valenciennes, 159
Valladolid, 74n.
Valle, 43–4
Vera, 132n., 133–4, 137
Villar de Puerco, 31
Villar Formoso, 65
Vimeiro, 6n.
Viseu, 23–4, 29

Vittoria, 21n., 110–12, 123–9, 132, 139

Waterloo, 14, 16, 26–7, 64, 128n., 134, 150–1, 153, 159n., 161

Zadora, River, 123

REGIMENTS (British and Allied)
Cavalry
Royal Horse Guards, 119, 120 and n.
Life Guards, 119, 120 and n., 127
1st (Royal) Dragoons, 67, 153, 156
10th Hussars, 127–8
13th Light Dragoons, 110
14th Light Dragoons, 28, 30, 31, 64–6, 106
16th Light Dragoons, 23, 28, 30, 66
23rd Light Dragoons, 19
Infantry
Coldstream (2nd Foot Guards), 36 and n., 66, 68
3rd Foot Guards (Scots), 36 and n., 66, 68
2nd (Queen's Royal), 69, 70
4th (King's Own), 69, 70, 99
5th (Northumberland Fusiliers), 74, 97
27th (Inniskilling), 24
31st (Huntingdonshire), 14
32nd (Cornwall), 14
40th (2nd Somersetshire), 77

43rd (Monmouthshire), 17, 31, 43, 75, 133, 147–8, 159
52nd (Oxfordshire), 17, 31–4, 43–4, 68, 75, 77, 85–6, 93, 133, 140, 143
58th (Rutlandshire), 38
61st (South Gloucestershire), 102
68th (Durham) Light Infantry, 38
69th (South Lincolnshire), 6n.
77th (East Middlesex), 74
79th Highlanders, 68
81st (Loyal Lincoln Volunteers), 154, 156
83rd (County of Dublin and Royal Irish Rifles), 100
85th (Bucks Volunteers), 38, 67
87th (Prince of Wales's Own Irish), 38
88th (Connaught Rangers), 82, 97, 100, 125
95th Rifles (later The Rifle Brigade), 2, 75, 82, 83, 94, 100, 131 and n., 140–1, 144
King's German Legion 23–5
1st Hussars, 51 and n., 52, 66, 122
3rd Hussars, 28, 30, 31, 33
Brunswick Oels Jäger, 46 and n., 47
Portuguese
1st Caçadores, 28
3rd Caçadores, 28, 44
Ordenança, 37
Dublin Militia, 1
Lincoln Militia, 8
'Belem Rangers', 38, 122